Pioneers of Science

Alfred Bernhard Nobel 1833–1896

Pioneers of Science

Nobel Prize Winners in Physics

Robert L Weber

Edited by J M A Lenihan

The Institute of Physics, Bristol and London

Published by The Institute of Physics
Techno House, Redcliffe Way, Bristol BS1 6NX, and
47 Belgrave Square, London SW1X 8QX.

British Library Cataloguing in Publication Data

Weber, Robert Lemmerman
          Pioneers of Science.
          1. Physicists – Biography
          I. Title   II. Institute of Physics
          530′.092′2   QC15
          ISBN 0–85498–036–9

The first 99 portraits are reproduced from *College Physics* by R L Weber,
K V Manning and W M White. Copyright © 1974 McGraw-Hill. Used
with permission of McGraw-Hill Book Company.

The frontispiece photograph of Alfred Nobel is reproduced by courtesy
of the Nobel Foundation, Stockholm, Sweden.

Text set in 10/12 point Linotron 202 Palatino
Printed and bound in Great Britain by
The Pitman Press, Bath

To Marion, Rob, Karen, Meredith and Ruth

Preface

Now that you have in hand this volume, I hope that you will find it as enjoyable as many readers, perhaps yourself included, found the first general-interest book published by The Institute of Physics, *A Random Walk in Science*. Some aspects of this later book might also be considered random. In it the biographical notes of the Nobel laureates are arranged in the order of the date of the award, although few or many years may have elapsed between the time the award-winning work was performed and the date of the Nobel Prize. Further, in any one year there seems to be an element of chance as to which of several eminent physicists will be struck by the lightning of Nobel recognition. However, taken together, the achievements of the Nobel Prize winners briefly described in this book highlight the progress of twentieth-century physics.

It was felt desirable that the biographies be held to their present short length and that they be written to interest the general reader. To that I mentally added 'students and prospective students of physics.' I recall that Aage Bohr addressed his Nobel lecture to 'Dear Students.'

Each biographical note seeks to identify the work for which the award was given and its place in modern physics. Here some 'physics jargon' may appear, but I trust that any technical discussion will be as acceptable as that, say, in the *Scientific American*. In the biographies you may note the sort of family background, education, apprenticeship, and work habits which may distinguish a successful scientist. You may also note that some scientists are loners, while others enjoy interaction with colleagues and feel a social responsibility.

As the drafts of the biographies were completed, I sent each living Nobelist a copy of his, requesting suggestions for its improvement. In the case of shared awards, each recipient saw the other biographies and had opportunity to comment on how the physics was divided. The biographies in their present form have greatly benefited from the generous help I have received from the laureates. In their replies they made corrections, suggested viewpoints, and provided up-dating information on their current interests. Some were historic documents in themselves. Also, I welcomed the warm approval they expressed for the preparation of this book.

In a lecture to students at the Claremont Group of Colleges in 1960, Dr I I Rabi described the life of a physicist before World War II and nuclear weapons clouded his public image: 'The history of a physicist's life was very simple. He was born; he became interested in physics in some way, either through reading or through the personal influence of a teacher or a lecturer; he wrote his thesis and received his PhD degree; he died. The rest and essential part of this biography could be read only in the scientific journals, in which were described his own work and the work of his students and colleagues. It was an eminently satisfactory life, to my mind the only serious occupation for a gentleman. The drama in which he played his role was epic in quality: the drama of man's unfolding discovery of the world in which he finds himself . . . The stage on which he played his role was the globe . . . He had no counterpart to the art critic, the music critic, the literary critic, or the dramatic critic to plague him. No one stood between him and his public because his public were his colleagues. With all the fringe benefits which I have tried to describe so alluringly, you will not be surprised to learn that his actual take-home pay was not large. Plain living and high thinking were the order of the day . . .'

The Artists

The portrait drawings of the 49 physicists who received Nobel awards from 1901 to 1945 were made by the Princeton artist and pianist Carola Spaeth Hauschka (1883–1948), widow of Hugo Hauschka, of Vienna. She had two brothers: Duncan Spaeth, a Princeton professor who in his spare time coached crews on Lake Carnegie, and Sigmund Spaeth, a music critic known as the 'tune detective' of radio.

In 1905 Mrs Hauschka went to Europe for piano studies and was a pupil of the famous Polish teacher, Theodore Leschetizky, in Vienna. After 1921 she was a resident of Princeton where she was a frequent accompanist on the piano of Albert Einstein. During World War II Mrs Hauschka was active as a grey lady for the Red Cross, and visited many hospitals where she made sketches of wounded soldiers. She was a well known member of the art colony at Boothbay Harbor, Maine, where she had a summer home. In her artwork Mrs Hauschka used oil and water-colours and also made pastel and charcoal sketches. She was an excellent teacher.

Mrs Hauschka encountered afflictions which she bore with fortitude. However, about two years before her death, illness, loss of her home, and the discovery that she had cataracts, led to a nervous breakdown.

In her correspondence with me about the Nobel portraits, Mrs Hauschka referred to the subjects as 'my noble physicists' (some of whom she knew personally). Her respect and affection for them is apparent in her drawings, and I consider this book as a memorial to Mrs Hauschka.

Mr Peter Geoffrey Cook, also a Princeton artist, kindly consented to continue the series of portraits of the Nobel laureates (1946–1972) in a style consistent with Mrs Hauschka's drawings.

Mr Cook was a 1937 graduate of Princeton University with an AB in architecture, and was a student of the National Academy School and the Art Student League. Mr Cook has taught painting at the National Academy School in New York, at New Hope, Pennsylvania, at Clearwater, Florida, and at Princeton, New Jersey. He is a member of the National Academy of Design and has won some 15 prizes for figure, landscape and portrait painting.

The latest of the portraits (1972–1979) have been made by Mr John B Fleming who, until his recent retirement, was Registrar of Glasgow School of Art, where he had been a member of the full-time teaching staff for almost 30 years. He is well known as a freelance illustrator and has collaborated with several authors on numerous books and newspaper articles.

Acknowledgments

I would like to express my warm gratitude to the Nobel laureates who so kindly corrected and up-dated their biographical notes and offered encouragement for the completion of this book. For its unique feature, the portrait drawings, I acknowledge the beautiful work of the artists mentioned above. Some of these portraits were originally commissioned for *College Physics* by Weber, White and Manning. The Institute of Physics and I thank the McGraw-Hill Book Company for permission to reproduce those drawings in this book.

I would like to express my gratitude to Mr Neville Hankins, Miss Valerie Jones and Mrs Terry Poole for their painstaking work in the preparation of the text and in the design of this book.

Robert L Weber

Contents

Introduction

Alfred Nobel and His Prizes

Alfred Bernhard Nobel (1833–1896) was the son of a Swedish inventor. Never in good health, he was taught chiefly by tutors. He studied engineering at St Petersburg and for about a year in the United States, under John Ericsson. While experimenting in his father's factory, Nobel found that when nitroglycerine is dispersed in an inert material such as fuller's earth or wood pulp the explosive (dynamite) can be handled more safely. He also invented and patented other explosives and detonators.

Nobel acquired an immense fortune from the manufacture of explosives and the exploitation of the Baku oilfields. He never married; he is reputed to have held feelings of guilt and loneliness. He had a sardonic view of his fellow men, tempered with benevolence and hope for the future of mankind.

In his will, Nobel set up a fund of $9 million, 'the interest on which shall be annually distributed in the form of prizes to those who, during the preceding year, shall have conferred the greatest benefit on mankind. The said interest shall be divided into five equal parts, which shall be apportioned as follows: one part to the person who shall have made the most important discovery or invention within the field of physics; one part to the person who shall have made the most important chemical discovery or improvement; one part to the person who shall have made the most important discovery within the domain of physiology or medicine; one part to the person who shall have produced in the field of literature the most outstanding work of an idealistic tendency; and one part to the person who shall have done the most or the best work to promote fraternity between nations, for the abolition or reduction of standing armies and for the holding and promotion of peace congresses.

'The prizes for physics and chemistry shall be awarded by the Swedish Academy of Sciences, that for physiological or medical works by the Karolinska Institute in Stockholm, that for literature by the Academy in Stockholm, and that for champions of peace by a committee of five persons to be elected by the Norwegian Storting [Parliament].'

1

Nobel's estate was bequeathed to a foundation that did not yet exist, and when his will was read in January 1897 it was contested by some of his relatives. Some of the designated prize-awarding bodies (none of whom had been consulted in advance) were hesitant initially to assume the formidable task, but after three years the problems were settled, the Nobel Foundation was created as legatee in June 1900, and by December 1901 the first set of prizes was awarded.

Nobel's stipulation that awards be made for work done 'during the preceding year' was set aside from the start; the selection committee felt that it often takes years to establish the value of a contribution to physics. A Nobel Prize is not awarded for a lifetime's work, but rather for a particular achievement. Arne Tiselius, when head of the Nobel chemistry committee, wrote: 'You cannot give a Nobel Prize for what I call "good behaviour in science." There are . . . great names who have played roles as teachers, organisers, and as sources of inspiration, but when you try to find a particular contribution, a particular discovery, you may fail to do so.'

Nobel awards are made only to living persons, and by tradition no single Nobel Prize has ever been awarded to a group larger than three persons. Each autumn nominations for the Nobel Prizes in science are solicited in some 650 letters sent to members of the Royal Swedish Academy of Sciences, members of the Nobel committees for physics and chemistry, past physics and chemistry prize winners, professors of physics and chemistry at eight Swedish universities and at some 40–50 universities or institutions selected by the Academy, and to other scientists in foreign academies and large research institutions. Some 60–100 physicists may thus be nominated. The Nobel selection officials, an extraordinarily conscientious group, then undertake the staggering spare-time workload of investigating the nominees. A committee chairman has said: 'You cannot define who is best. Therefore you are left with the only alternative: to try to find a particularly worthy candidate.'

Ernest Rutherford 1871–1937

Many physicists assume that Ernest Rutherford received a Nobel Prize. He did, but for chemistry, so the title of this book logically excludes him. Mention of Rutherford in this Introduction is an attempt to compromise an arbitrary limitation and is a recognition of Nobelist Rutherford as the father of nuclear physics.

Ernest Rutherford (Lord Rutherford of Nelson) received the 1908 Nobel Prize for chemistry 'for his investigations into the disintegration of the elements, and the chemistry of radioactive substances.' Rutherford himself found amusement in his transformation to a chemist.

Rutherford was born near Nelson, New Zealand, the fourth of eleven children. His ability in mathematics and physics enabled him to obtain scholarships to Nelson College, Canterbury College, and then Cambridge University. There at the Cavendish Laboratory in 1896 Rutherford and J J Thomson showed that the electrical conductivity produced in air by the newly discovered x-rays could be explained as being due to their producing equal numbers of positively and negatively charged molecules (ions). Electrical conduction and saturation current were explained in terms of the mobility and recombination of these charged particles. Rutherford then investigated the conductivity produced by radioactive materials, and showed that they emitted at least two kinds of radiation which he called alpha (identified as helium nuclei) and beta (electrons). The permanence of atoms was challenged by the view that radioactive atoms were unstable, spontaneously emitting particles, losing mass, and changing their properties as they decayed toward a stable structure.

Rutherford moved to the University of Manchester in 1907. To probe the structure of atoms he suggested to graduate students Hans Geiger and E Marsden an investigation of the scattering of energetic alpha particles by thin metal foils. When they reported that one particle in 8000 striking a platinum foil was deflected by more than a right angle, Rutherford expressed his amazement in saying later it was 'as if you fired a 15-inch naval shell at a piece of tissue paper and the shell came right back and hit you.' These large deflections were explained by Rutherford as arising from a single encounter of an alpha particle and a small, positively charged *nucleus* in the atom. Earlier speculations, by J J Thomson and others, that an atom contained a diffuse positively charged cloud were thus replaced by the nuclear atom model: the positive charge is associated with a massive nucleus of diameter 10^{-5} that of the atom, and is balanced by the negative charge of a surrounding cloud of electrons. This theory was carried further by Niels Bohr, who spent three months with Rutherford and showed how a planetary model for the atom could account for the observed spectrum of hydrogen.

Rutherford's experiments characteristically used simple apparatus and reflected his remarkable intuition in conceiving simple ideas which proved to be correct. To explain why atomic mass increases more rapidly than atomic number, he suggested the existence of a neutral particle, the *neutron*. Chadwick later verified its existence, and the bombardment of nuclei with neutrons opened the way to transmutation of elements and the release of nuclear energy.

Rutherford was a remarkable team leader; nuclear physics research in many universities throughout the world was initiated by men trained at the Cavendish Laboratory by Rutherford. On the occasion of one of his discoveries, a friend said to him, 'You are a lucky man, Rutherford, always on the crest of the wave.' Rutherford smilingly replied, 'Well, I made the wave, didn't I?' He then added, 'At least to some extent.'

In 1915 Rutherford expressed the 'hope that no one discovers how to release the intrinsic energy of radium until man has learned to live at peace with his neighbour.' After his death in 1937, Rutherford's ashes were placed close to Newton's tomb in Westminster Abbey.

Chemistry Laureates Prominent in Physics

Scientists who have done outstanding work in physics and have received a Nobel Prize for chemistry include:

1909   Ernest Rutherford: nuclear atom model
1911   Marie Curie: discovery of radium and polonium
1920   Walther Nernst: infrared investigations, third law of thermo-dynamics
1921   Frederick Soddy: origin and nature of isotopes
1922   Francis William Aston: mass spectroscopy
1932   Irving Langmuir: vacuum phenomena, tungsten filaments, seeding of clouds
1934   Harold C Urey: discovery of heavy hydrogen
1935   Frédéric Joliot and Irène Joliot-Curie: synthesis of new radioactive elements
1936   Peter J W Debye: dipole moments, diffraction of x-rays
1943   Georg von Hevesy: use of isotopes as tracer elements
1944   Otto Hahn: discovery of the fission of heavy nuclei
1949   William Francis Giaque: low-temperature research
1951   Glenn T Seaborg and Edwin M McMillan: production of trans-uranic elements
1966   Robert S Mulliken: spectroscopy, electronic structure of molecules
1968   Lars Onsager: relations fundamental to thermodynamics of irreversible processes
1971   George Herzberg: electron structure and geometry of molecules

Uncrowned Nobel Laureates

Each year more scientists are eligible for Noble Prizes than can receive them. So there are 'uncrowned' laureates who are the peers of prize winners in every respect save that of having the award. These scientists, like the 'immortals' who happen not to be among the forty in the French

Academy have been said by sociologists R Merton and H Zuckerman to occupy the 'forty-first chair.' For some there is still a chance of being elected for a Nobel Prize; for others death precludes election.

Nobel laureates whom I invited to name physicists who should have been or should be awarded a Nobel Prize were cautious in their replies. From them and other sources one might compile a list, certainly not inclusive and probably not completely acceptable to others.

Dmitri I Mendeleev (1834–1907): periodic law, table of the elements
Arnold Johannes Wilhelm Sommerfeld (1868–1915): atomic spectra
Paul Langevin (1872–1946): theory of paramagnetism
Henry Gwyn Jeffreys Moseley (1887–1915): Moseley's law, x-ray evidence for the periodic table
Samuel Abraham Goudsmit (1902–1978): electron spin, atomic structure and spectra
Erwin W Mueller (1911–1977): field emission microscope, field ion microscope, atom-probe field ion microscope
John Archibald Wheeler (1911–   ): atomic and nuclear physics, relativity, geometrodynamics, mu-meson

Wilhelm Conrad Röntgen

1845–1923

Awarded the first Nobel Prize for physics, in 1901, for his discovery of x-rays.

Wilhelm Röntgen first observed on 8 November 1895 that an unidentified radiation from an evacuated glass bulb through which he was passing a high-voltage electric current caused a glow in a little barium platinocyanide screen lying on the bench. In succeeding weeks of intense, isolated activity, Röntgen determined most of the characteristics of these x-rays which would be known in the next 16 years. These he methodically set down in 17 numbered sections in a paper *On a New Kind of Rays, a Preliminary Communication* which he handed to the secretary of the Wurzburg Physical-Medical Society several days after Christmas, for publication in the *Sitzungsberichte*. On the first of January, he mailed reprints of this publication, and some x-ray photographs, to scientists in several countries. 'Then hell broke loose!' as Röntgen later wrote to his friend Zehnder. 'Our domestic peace is gone,' observed Frau Röntgen.

Röntgen's discovery amazed and excited physicists worldwide; many hurriedly used available Crookes tubes and induction coils to repeat his experiments. Newspapers hailed the discovery of x-rays and also showered the public with rumours, fanciful speculations, absurd claims, and some humorous reactions.

Röntgen did not patent his apparatus nor seek financial gain from his discovery. Commercial apparatus quickly became available, and within a few months x-rays were being used in clinics to detect

7

foreign bodies in patients and to help in setting fractured bones. When Röntgen made an x-ray picture of his wife's hand, showing its bones and two rings on her finger, she reacted with apprehension, as did others later, associating the skeletal view with death. Her fears were justified; many experimenters suffered severe skin burns, impaired vision, and other injuries from protracted exposure to x-rays.

Röntgen was born in 1845 in Lennep in the Rhineland, Germany, the indulged only child of a textile merchant; Wilhelm's mother was his father's first cousin. Röntgen spent most of his childhood in Holland, his mother's native country. He graduated as a mechanical engineer from the Federal Polytechnic School of Zürich in 1868, received his PhD there in 1869, and was influenced by Clausius and Kundt to pursue physics.

Röntgen accompanied Kundt first to the University of Würzburg as his assistant, and in 1872 to Strasbourg (then in Germany) where he advanced to associate professor. In 1879 Röntgen became professor of physics at the University of Giessen. His success in many branches of physics (18 papers published by this time, 58 during his lifetime) was largely due to Röntgen's tremendous knowledge of physics literature and his ready progress from theoretical conception of a problem to experimental proof.

When Röntgen was 43, he was invited to succeed F Kohlrausch as professor of physics and director of the new physical institute of the University of Würzburg. He shared with Kohlrausch and Michelson a talent in highly precise physical measurements. For 40 years Röntgen was interested in specific heats and other physical properties of crystals, and at the age of 76 he published an extensive paper on the electrical conductivity of crystals.

Röntgen received 17 out of 29 nominations for the first Nobel Prize awarded in physics. He did not give a Nobel lecture. The only lecture which Röntgen gave on x-rays to a large audience, it seems probable, was a memorable lecture demonstration given on 23 January 1896 in response to appeals from his Würzburg colleagues. At its close, His Excellency Albert von Kölliker told the applauding audience that in 48 years he had never attended a scientific presentation of greater significance. Leading the audience in a cheer, he proposed that henceforth the rays be called 'Röntgen's rays.'

In 1872 Röntgen married Bertha Ludwig, whom he had met in Zürich; they had no children, but in 1887 took Bertha's six-year-old niece to live with them. They shared a love of mountain climbing. Röntgen was an excellent shot, although when hunting it was difficult for him to distinguish red deer against green foliage because of his colour blindness.

Röntgen survived his wife, who died in 1919, and many friends, and in his later years he wrote: 'Loneliness lies heavily upon me. . .' As a result of Germany's defeat in World War I and the inflation of currency, Röntgen lost most of his savings. He had given his Nobel Prize money to the University of Würzburg to advance science and designated other funds for scholarships.

A lifelong friend Margret Boveri wrote of Röntgen: 'His outstanding characteristic was his absolute integrity. Perhaps one can say that Röntgen was in every sense the embodiment of the ideals of the nineteenth century: strong, honest and powerful, devoted to his science and never doubting its value; in spite of self-criticism and great humour, perhaps endowed with some unconscious pathos; of a really rare faithfulness and sense of sacrifice for people, memories, and ideals . . . but open-minded in his acceptance of new ideas . . .'

Pieter Zeeman

1865–1943

Shared the 1902 Nobel Prize for physics with Lorentz for their research on the effect of magnetism on radiation phenomena.

At the Kamerlingh Onnes Laboratory of the University of Leiden is an unusual memorial to an experiment: a stained-glass window whose three panels picture the apparatus and, according to the inscription, 'commemorate the fortunate discovery which became known as the Zeeman effect and which . . . offered a glorious example of the power of cooperative efforts in lifting the spirit.'

        Maxwell's theory of light as electromagnetic in nature led Faraday, Larmor, Lorentz and others to look for effects which a magnetic field might have on light. Before electrons were identified, Larmor showed theoretically that revolving or vibrating atoms constituted an electric current and would be influenced by a magnetic field so as to shift the frequency radiated. Instead of looking for this effect, Larmor stayed with theory: he calculated what line splitting might be expected, found it too small for experimental detection (by a factor of about 2000), and gave up the quest.

        Zeeman independently examined the spectrum of a sodium flame situated in a strong magnetic field using a concave Rowland grating ten feet in radius, and found that the lines were indeed split by the field. The magnitude of the Zeeman effect proved that the *electron* was the radiator, not the atom, as Larmor had assumed. In a lecture entitled 'States of Mind Which Make and Miss Discoveries,' Sir Oliver Lodge in 1929 commented on Zeeman's 1896 discovery and pointed a moral: 'An experimenter should seldom be deterred by a theoretical difficulty for the data on which the theory is dependent *may* be erroneous . . .'

Zeeman's was the third example of the influence of a magnetic field on light to be discovered. In the Faraday effect (1845) when plane-polarised light traverses an isotropic transparent medium placed in a magnetic field which has a component in the direction of the light ray, the plane of vibration is rotated. In the Kerr effect (1875) when plane-polarised light is reflected from a highly polished pole of an electromagnet, the light becomes elliptically polarised.

The discovery of the Zeeman effect may also be considered to have been one of four independent discoveries of the *electron* made within the span of a year, 1896–7. Zeeman's calculation of e/m for the negatively charged particle responsible for the radiation he studied agreed with Thomson's determination of e/m for electrons in deflection experiments.

Pieter Zeeman was born in Zonnemaire, Zeeland, Holland, in 1865, the son of Catharinus Farandinus Zeeman, a Lutheran minister, and Wilhelmina Worst. In 1885 he went to the University of Leiden where he studied under Lorentz and Kamerlingh Onnes and became Lorentz's assistant in 1890. He received his PhD in 1893, with a dissertation on the Kerr effect, for which he won a gold medal. After a semester at the Kohlrausch Institut in Strasbourg, Zeeman returned to Leiden as a *Privatdozent*. In 1895 he was married to Johanna Elisabeth Lebret; they had a son and three daughters.

Zeeman left Leiden to go to the University of Amsterdam in 1897, as a lecturer. He became a professor in 1900, succeeded van der Waals as director of the physical institute in 1908, and in 1923 became director of what was later renamed the Zeeman Laboratory where he worked until his retirement in 1935. In his earlier years at Amsterdam Zeeman was handicapped by equipment inferior to that he had had at Leiden. Until 1907 he worked in a building so shaken by traffic that few of his spectrograms were usable.

In addition to his chief work in magneto-optics, Zeeman made skilful measurements of the speed of light in moving media, essentially repeating in 1915 the Michelson–Morley experiment in water. He showed that the light suffered a velocity change which depended not only on the speed of the water and its index of refraction, but also on how that index varied with wavelength—the dispersion. He also did some isotope research with J de Gier. A master experimentalist, and also an excellent linguist, Zeeman was most effective as a teacher in his regular informal discussions with graduate students. He was never dogmatic, avoided controversy, but had strength of character. He was genial, inspired confidence, and had many sincere friends.

Hendrik Antoon Lorentz

1853–1928

Shared the 1902 Nobel Prize for physics with Zeeman for their investigations regarding the influence of magnetism on the phenomena of radiation.

A survey of Lorentz's whole life's work is, to paraphrase Larmor, a liberal education in the history of physical science during a half century that introduced a new era in physics. Also, Lorentz was one of the most cosmopolitan men of science of all times in a country which since the middle ages had been a seat of productive intellectual activity.

Hendrik Lorentz was born in Arnhem, Holland, in 1853. At the age of 22 he received his doctorate from the University of Leiden. The subject of his thesis was 'The Theory of the Reflection and Refraction of Light,' a prominent problem of the electromagnetic theory of light which Maxwell had left unsolved. Lorentz found the correct conditions to be satisfied at a boundary.

In 1892 Lorentz put forward the theory of electrons which profoundly influenced the development of theoretical physics. In 1895 he published his mathematical investigation of the effect on the shape of a body produced by its moving with speed v through the ether. In it he confirmed FitzGerald's hypothesis that the body would contract by a factor $\sqrt{1 - v^2/c^2}$, where c is the speed of light. Ten years later this result was shown to follow from the theory of relativity.

One deduction from Lorentz's electron theory of matter was that the mass of an electron increased with its velocity. Later experiments with beta rays from radioactive elements confirmed quantitatively his prediction, and once again Lorentz anticipated a finding of the theory of relativity.

When in 1896 Zeeman discovered that the frequencies of spectral lines are altered when the emission occurs in a strong external magnetic field, Lorentz provided the theoretical explanation for the simplest type of this effect. Explanation of the 'anomalous' Zeeman effect, a more complex splitting, required the concepts of quantum mechanics and electron spin as developed by Goudsmit, Uhlenbeck, Dirac and others. But contemporary opinion saw so much of promise in the importance that electron theory would have in understanding spectra and atomic structure that the 1902 Nobel Prize was divided between Zeeman and Lorentz.

In 1904 Lorentz made his greatest contribution to theoretical physics when he showed that James Clerk Maxwell's electromagnetic equations were not invariant with respect to velocity when transformed from one reference frame to another by the hitherto universally accepted Newtonian transformation formulae. These related the time and position coordinates of an event in one reference frame to those assigned to the same event viewed in another frame. Lorentz devised alternative transformation formulae which made Maxwell's equations invariant. Einstein, refusing to believe that there could be one set of such formulae (Newton's) for mechanical relationships and another (Lorentz's) for electrical, accepted Lorentz's transformation formulae as universally applicable. The special or restricted theory of relativity followed from that acceptance.

Most of Lorentz's career was spent at the University of Leiden where he became a professor of physics at the early age of 24. He retired from that university in 1912 when he was appointed director of the Teyler Laboratory at Haarlem, but he continued to go to Leiden once a week to deliver lectures and discuss problems with students. He wrote voluminously for Dutch, French, English and German journals.

In his later years, much of Lorentz's energy went into guiding international scientific gatherings, such as the Solvay Conferences in Brussels. As president, his linguistic abilities, wisdom, charm and modesty led discussions into fruitful channels. After World War I he fostered scientific relations among the former belligerents.

Lorentz was much concerned with education. The Senate of the University of Leiden in 1926 made him an honorary doctor of medicine in appreciation of his attention to the instruction of medical students. He was also concerned with such national undertakings as the draining of the Zuider Zee.

In 1881 Lorentz married Alletta Catherina Kaiser; they had three children. His wife took an active interest in his work and accompanied him on his journeys.

Lorentz was intellectually active until his sudden death at the age of 74. When his funeral took place at Haarlem at noon on Friday

10 February 1928, the State telegraph and telephone services of Holland were suspended for three minutes as a tribute to the greatest man Holland had produced in a generation. Sir Ernest Rutherford, president of the Royal Society, made an oration at the graveside.

Antoine Henri Becquerel

1852–1908

Shared the 1903 Nobel Prize for physics with Pierre and Marie Curie for his discovery of spontaneous radioactivity.

Henri Becquerel was born into a distinguished French scientific family. His grandfather, father, and Henri, each in his turn, were members of the Academy of Sciences and professors of physics at the Museum of Natural History. Henri also held chairs of physics at the Ecole Polytechnique and at the Conservatoire National des Arts et Métiers— and became chief engineer in the National Administration of Bridges and Highways.

In 1874 Becquerel married Lucie-Zoé-Marie Jamin, daughter of a physics professor. She died in 1887, a few weeks after the birth of their son Jean.

Becquerel's early optical researches were concerned with the rotation of plane-polarised light by magnetic fields (the Faraday effect), infrared spectra, and absorption of light in crystals, particularly its dependence on the plane of polarisation and direction of propagation. With this research he obtained his doctorate from the Faculty of Sciences of Paris (1888) and election to the Academy of Sciences (1889). He then became relatively inactive in research.

Becquerel married his second wife in 1891; she was the daughter of E Lorieux, inspector general of mines. By 1894 Becquerel had succeeded to his father's two chairs of physics, at the Conservatoire and the Musée; he was also lecturing at the Polytechnique and serving as chief engineer for Bridges and Highways.

15

In 1896 Becquerel learned of Röntgen's discovery of x-rays and that they seemed to originate at a fluorescent spot where the electron beam impinged on the wall of the glass tube. Becquerel was acquainted with luminescent crystals, and began to hunt for a crystalline emitter of penetrating radiation, similar to x-rays. In March 1896 he reported to the Academy of Sciences that crystals of potassium uranyl sulphate made a record on a photographic plate wrapped in black paper, even though both crystals and plate lay in total darkness. This was puzzling since the luminescence of this salt ceases immediately when the sunlight (ultraviolet radiation) that excites it is removed. He then tested non-luminescent compounds of uranium and found that they too emitted the penetrating rays. When in May he found that a disc of pure uranium metal also produced the penetrating rays, Becquerel's discovery of radioactivity was established.

Becquerel had little enthusiasm for physical theories, but when he did follow a hypothesis his critical power enabled him, when necessary, to redirect his investigation. Thus while he searched for x-rays in phosphorescence, he managed to discover the radioactivity inherent in uranium.

Only gradually was it realised that other elements might emit such radiation. Marie Curie and G C Schmidt found that thorium was a ray-emitter. Marie and Pierre Curie looked for unknown elements with this property, and so discovered polonium and radium. The Curies coined the term *radioactivity* for the spontaneous disintegration of certain unstable atoms (nuclei) with emission of the 'radiations' not then fully identified. So Becquerel's rays became known as radioactive radiation.

When Becquerel obtained a small specimen of radium bromide from the Curies, he subjected the rays it emitted to the influence of an electromagnet. By this means he found three categories: (1) rays which were positively charged particles of the dimensions of an atom (alpha rays), which were scarcely deflected by the magnet; (2) rays (now recognised as electrons) which were deflected considerably by the magnetic field in the opposite direction to alpha rays; and (3) rays which were not at all deflected by the magnet and which, like Röntgen rays, were probably electromagnetic waves. In 1901 he published the first evidence of a radioactive transformation of one element into another.

Becquerel became president of the Academy of Sciences in 1908 and in the same year he was elected to a more influential position as one of the Academy's two permanent secretaries, serving with Darboux who had taught him mathematics some 40 years earlier at the Lycée Louis-le-Grand. Becquerel died soon after at the ancestral home of his wife's family in Brittany.

Pierre Curie

1859–1906

Pierre Curie and Marie Curie shared the 1903 Nobel Prize for physics with Henri Becquerel for their work on the phenomena of the radiation discovered by Becquerel.

Pierre Curie's grandfather and father were physicians of relatively modest means. His family were close in affection and intellectual interests. His parents recognised that Pierre's independent and dreamy nature would not fit the usual schools, so he was taught at home, where he showed a love of nature. When given a tutor at the age of 14, Pierre showed on aptitude for both mathematics and physics, and at 16 he obtained his *licence.* He went to the Sorbonne for further studies, assisted in the preparation of physics lectures in the School of Pharmacy where his brother Jacques Paul was a chemical assistant, and in 1877 received his master's degree.

Curie taught for 22 years at the Ecole de Physique et Chimie in Paris where, for the twelve years before he obtained his doctorate, his salary was comparable to that of a labourer. His first research was with P Desains in the determination of the wavelengths of infrared rays, using a novel system of a thermocouple and a wire grating (1880). Pierre was always close to his brother, Jacques Paul, three years older than he. In collaboration they discovered that 'some crystals when compressed in particular directions show positive and negative charges on . . . their surfaces, the charges being proportional to the pressure and disappearing when the pressure is withdrawn.' They published accurate measurements for the 'piezoelectric' effect in quartz and tourmaline in 1881. In

1882 they verified Lippmann's prediction of a converse effect: the production of a minute compression in a piezoelectric crystal by an electric field. They then developed a practical application, by designing a piezoelectric quartz electrometer—the forerunner of modern quartz controls for timepieces and radio transmitters. This first period of collaboration in Curie's career ended when in 1883 Jacques left for a post at the University of Montpelier.

Curie then started a second period in his career, conducting isolated but fruitful research on crystals and magnetism. In 1885 he published the first of his papers on the theoretical relations between crystallography and physics.

At the age of 35 Curie obtained his doctorate with a thesis on the magnetic properties of materials. The Curie law states: 'The properties of diamagnetic materials are generally independent of temperature but for paramagnetic materials the susceptibility is inversely proportional to the absolute temperature.' The temperature at which the transition from ferromagnetism to paramagnetism takes place has become known as the 'Curie point'.

In 1895 Pierre married Marie Sklodowska in a civil ceremony, since he professed no religious creed. Two daughters were born to them, Irène in 1897 and Eve in 1904. For her doctoral thesis at the Sorbonne, Marie studied the phenomenon of the penetrating radiation emitted by uranium compounds which Becquerel had discovered.

Pierre entered a third period in his career, working with Marie on the isolation of the new element radium, which was announced in 1898. In 1899 André Debierne, a student of Pierre Curie, discovered actinium, and in the same year the Curies discovered induced radioactivity in the action of polonium or radium on inert substances. Pierre published two papers on the physiological action of radium rays after subjecting his arm to a burn, and studying their toxic effects on mice and guinea pigs. In 1903 Pierre found that 1 g of radium salts released 22 500 cal/h. The heat which Curie first identified with atomic energy (spontaneous decay) is much less than that now produced by induced nuclear fission. In Stockholm, Pierre expressed concern about radium in criminal hands. But, 42 years before Hiroshima, he said: 'The question therefore arises whether it be to the advantage of humanity to know the secrets of nature . . . I am among those who believe with Nobel that humanity will obtain more good than evil from future discoveries.'

On 19 April 1906, while crossing the Place Dauphine in a rainstorm, Curie slipped and fell beneath the wheels of a dray which killed him instantly. Those who knew Pierre Curie valued him as a man of the very highest character, kindly, of great gentleness and completely free from vanity. With 58 publications, Curie's worth in science was first recognised abroad and only late in his career did he receive a Sorbonne professorship and financial support which, if it had been available earlier, could have relieved the wretched conditions under which he and Marie performed much of their research.

Marie Sklodowska Curie

1867–1934

Marie Curie shared the 1903 Nobel Prize for physics with Pierre Curie and Henri Becquerel; she was also awarded the 1911 Nobel Prize for chemistry for her discovery of radium and polonium.

Maria Sklodowska was born in 1867, the fourth daughter in the family of a Warsaw school teacher, and was left motherless at four. Her parents, descendants of Catholic landowners, were intellectuals but their opportunities were restricted by the Russian domination of Poland. Her father took boarders into his home; Marie helped with housework and became a governess for six years so that her sister Bronie might study in Paris and become a medical doctor. In 1891 Marie also went to Paris and after four years of spartan living and intense study she received a *licence* or master's degree in physics, rank first (1893) and in mathematics, rank second (1894).

In 1895 Marie was married to Pierre Curie in a civil ceremony, followed by a honeymoon which was a three-week bicycle tour. Living in near poverty they gave up recreation and social contacts for their devotion to research. Marie's first scientific work was on the magnetic properties of tempered steel (1898). Then, learning of Becquerel's discovery, she selected the radiation from uranium for her doctor's thesis. From the observation that uranium ore (pitchblende) was several times more radioactive than uranium, the Curies came to believe that the ore contained a new element or elements more active than uranium.

Working under miserable conditions in a shed, the Curies

carried out the chemical concentration of some 100 kg of uranium ore supplied by the Austrian government to obtain at last a specimen from which spectroscopic identification was made of a new element which they called *polonium*, chemically similar to bismuth but radioactive. Marie later discovered a second element in pitchblende, which she named *radium*. By 1902 she had isolated 0·1 g of pure radium salt and had determined the atomic mass of radium as 225 (226 now accepted). In 1910 with the help of André Debierne she finally obtained 1 g of the pure radium metal. The Curies also determined that the beta rays emitted by radium were negatively charged particles (electrons).

A daughter Irène was born to the Curies in 1897. In 1904, a month before the birth of their second daughter Eve, Marie was finally named as Pierre's assistant at the Faculté des Sciences where she had long worked without pay.

Confident of medical and industrial applications, a French industrialist named Armet de L'Isle constructed a factory near Paris for the extraction of radium from pitchblende. The Curies took out no patents and claimed no royalties, thereby renouncing a fortune. After Pierre's death in a road accident in 1906, Marie's life was even more circumscribed, devoted to raising her daughters and continuing her research. The physics chair created for Pierre (1904) was bestowed on Marie in 1906 and for the first time a woman taught at the Sorbonne. As had Pierre, Marie declined the recognition of the Légion d'Honneur (1911), asking only for the means to work. She was nominated for the French Academy of Sciences (1911), but was rejected by one vote after a slanderous campaign which labelled Marie a Jewess to Catholic supporters of her competitor Edouard Branly, and labelled her a Catholic to free-thinkers. Further, 'Women cannot be part of the Institute of France,' declared M Amagat. Marie's co-workers were stunned by this defeat but she made no comment on her rejection for extra-scientific reasons.

Marie worked with the Radiology Congress in Brussels in 1910 to establish official standards for radium needed in research and therapy. The Congress defined the *curie* as the unit of radioactivity. During World War I Marie, with the aid of private gifts, equipped ambulances (which she could drive) with portable x-ray equipment; she became head of radiological services for the Red Cross. Her wartime experience led her to write the book *La Radiologie et la Guerre* (1920).

Through the Radium Institute (Warsaw, 1913), the Curie Foundation (1920), and her membership of the Academy of Medicine (1922), Marie Curie pursued goals Pierre had sought, such as 'curietherapy' and the establishment of safety standards for workers. Marie Curie has been honoured more than any other scientist on the postage stamps of many nations; many picture the benefits of x-ray diagnosis, the use of radium in the treatment of cancer, and the gift of 1 g of radium to Madame Curie by grateful women of America in 1921.

Madame Curie's health declined. She had cataract operations and suffered from lesions on her fingers and from anaemia, lethal effects of her prolonged exposure to nuclear radiations. She died in a sanatorium in the French Alps in 1934.

John William Strutt (Third Baron Rayleigh)

1842–1919

Awarded the 1904 Nobel Prize for physics for his investigations on the density of the more important gases and for his discovery of argon, one of the results of those investigations.

Rayleigh was interested in Prout's hypothesis (1815) that all atomic weights were exact multiples of that of hydrogen. However, the best value for the density of oxygen relative to hydrogen known to Rayleigh was 15·96, not exactly 16 as required by Prout's hypothesis. So, for more than 20 years Rayleigh conducted what he called 'stand-by' research on refining measurements of gas densities. Discrepancies in the apparent density of nitrogen derived from air and from ammonia led Rayleigh (1895) to identify as an impurity in air a new element which he named *argon* (Greek, 'inactive'). In the same year Rayleigh's collaborator W Ramsay, looking for possible argon compounds, found *helium* (Greek, 'sun'), so named because it was responsible for a bright yellow line in the solar spectrum which, N Lockyer observed in 1868, did not correspond to any known terrestrial element.

Lord Rayleigh was born John William Strutt at Terling Place in Witham, Essex, in 1847, the son of James Strutt, second Baron Rayleigh, and Elizabeth (Vicars) Strutt. His early education was interrupted by ill health. He studied at Trinity College, Cambridge, under the mathematician E J Routh, obtained a scholarship to study astronomy in 1864, and received his BA degree in 1865 as senior wrangler and first Smith's Prizeman. He held a fellowship at Trinity College from 1866 to 1871. In 1868, he made a trip to the United States, then in reconstruction after the Civil War. In 1871, Strutt married Evelyn Balfour, sister of Arthur James Balfour; they had three sons.

Much of Rayleigh's experimental work was performed at the family estate at Terling. Cambridge University first established a professorship in experimental physics in 1871; the Cavendish Laboratory was opened in 1874, with James Clerk Maxwell as its first director. Following Maxwell's untimely death in 1879, Lord Rayleigh accepted the Cavendish professorship, perhaps influenced by a loss of income from his estate due to the agricultural depression of the late 1870s.

Rayleigh worked vigorously in pioneering elementary laboratory instruction at Cambridge. To foster a spirit of community among the advanced students he sought to identify the laboratory with a project in which a combination of workers was necessary: the standardisation of electrical units. Further, a tea break was introduced to encourage informal discussions. Tea was served in a room where other experiments were kept going and invited attention.

Rayleigh's professional activities were prodigious. He maintained voluminous correspondence with active colleagues such as Lord Kelvin and Sir Arthur Schuster. He was influential in the establishment of the National Physical Laboratory at Teddington, in 1900. He served for eleven years as secretary of the Royal Society of London and was its president from 1905 to 1908. In 1887 Rayleigh was appointed professor of natural philosophy at the Royal Institution of Great Britain, founded in 1800 by the American Benjamin Thompson, Count Rumford, to encourage popular interest in science and its useful applications. There Rayleigh gave over 110 popular lectures in the afternoon series, mainly on sound, light, and aspects of electricity and magnetism in which he was doing research.

From its inception in 1909, Rayleigh was president of the Advisory Committee on Aeronautics, whose actions were important in World War I. Rayleigh served on the governing bodies of some six educational institutions, and from 1908 until his death he was chancellor of Cambridge University. When he was awarded the Nobel Prize in 1904, Rayleigh gave the prize money to Cambridge for an extension to the Cavendish Laboratory.

In addition to the two-volume *Theory of Sound* (1877), the collected edition of Rayleigh's scientific publications includes 445 papers covering almost every branch of physics. Two of his favourite fields were light and sound. His name is associated with the Rayleigh–Jeans law governing radiation from a black-body source, and Rayleigh's law of scattering which states that the scattering of sunlight by particles in the atmosphere is proportional to the inverse fourth power of the wavelength—the reason why the sky appears blue.

Rayleigh was able to continue his work until the very end of his life. When he died at Terling in 1919, three recently completed scientific papers were still unpublished, the very last one on acoustics.

Rayleigh, together with Kelvin, Maxwell and Stokes, formed the great group of nineteenth-century physicists who made British science famous worldwide.

Philipp Lenard

1862–1947

Awarded the 1905 Nobel Prize for physics for his work on cathode rays.

Philipp Lenard was one of the most skilful experimental physicists of his time, but the consequences of his work were repeatedly anticipated by others in making solid additions to the theoretical structure of physics. He was born at Pozsony (later Pressburg and Bratislava), Czechoslovakia, the only son of a wealthy wine merchant who would have preferred to have his son continue that business. Lenard studied at the universities of Budapest, Vienna, Berlin and Heidelberg, under Bunsen, Helmholtz, Königsberger and Quincke. After receiving his doctorate *summa cum laude* at Heidelberg in 1886, Lenard taught at Breslau, Aachen and Kiel. In 1907 Lenard succeeded Quincke as professor of experimental physics at Heidelberg, where he remained for most of his life.

In an early paper (1887) Lenard had explained why air near a waterfall is negatively charged while the water is positively charged, through the spraying and bursting of water drops. He devised a bismuth wire detector for measuring magnetic fields (1888), investigated ionisation by ultraviolet light (1899), and the electrical properties of flames (1902). He showed that an electron must possess a certain minimum energy before it can ionise an atom, and he made a respectable estimate of 11 volts as the ionisation potential of hydrogen.

Lenard is chiefly known for his pioneering work on cathode rays. Hertz showed in 1892 that these rays could pass through thin metal foil. Lenard, then Hertz's assistant, made a cathode-ray tube with

26

a 'Lenard window' through which he obtained outside the tube a beam of cathode rays. He measured their absorption in various specimens, showed that it was roughly proportional to density, and that the rays became more penetrating with increasing voltage. Like Perrin, Wien and Thomson, Lenard established that cathode rays consisted of negatively charged particles, a discovery for which he claimed priority.

When Lenard found that high-energy cathode-ray particles could pass through atoms, he proposed that the positive and negative charges within the atom were grouped in tight couplets, which he called 'dynamids.' Lenard was right in suspecting that the space within an atom was relatively empty, but it was Rutherford who suggested the planetary structure which became the accepted model of the atom. Lenard was profoundly disappointed that in his experiments with cathode-ray tubes he had not discovered x-rays, rather than Röntgen. In studying light emission, Lenard thought that the release and return of an electron was involved, but it was Bohr's model that was accepted. In 1902, while at Kiel, Lenard discovered some important properties of the photoelectric effect, which Einstein interpreted in 1905 using the concept of light quanta.

At the outbreak of World War I, Lenard was ultra-nationalistic, writing that the work of German researchers was continually hidden and plagiarised by British scientists. After Germany's defeat, Lenard incited his students against the Weimar Republic and toward rearmament.·

Lenard, an experimentalist, found repugnant the mathematically difficult theories which came to play an important part in physics. The new theories he labelled 'dogmatic Jewish physics.' In the preface to his four-volume *Deutsche Physik* (1936–37) Lenard wrote: 'German physics? one will ask—I could have said Aryan physics or physics of the Nordic man, physics of the reality explorers, of the truth seekers, the science of those who have founded natural science . . . Science, like everything man produces, is racially determined.'

When Hertz died in 1894 at the age of 36, Lenard generously devoted time to publishing his collected works. But when in 1929 Lenard published *Grosse Naturforscher* (translated as *Great Men of Science*, 1935) he had already developed his racial ideology and he revealed that he had detected a split personality in Hertz, whose father's family was Jewish; Hertz's theoretical works, thought Lenard, were a product of his Jewish inheritance. At a 1920 conference on relativity at Bad Nauheim, according to Max Born, Lenard directed 'sharp, malicious attacks against Einstein, with an unconcealed anti-Semitic bias.'

Lenard was one of the early champions of National Socialism and Hitler came to value this Nobel laureate who, unlike other German scientists who treated Hitler as someone only half-educated, had supported him from the beginning. With Lenard as his physics adviser, Hitler occasionally referred to nuclear physics as 'Jewish physics' and delayed its support. This and his expulsion of Jewish scientists from the Third Reich had a damaging effect on German efforts to develop nuclear weapons.

After World War II, Lenard, who was 83, left Heidelberg to live in the small village of Messelhausen, where he died in 1947.

Sir Joseph John Thomson

1856–1940

Awarded the 1906 Nobel Prize for physics for theoretical and experimental investigations of the passage of electricity through gases.

Vortex rings, of which smoke rings are an example, appealed to nineteenth-century physicists, including Helmholtz and Lord Kelvin, as models for atoms and molecules: if vortex rings are linked together they will retain the linking. J J Thomson wrote a prize-winning essay (1883) on the theory of vortex rings and this led to his experiments on gaseous discharges. Thomson seized on x-rays, discovered by Röntgen in 1895, as a convenient way of making a gas conducting—he used the word *ionisation*—and he was on his way to the discovery of the electron.

There had been electron theories of a sort in the nineteenth century: that of Lorentz had explained the Zeeman effect (1896), and G J Stoney had coined the name *electron* for a hypothetical unit of charge suggested by Faraday's laws of electrolysis (1833). For certain cathode rays, Thomson measured the magnetic deflection and then the heating effect that corresponded to the transport of a unit of charge. The first gives e/mv, and the second e/mv^2, from which e/m and v can be calculated. He found that for these particles e/m was more than about 2000 times larger than the charge to mass ratio Faraday had found for the lightest atom. Further experiments at the Cavendish Laboratory using deflections by electric and magnetic fields and path-tracing in the Wilson cloud chamber completed the identification of the electron. It was established that all matter contains at least this one common constituent.

Joseph John ('J J') Thomson was born in Cheetham, a suburb of Manchester, in 1856. His father, of Scottish origin, was a bookseller and publisher. At the age of 14 Thomson entered Owens College, and in three years of engineering courses Osborne Reynolds taught him to approach a new problem 'by independent thinking rather than by consulting a bibliography.' In 1880 Thomson received his BA from Trinity College, Cambridge; he was second wrangler in the mathematics tripos and second Smith's Prizeman.

Soon after, in a paper on energy transformations, Thomson concluded that energy must have both mass and momentum, a partial forecast of the dual nature of moving charged particles and Einstein's $E = mc^2$. Later, Thomson's study of the scattering of x-rays by the electrons in atoms, combined with Barkla's results, showed that the number of electrons in an atom is about one half the atomic weight, pointing toward the importance of atomic number. He made advances in optics, electricity and magnetism, radioactivity, photoelectricity and thermionics. His suggestion of a 'spotted wave front' anticipated Einstein's treatment of light quanta.

Thomson was Cavendish Professor of experimental physics, Cambridge University (1894–1919), became master of Trinity College in 1918, and was professor of natural philosophy, Royal Institution of Great Britain (1905–1918). During World War I Thomson was adviser to various government departments and a member of the Bureau of Inventions and Research.

'J J' was humble, devout, generous, a good conversationalist in many fields, and had an uncanny memory. He enjoyed popularity with both dons and servants. He valued and inspired enthusiasm in his students. They had the custom of honouring him at their annual dinners; the 'Postprandial Proceedings of the Cavendish Society' featured songs about physics and physicists. Thomson's inspiration built a research school in physics whose students went out from Cambridge to become professors in some 55 of the world's universities. Seven of Thomson's trainees became Nobel Prize winners in their turn. When his superbly useful life ended, Thomson was buried in Westminster Abbey close to Newton, Darwin, Lord Kelvin, Herschel and Rutherford.

Albert Abraham Michelson

1852–1931

Awarded the 1907 Nobel Prize for physics for his optical instruments of precision and the spectroscopic and metrologic investigations which he carried out by means of them.

A man of medium size, rugged physique, and black hair and eyes, Albert Michelson was once described by Einstein as the artist in science: 'His greatest joy seemed to come from the beauty of the experiment itself, and the elegance of the method employed.' Devising instruments sensitive to one part in 4×10^9, he was 'the man who taught the world to measure.' Professor K B Hasselberg, a member of the selection committee for the Nobel Prize, made this remarkable statement: 'I am also of the opinion that this choice . . . is the best of all which have been made to this date. Our earlier laureates . . . are indeed men of eminent scientific merits, but for my part I must consider the work of Michelson as more fundamental and also by far more delicate . . .'

Born in 1852 at Strelno in Prussia, Albert was taken to America at the age of four by his parents, Samuel and Rosalie Michelson. In 1869 Michelson travelled from San Francisco to Washington, saw President Grant, and gained a special appointment to Annapolis. Following his graduation, Ensign Michelson was assigned to Annapolis as an instructor under his former professor, Commander W T Sampson whose niece, Margaret Heminway, Michelson married in 1877. They had three children and were later divorced. Michelson demonstrated to midshipmen the measurement of the velocity of light. He pursued this measurement, important for theory and for navigation, with increasingly refined equipment for the rest of his life.

During 1880–82 Michelson studied in Berlin, Heidelberg and Paris. In Helmholtz's laboratory, with funds from Alexander Graham Bell, Michelson designed and had built an 'interferential refractometer.' This he used to test for an 'aether wind' associated with the progress of the Earth in its orbit. The instrument permitted comparison of the speed of two pencils of light split from a single monochromatic beam, made to travel paths at right angles to each other, and reunited. The entire instrument, floated on mercury, could be rotated between observations. At different angles it was expected that the interference fringes formed by the reunited pencils would shift past a reference mark, thereby giving data from which could be calculated the 'absolute motion' of the Earth, relative to the 'aether.' No significant fringe shift was found. This null result called into question the hypotheses of A J Fresnel about a universal stationary aether, and that of G G Stokes about astronomical aberration. Michelson was awarded the Rumford Premium in 1888, 'not only for what he has established, but also for what he has unsettled.'

In 1881, after twelve years of service, Michelson resigned from the Navy. In 1882 he was appointed professor of physics in the new Case School of Applied Science in Cleveland, Ohio, where he continued precision optical measurements. From measurement of indices of refraction he obtained strong evidence for the wave theory of light. In collaboration with E W Morley, professor of chemistry, Michelson repeated a much-perfected version of the experiment to detect aether drift. The 1887 'Michelson–Morley experiment' also gave a null result. In searching for a suitable wavelength in terms of which to evaluate the metre, Michelson discovered the fine structure of spectral lines, which became important in modern atomic theory.

When Michelson was appointed head of the department of physics at the University of Chicago (1892–1930), President Harper provided an environment that approached Michelson's ideals for graduate-level education and financial support for research that interested him. His remarkable judgment in selecting staff is indicated by the later careers of S W Stratton, G E Hale, R A Millikan and A H Compton. Michelson devised the echelon spectrograph (1898) to investigate the Zeeman effect, developed astrophysical spectroscopy, performed with G H Gale the Earth-tide experiment (1916), and produced excellent optical gratings (one had a resolving power of 600 000 in the sixth order).

In the 1920s Michelson began to spend more time in California; there he worked in the laboratories at Mount Wilson and at the California Institute of Technology, and enjoyed tennis, chess, billiards and water-colour painting. With F G Pease in 1921 he extended the interferometer method to determine the diameter of α Orionis (Betelgeuse) with a margin of error equal to an angle that could be subtended by the diameter of an ordinary pinhead laid between radii

1000 miles in length.

Michelson's second marriage (1899) was to Edna Stanton, of Lake Forest. They had three daughters.

Today, Michelson is most often called to mind for the relations between his experimental work and Einstein's theories of relativity. The influence of the aether-drift tests on Lorentz, FitzGerald, Poincaré, Lord Kelvin, Larmor, and other theoreticians around 1900 is quite apparent. But in response to an enquiry in 1954, Einstein said of the Michelson–Morley experiment '. . . not a considerable influence. I even do not remember if I knew of it at all when I wrote my first paper on the subject [1905].'

When asked why he made the considerable effort to measure c over a 22 mile path between Mount Wilson and Mount San Antonio (1926), Michelson started a half-hearted defence of its value to science, then added laughingly, 'But the real reason is because it is such good fun!' Michelson died in 1931 after several strokes suffered during preparations to measure c in a three-foot diameter pipe a mile long which could be evacuated.

Gabriel Lippmann

1845–1921

Awarded the 1908 Nobel Prize for physics for his method of photographic reproduction of colours, based upon the phenomenon of interference.

In his brief Nobel lecture at the Royal Swedish Academy of Sciences, Lippmann described his method of producing photographs in natural colours: 'A plate covered with a sensitive photographic layer is placed in a holder containing mercury. During the exposure the mercury is in contact with the sensitive layer, forming a mirror. After the exposure the plate is developed in the usual manner. When it is dry the colours appear, seen by reflection, and are permanent.

'This result is due to an interference phenomenon taking place inside the sensitive layer. During the exposure interference takes place between the incident rays and those reflected by the mirror, with the formation of interference fringes at a distance of half a wavelength. It is these fringes that are impressed photographically within the thickness of the film and there form a sort of cast of the luminous rays. When the photograph is afterward viewed by white light, the colour is seen because there is selective reflection; the plate at each point sends back to the eye only that simple colour which has been impressed on it, the other colours being destroyed by interference. Thus the eye sees at each point the colour present in the image; but it is only a phenomenon of selective reflection, as in the case of the soap bubble or mother of pearl, the photograph itself being formed of colourless material . . .

'This explanation can be verified by an experiment . . . Here is a photograph of the spectrum, which I will project on the screen: you see the colours are brilliant. We now moisten the photograph: now there is no colour; this is because the gelatine has swollen and the intervals between the images of the interference fringes have become two or three times too great. Wait a minute while the water evaporates: we see the colours reappear as the drying proceeds; and they reappear in an order we might have foreseen: the red, corresponding to the longest wavelength, reappears first . . .'

Because Lippmann's method required relatively long exposure times and produced unsaturated colours it was eventually replaced by three-colour dye processes using absorbing dyes, as suggested by Maxwell.

Gabriel Lippmann was born in Hollerich, Luxembourg, in 1845. His parents were French and settled in Paris while he was still a boy. Early in his career Lippmann helped Bertin in the publication of *Annales de Chimie et de Physique*, by abstracting German papers, thereby developing an interest in research in electricity. In 1873 he was appointed to a scientific mission and visited Germany. At Heidelberg, W Kühne, professor of physiology, showed him an experiment in which a drop of mercury covered with dilute sulphuric acid contracts on being touched lightly with an iron wire and regains its original shape when the wire is removed. Lippmann recognised that there was a relation between the contact voltage and surface tension. His systematic study of the phenomenon led to his invention of a capillary electrometer capable of measuring changes of potential of the order of 0·001 volt.

Lippmann showed that the electro-capillary phenomena are reversible. Using them he built an engine which turned when a current was supplied to it, but produced a current when it was turned by hand. Also, from the existence of piezoelectricity he deduced that a crystal should lengthen in an electrostatic field, a result which was confirmed by Pierre and Jacques Curie. In as early as 1879, Lippmann reported to the French Academy that there was an apparent increase in the mechanical inertia of a charged body.

In 1883 Lippmann was appointed professor of mathematical physics in the Faculté des Sciences in Paris and in 1886 director of the Research Laboratory. He made contributions to the design of instruments for seismology and astronomy; most notable was his invention of the coelostat. Lippmann died at sea while returning from a visit to the United States and Canada, in 1921.

Guglielmo Marconi

1874–1937

Shared the 1909 Nobel Prize for physics with Ferdinand Braun for their development of wireless telegraphy.

In his Nobel lecture, delivered in English, Marconi told his audience: 'I never studied physics or electrotechnics in the regular manner, although as a boy I was deeply interested in those subjects . . . I was acquainted with the works of Hertz, Branly and Righi.' Guglielmo Marconi was born in Bologna, Italy, the second son of Guiseppe Marconi, a wealthy landowner, and his second wife, Irish-born Annie Jameson.

When in 1894 Marconi learned of Hertz's laboratory experiments with electromagnetic waves, he was immediately curious to know how far the waves might travel, and he began to experiment, with the assistance of Professor A Righi. His initial apparatus resembled Hertz's in its use of a spark-gap oscillator and dipole antennae, but it replaced Hertz's spark-gap ring detector with a Branly coherer to which Marconi added a tapper, similar to that of an electric bell, to tap the coherer back to its non-conducting state after signal reception. In 1895 he achieved a transmission distance of 1·5 miles on his family's estate, and at about this time he conceived of 'wireless telegraph' communication by keying the transmitter in telegraph code.

In 1896 Marconi moved to London. He successfully demonstrated his apparatus for Sir William H Preece, engineer-in-chief of the Post Office, and in 1897 a message was sent from Queen Victoria to the Prince of Wales on the royal yacht. In the same year Marconi founded Marconi's Wireless Telegraph Ltd, and in 1899 he went to America to report on the 1900 elections using his wireless equipment. In Newfoundland he received the signal 'S' sent from Cornwall, England. This 1901 achievement was made possible by refraction and reflection of the signal in a conduction layer in the upper atmosphere, suggested Heaviside and Kennelly. Marconi established wireless telegraph communication across the Atlantic Ocean in 1902 and provided a daily news service for trans-Atlantic liners in 1904.

Marconi combined remarkable physical intuition, engineering skill, and business acumen. He very soon increased the range of the spark-coil transmitter by grounding one terminal and connecting the other to a tall antenna. He produced a tunable, syntonic system in 1901 by inserting capacitance and variable inductance between earth and the antenna. Without much mathematics, he shaped his antennae to beam the signals, thus increasing their range. After radio amateurs discovered that short waves even from low-power transmitters were effective, Marconi threw himself into developing a reliable worldwide network of communication. Wireless telegraphy was a welcome aid to maritime safety, in direction-finding for ships, and in rescue operations. From 1921 onwards, Marconi used his steam yacht *Elettra* as his home, laboratory and mobile receiving station.

Marconi's first wife, Beatrice O'Brien, was of an aristocratic Irish family. His second wife was Contessa Criltina Bezzi-Scali.

Marconi was predominantly interested in the practical applications of scientific knowledge. He was an engineer in the definition of the Institution of Civil Engineers: 'one who utilises and controls the energies of Nature for the assistance and benefit of mankind.'

Carl Ferdinand Braun

1850–1918

Shared the 1909 Nobel Prize for physics with Guglielmo Marconi for their development of wireless telegraphy.

Even while pioneers were increasing the range of wireless telegraphy, most experiments were of the cut-and-try variety. Braun approached the problem as a scientist. For example, no one knew the wavelength of the waves generated by the Marconi transmitter. It was thought that short waves, of the order of 1 m, were generated at the spark gap in the oscillator. Braun recognised that the antenna, grounded through the spark gap, should be considered as a whole and that the broadcast waves were much longer.

To further his studies, in 1897 Braun invented the cathode-ray tube (or Braun tube) in which a narrow cathode-ray (electron) beam produced a glowing spot on a fluorescent screen. By allowing the varying voltage or magnetic field of the wave being investigated to control the deflection of the beam, Braun caused it to draw glowing patterns of wave phenomena. This invention (his original tube had a cold cathode) probably ranks second only in importance to de Forest's radio tube (audion) in the field of communication, and is indispensable in television receivers and in many analytical instruments.

Ferdinand Braun was born in 1850 in Fulda, Principality of Hesse, Germany, the son of Konrad and Franziska (Gohring) Braun. He studied at the universities of Marburg and Berlin and left there with Quincke to become his assistant at Würzburg. He received his doctorate from Berlin, and later became headmaster of the Thomas School in

Leipzig. He was one of the few high school teachers who had enthusiasm and energy enough to be active in science despite strenuous teaching responsibilities. Braun had broad interests and simple, even democratic, tastes. He enjoyed travelling, painting and sketching. As a by-product of his travels, Braun wrote a book of juvenile fiction on the American Indian in 1891. Braun was married to Amelie Büchler in 1885; they had two sons and two daughters.

Braun was professor of theoretical physics successively at Marburg 1876, Strasbourg 1880, and Karlsruhe 1883, and professor of experimental physics at Tübingen. He set up an institute of physics at that university and then returned to the faculty at Strasbourg in 1895. Braun had extraordinary talent and originality in devising experimental apparatus. For example, to study the dielectric constant of rock salt, he devised the Braun high-tension electrometer. After early work in mechanics and thermodynamics, Braun was chiefly occupied in electrical research. He found that crystals of mineral sulphides conducted a current in only one direction—a discovery employed many years later in crystal radio receivers. He inspired the help of able assistants, men like Cantor and Zenneck, who became president of the Deutsche Museum in Munich.

It was at Strasbourg that Braun made great advances in wireless telegraphy. He showed how to produce waves that were more powerful and less damped, and how to separate signals from different sending stations at a receiver. The Marconi transmitter operated with an *open* oscillatory circuit; this acted as a good radiator but could not generate much power. Braun devised a transmitter which consisted essentially of a *closed* circuit of a capacitor and spark gap (driven by an inductor) coupled to an antenna that contained no spark gap. Oscillations in the capacitor circuit generated substantial currents in the radiating antenna. By 'tuning' a transmitter to a narrow frequency band Braun minimised interference among different transmitters. He developed directional antennae to conserve power by beaming the signal in the desired direction. He measured for the first time the field strength of radio waves, received in Strasbourg from the Eiffel Tower in Paris. Braun's assistants invented the first practical (Köpsel–Dönitz) wavemeter consisting of a tuned circuit employing an inductor, calibrated capacitance and thermic current indicator. Present-day wavemeters are similar.

When World War I broke out, a patent suit was brought against the Sayville, Long Island, radio station in an attempt to close it and cut off all communication between the US and Germany. Braun was asked to appear in New York to testify about experiments he had made. Hoping to be of use to his country, Braun, at the age of 64 and in ill health, made a mid-winter trip through the British blockade. The suit was postponed. When the US entered the war, Braun was not permitted to return to Strasbourg. He stayed in his son's home in Brooklyn where he died, on 20 April 1918.

Johannes Diderik van der Waals

1837–1923

Awarded the 1910 Nobel Prize for physics for his work concerning the equation of state of gases and liquids.

Johannes van der Waals was born in Leiden in 1837, the son of Elisabeth van den Burg and Jacobus van der Waals. Probably for economic reasons he did not initially prepare for a university education but taught physics in schools at Deventer and The Hague. In 1864 he married Anna Magdalena Smith, who died a few years later after giving birth to three daughters and a son, Johannes Diderik junior.

When van der Waals eventually obtained an exemption from the requirements of Greek and Latin, he obtained his doctoral degree from the University of Leiden, at the age of 36. His dissertation *On the Continuity of the Gaseous and Liquid States* received an enthusiastic review by James Clerk Maxwell in *Nature* in 1874 and was subsequently translated from Dutch into German (1881), English (1888) and French (1894). In 1877 van der Waals was appointed professor of physics at the University of Amsterdam, where for 20 years he was the only teacher of physics, with heavy responsibilities for physics, chemistry, philosophy and medical students, and yet he continued to publish important scientific papers.

Van der Waals acknowledged inspiration from an 1857 paper by Clausius on the kind of motion we call heat. A gas is pictured as consisting of a myriad of material points bouncing about at great speed. As developed by Maxwell and Boltzmann, the kinetic theory explains how a gas exerts pressure on its container and how the pressure p depends on the volume v and absolute temperature T. As an ideal or first approximation, $pv = RT$, where R is constant for all gases, if the density is not too high.

Van der Waals' idea of *continuity* was that there is no essential difference between gaseous and liquid states of matter, although one must consider other factors in addition to motion of the molecules in the determination of pressure. The important factors are the attraction between particles and their proper volume (both neglected in the ideal gas model). From these considerations van der Waals arrived at the equation

$$\left(p + \frac{a}{v^2}\right)(v - b) = RT,$$

where a expresses the mutual attraction of the molecules, and b is their volume (a and b have different values for different gases). Other experimenters have suggested different models and equations of state, but van der Waals' model is probably the most useful because it emphasises the essential features of molecules that determine liquidity, without introducing too many 'realistic' complications. Van der Waals' work is a valuable example of how a shrewd scientist can by appropriate simplifying assumptions arrive at the heart of a complex phenomenon, and thereby open up a new field of theoretical and experimental research.

A gas cannot be liquefied by a mere increase in pressure unless its temperature is below a certain *critical temperature* (31 °C for CO_2; $-267 \cdot 9$ °C for He, etc). From van der Waals' equation the critical temperature T_c, and associated critical volume v_c and pressure p_c, can be calculated in terms of constants a and b. Further, van der Waals' law of corresponding states says that as soon as the behaviour of a single gas and the corresponding liquid is known at all temperatures and pressures, then the state of any gas or liquid at any temperature and pressure can be calculated if the state at the critical temperature is known (that is, if T_c, p_c and v_c are known). Obviously an important practical application of the theory is the prediction of conditions necessary for the liquefaction of a gas; this was an important guide in the liquefaction of the 'permanent' gases.

Van der Waals was of small stature and had clear blue eyes. It is said that while he had a religious inclination he did not join any established church. He lived a simple life, keeping to a regular schedule. He enjoyed walking, reading, solitaire card games and playing billiards (as did several other pioneers of the kinetic theory of gases).

Wilhelm
Carl Werner
Otto Fritz Franz
Wien

1864–1928

Awarded the 1911 Nobel Prize for physics for his discoveries regarding laws governing the radiation of heat.

Wilhelm Wien was born in rural Germany at Gaffken, East Prussia, in 1864, the only child of Carl Wien, a farmer, and Caroline (Gertz) Wien. When Wien was two, the family moved to a farm at Drachenstein. His mother's knowledge of history and literature stimulated Wien's lifelong interest in those subjects. He received private tutoring and spoke French before he could write German. Encouraged mainly by his mother, Wien entered the University of Göttingen in 1882 to study mathematics and natural science. But, an introvert and independent, he left after one semester, to travel. In 1884 at the University of Berlin Wien 'really came into contact with physics for the first time' in Helmholtz's laboratory. He received his doctorate in 1886.

That summer Wien returned to Drachenstein to help his parents, feeling an obligation as an only son to prepare to operate the estate, yet wanting to pursue scientific research. His dilemma was resolved when in 1890 drought forced his parents to sell the farm. Wien thereupon became an assistant to Helmholtz at the Physikalische-Technische Reichsanstalt in Charlottenburg; his parents moved to Berlin.

After appointments at the University of Berlin, at the technical high school in Aachen, and at the University of Giessen, Wien became Röntgen's successor at Würzburg (1900–1920). He succeeded Röntgen again in 1920, at the University of Munich where he remained until his death in 1928.

Wien's major work dealt with the distribution of radiant energy in the spectrum and the effect of a change in temperature on this distribution. Wien and Otto Lummer devised the first practical black-body or cavity radiator to provide the 'full radiation' needed for their experiments. Wien announced his displacement law in 1893: $\lambda_{max}T =$ constant, which states that the wavelength at which the intensity of the radiation is a maximum shifts to shorter wavelengths as the temperature of the source increases. Something of this sort can be easily seen as a carbon rod is heated: when it first becomes visible by its own radiation it is dull 'red hot'; as the temperature increases the rod becomes bright red, orange, yellow, and finally white, corresponding to a gradual shift of λ_{max} toward the blue end of the spectrum.

Wien next investigated the problem of the distribution of energy among the wavelengths in black-body radiation. Thermodynamical reasoning was not sufficient. Wien made some arbitrary assumptions (within the framework of classical physics) about the role of molecules in the emission of radiation, and arrived at the formula

$$E_\lambda = \frac{c_1}{\lambda^{-5}\exp(-c_2/\lambda T)},$$

where E_λ is the energy at wavelength λ over a unit range of wavelength, and c_1 and c_2 are constants, which he determined by curve-fitting. Wien's formula predicts intensities a little lower than experimental values for large values of λT. The search for a better formula led Max Planck to formulate the quantum theory of radiation. Satisfyingly, Planck's theory gives c_1 and c_2 in terms of fundamental physical constants, but oddly, Planck's equation differs from Wien's in form only by the addition of a (−1) in the denominator. In temperature measurements with an optical pyrometer, Wien's equation is still often used; the calculations are simpler and sufficiently accurate.

In 1898 Wien married Louise Mehler whom he met in Aachen. They had four children: Gerda, Waltraut, Karl and Hildegard. In 1904 Wien visited Norway, Spain, Italy and England; he visited Greece in 1912. In 1913 he went to Columbia University to deliver six lectures on recent problems in theoretical physics and also visited Harvard and Yale. The war affected Wien deeply, as did Germany's situation in the 1920s, marked by 'war tribute and socialism.'

Wien had outstanding general competence in both experimental and theoretical physics. For his doctoral thesis he studied the diffraction of light at a metal foil and showed that one needed to consider interaction with the molecules. In his study of conduction of electricity in gases he showed that the positive or 'canal' rays (discovered by Goldstein) were positively charged atoms. His apparatus for deflecting these (1898) provided a basis for the development of the mass spectrometer. In 1905–6 Wien made the first energy measurements of x-rays and obtained a good approximation for their wavelengths.

Editing was another important contribution Wien made to physics. From 1906 until his death in 1928, Wien and Planck edited the *Annalen der Physik*. Wien and F Harms were editors of the *Handbuch der Experimental Physik*, the first volume of which appeared in 1926.

Wien is said to have been a fine teacher and lecturer who was held in esteem and affection by his students. His enthusiasm and ingenuity were characteristics of his entire career.

Nils Gustaf Dalén

1869–1937

Awarded the 1912 Nobel Prize for physics for his invention of the automatic regulators that can be used in conjunction with gas accumulators for lighting beacons and light buoys.

Nils Gustaf Dalén, 'benefactor of sailors,' was born in 1869 at Stenstorp in southern Sweden. His father was occupied with agriculture, horticulture and dairy-farming, but Nils leaned toward an engineering career. After private study, he entered the Chalmers Institute at Göteborg and graduated as a mechanical engineer in 1896. After a year at the Federal Polytechnic at Zürich, Dalén returned to Sweden and undertook experiments on hot-air turbines, compressors and air-pumps. Some experiments were carried out in workshops of the de Laval Steam Turbine Company in Stockholm.

From 1900 to 1905 Dalén was a member of the engineering firm Dalén and Alsing, founded for the purpose of exploiting inventions. For two years he was works manager for Swedish Carbide and Acetylene Company, which in 1909 became Swedish Gas Accumulator Company, with Dalén its managing director.

Dalén set out to make acetylene useful for lighting unattended navigational aids. He dissolved acetylene in acetone and then forced this into a porous mass, 'aga,' in a steel container at ten atmospheres. The container then held 100 times its own volume of acetylene and could be handled, without danger of detonation from shock, as a practical light source for a lighthouse or buoy. Dalén invented a valve for producing light flashes, whose duration could

45

identify the source.

To conserve gas, Dalén invented a sun-valve to extinguish the light at sunrise and relight it at nightfall. The valve depended on differential expansion, plus the fact that a black surface absorbs radiation more than a bright one. Dalén's valve consisted of four metal bars enclosed in a glass bulb. The inner bar was blackened, the others gilded; all four were fastened at their upper ends. Sunlight absorbed by the black bar heated it and its expansion closed the gas valve. When daylight failed, the black bar came to the same temperature as the other three and its contraction reopened the valve.

Ronald W Clark, in his 1977 biography of Thomas Alva Edison, states that the Nobel Prize selection committee considered awarding the 1912 physics prize to the inventors Edison and Nikolai Tesla, but Tesla refused to be honoured with Edison, with whom he had had a bitter financial misunderstanding. So the award went to inventor Dalén.

In 1912 Dalén was seriously injured in an explosion while carrying out tests and lost his sight. A few weeks later his brother, a medical professor, attended the Nobel ceremony in his place. Dalén gallantly continued to supervise research in his factories until his death in 1937.

Heike Kamerlingh Onnes

1853–1926

Awarded the 1913 Nobel Prize for physics for his investigations into the properties of matter at low temperature which led, among other things, to the production of liquid helium.

Kamerlingh Onnes was born in the university town of Groningen in the Netherlands in 1853. He and his brothers were raised in a home where 'all was made subservient to one central purpose, to become men.' His father, owner of a tile factory, and his mother taught diligence by example and led the family in reading and discussions.

Onnes entered the University of Groningen in 1870, and in the following year he submitted an essay on vapour density in a contest sponsored by the University of Utrecht and won a gold medal. At Heidelberg (1871–73) Onnes studied under Bunsen and was one of two students allowed to work in Kirchhoff's private laboratory. Onnes returned to Groningen for his doctorate. When in 1879 he presented his defence of his thesis *New Proof of the Earth's Rotation*, the examiners burst into applause and voted him the degree *magna cum laude*.

In 1882 Onnes was appointed professor of physics and director of the laboratory at Leiden. He held this post for 42 years while making Leiden the world centre for low-temperature physics research. To give experimental support to van der Waals' theory of the behaviour of gases, and especially 'the law of corresponding states,' Onnes sought to extend measurements to the lowest temperatures attainable. To reach very low temperatures one must remove heat from the specimen; this is most conveniently done by immersing the specimen in a liquefied gas

47

which removes heat as it boils. To liquefy the gas, one compresses it and cools it below the critical temperature. If now the gas is allowed to do external work against a piston, or internal work by expanding into a vacuum, further cooling occurs, resulting in liquefaction of some of the gas.

To liquefy the most stubborn of the 'permanent' gases, helium, Onnes built an elaborate system using a jacket of evaporating liquid hydrogen to cool the helium, after which the throttled expansion would result in final cooling and liquefaction of some of the helium. Of a memorable day in 1908 Onnes said, 'I was overjoyed when I could show liquefied helium to my friend van der Waals, whose theory had been my guide in the liquefaction up to the end.'

Onnes enjoyed the title respectfully bestowed on him by intimate friends, 'the gentleman of absolute zero,' but his experiments in approaching absolute zero were not stunts. He carefully explored the optical and magnetic properties of substances at low temperatures. His discovery of superconductivity (the sudden disappearance of electrical resistance) and the discovery of helium II were important in the development of a theory of electrical conduction in solids.

Onnes worked at a time of transition in physics. The mechanistic image of physics was losing against Maxwell's theory of electromagnetism; physicists were also coming to believe that matter was not a continuum but had a corpuscular nature. Recognition of the importance of experimental physics was demonstrated in Onnes' appointment to the first chair of experimental physics in the Netherlands. In his inaugural address at Leiden (1882) 'The Significance of Quantitative Research in Physics,' Onnes declared: 'I should like to write "Door meten tot weten" [Through measuring to knowing] as a motto above each physics laboratory.'

Max Theodor Felix von Laue

1879–1960

Awarded the 1914 Nobel Prize for physics for his discovery of the diffraction of Röntgen rays in crystals.

Max Laue was born at Pfaffendorf, near Koblenz, Germany, in 1879, the son of Julius Laue, an official in the military court system, and Minna (Zerrenner) Laue. He began studying physics at the University of Strasbourg in 1898 while still in military service. The following year at Göttingen he developed an interest in theoretical physics, especially in optical problems, and he received his doctorate under Max Planck at the University of Berlin in 1903. Planck offered Laue an assistantship in 1905, and the two formed a lifelong friendship.

Laue became one of the first adherents of Einstein's special theory of relativity; he wrote his first monograph on relativity in 1910. In 1851 Fizeau had discovered a formula to express his experimental results for the velocity of light in flowing water which could not be justified in terms of classical physics. In 1907 Laue demonstrated that the Einstein theorem for the addition of velocities readily yielded Fizeau's equation, thereby furnishing Einstein's theory with an experimental confirmation.

In 1909 Laue became a *Privatdozent* at the University of Munich in the Institute of Theoretical Physics directed by Arnold Sommerfeld. At this time it had not been proved that x-rays were short-wavelength electromagnetic radiation (although some had made the assumption), and while it was assumed that a regular structure of atoms was the characteristic property of crystals, the physical composition of crystals was debated. Laue suggested that if these assumptions were correct, x-rays on penetrating a crystal should behave somewhat like light on striking a diffraction grating. When Walter Friedrich and Paul Knipping performed the experiment in 1912, the irradiation of a copper sulphate crystal did indeed produce regularly ordered dark spots on a photographic plate placed behind the crystal: the first 'Laue diagram.'

The diffraction of x-rays by a crystal established the nature of x-rays as electromagnetic waves. Measurement of the photographic pattern produced by a crystal of known structure, such as NaCl, permitted determination of the wavelength of the x-ray beam. In turn, a beam of known wavelength could be used to explore the structure of crystals and polymers.

In 1910 Laue married Magdalene Degen. In 1912 he was appointed associate professor at the University of Zürich, and became full professor at Frankfurt in 1914. In the same year his father was elevated to the hereditary nobility. So in 1914 *Privatdozent* Max Laue became world famous Nobel Prize winner Professor Max von Laue.

During World War I von Laue worked with Wien at Würzburg on improving military communication equipment. After the war, as an elected member of the German Research Association, von Laue had a role in directing available funds to important research during the economic depression of the Weimar Republic. As chairman of the German Physical Society, von Laue protested vigorously against Einstein's dismissal following the Nazi seizure of power; he also blocked the regime's request to admit Hitler's follower Johannes Stark to the Prussian Academy. During World War II von Laue's house, where he lived with his wife and daughter Hildegard (his only son Theodor was in the United States), was visited by a few friends who thought as he did and by sons and friends of Dutch and Norwegian scientists sent to Germany as workers, by French prisoners, and others who needed help or advice.

Eventually von Laue lost his post as adviser to the Physikalische-Technische Reichsanstalt (PTR), but he continued as professor at the University of Berlin and as deputy director of the Kaiser Wilhelm Institut für Physik. He retired early from teaching and in 1943 moved to Würtemberg-Hohenzollern. Following the war he was active in refounding the German Physical Society and giving rebirth to the PTR as the Physikalische-Technische Bundesanstalt in Brunswick. In 1946 von Laue and Planck were invited to England to receive honours.

Sir William Henry Bragg

1862–1942

Shared the 1915 Nobel Prize for physics with his son William Lawrence Bragg for their study of crystal structure by means of x-rays.

William Henry Bragg was born on his father's farm near Wigton, Cumberland, in 1862, the eldest child of Robert John Bragg, a former officer in the Merchant Marines, and Mary Wood, daughter of a vicar. His mother died when he was seven and for six years Bragg lived with his uncle, a pharmacist. In July 1881 Bragg started his work at Trinity College, Cambridge, first reading mathematics intensively with Routh's coaching, and then attending lectures by Rayleigh and J J Thomson.

In 1885, through Thomson, Bragg received an appointment to teach mathematics and physics at the University of Adelaide, South Australia. There in 1889 he married Gwendoline, daughter of Charles Todd, postmaster-general and government astronomer. Bragg developed a friendly, comprehensible style of public and classroom exposition, he was active in university affairs, and he enjoyed a relaxed social life and was a fine golfer. His eldest son Lawrence caddied for him.

Bragg's rise to fame followed an invitation to give a presidential address for his section of the Australasian Association for the Advancement of Science, in Dunedin. In his talk, 'Some Recent Advances in the Theory of the Ionisation of Gases,' Bragg gave a critical review of the field, finding fault with some of the work and with many of the assumptions. Later that year (1904), with the assistance of R D Kleeman, Bragg began experiments on the absorption of alpha particles from radioactive sources. They found that the exponential decrease others had assumed was not justified, but rather the alpha particles fell into a few groups each of which had a definite range and thus a definite initial velocity. Each group corresponded to a different radioactive species in the source, so measurement of alpha particle ranges became a valuable tool in the identification of radioactive substances. Following this line of research until 1907, publishing a paper every few months, Bragg established his reputation—and was elected a fellow of the Royal Society.

Bragg moved to the University of Leeds in 1909 as successor to Stroud. He reoriented his research interest to the possibility that gamma and x-rays might be of a material nature, specifically neutral pairs consisting of an electron and an alpha particle. (This was a year before Rutherford found the alpha particle to be doubly charged.) A feud developed with Barkla. But in 1912 Bragg was convinced by Laue photographs that the patterns resulted from interference of x-rays scattered in a crystal and that x-rays indeed had a wave character. His son Lawrence, working at the Cavendish Laboratory, showed how the Laue pattern might be regarded as a reflection of x-rays from atom-rich planes in a crystal. He derived the famous Bragg relation, $n\lambda = 2d \sin \theta$, connecting the wavelength λ of the x-ray with the glancing angle θ at which such a reflection could occur (d is the distance between adjacent atomic planes, and n is the order of the spectrum).

In 1915 Bragg succeeded in detecting reflected x-rays with an ionisation chamber and he constructed the first x-ray spectrometer to investigate the spectral distribution of x-rays, relations between wavelength, Planck's constant, the atomic mass of emitter and absorber, etc. But he quickly adopted his son's interest in using a known wavelength to determine d, the distance between atomic planes, and hence the structure of a crystal mounted in the spectrometer. Their book *X Rays and Crystal Structure* appeared in 1915.

In 1915 Bragg became Quain Professor of physics at University College, London. During the war he served 'within the cumbersome, complicated, and capricious frame set up by the Government,' and in 1920 was knighted. His appointment as Superintendent of the House and Director of the Laboratory of the Royal Institution required residence there. Lady Bragg was a gracious hostess at the Institution; after her death in 1929 her daughter took over that responsibility.

Despite a late start, Bragg published 237 books and papers between 1891 and 1942. In research he regarded theories as 'no more than familiar and useful tools.' His frequently quoted 1928 quip concerning the nature of light was to the effect that the thing to do was to use the corpuscular theory on Monday, Wednesday and Friday, and the undulatory theory on Tuesday, Thursday and Saturday.

In his book *Science and Faith* (1941), Bragg expressed his religious beliefs and sense of reverence, doubtless with some feeling of liberation from the terror of eternal damnation, a religious experience which had infected his whole class during his final year at school in 1880–81. Bragg was strongly attached to his family. To others also he showed a spirit which was generous, warm and free from pretence. He was a lover of tradition and a respecter of craftsmanship.

Sir William Lawrence Bragg

1890–1971

Shared the 1915 Nobel Prize for physics with his father William Henry Bragg for their study of crystal structure by means of x-rays.

William Lawrence Bragg was born in Adelaide, South Australia. He was educated at St Peter's College and at the University of Adelaide where his father was a professor. When his father became professor of physics at the University of Leeds in 1909, Lawrence entered Trinity College, Cambridge, intending to become a mathematician. But during his second year he changed to physics and earned his degree with first class honours in 1912. In the autumn he began his investigation of von Laue x-ray patterns and published his first paper on that subject in November. During the next two years he at Cambridge and his father at Leeds collaborated in a study of crystal structure by means of x-rays, publishing their research jointly in the book *X Rays and Crystal Structure* (1915).

In 1914 Lawrence Bragg was elected fellow and lecturer at Trinity College, Cambridge. In 1919 he was made Langworthy Professor of physics at Manchester University, where he remained until 1937. He was director of the National Physical Laboratory (1937–38), Cavendish Professor of experimental physics at Cambridge University (1938–53), and Fullerian Professor of chemistry and director of the Royal Institution of Great Britain (1953–66). During World War I Bragg served as technical adviser on sound ranging at the Map Section, General Headquarters, France.

With his father, Lawrence Bragg originated the science of x-ray crystallography. In early work they showed that crystals of such substances as sodium chloride contain no actual molecules of NaCl, but only sodium ions and chloride ions arranged in geometric regularity. This discovery revolutionised theoretical chemistry, and in particular it influenced Debye's treatment of ion dissociation. In the year these results were published, Lawrence Bragg became a Nobel Prize winner at the age of 25.

Bragg married Alice Grace Jenny Hopkinson in 1921; their children were Stephen, David, Margaret and Patience.

Bragg turned his research to other fields, especially where his keen perception of geometric relations could stimulate progress. He elucidated the structure of silicates (1925), and his Baker Lectures, given at Cornell University in 1936, summarised the system of silicate chemistry built by him on the basis of distinctive geometric features. Bragg next tackled metallurgy with its problems of polymorphism and phase transitions. He developed the distinction between long-range and short-range order first suggested by Bethe and Peierls. To visualise the geometry of dislocations, Bragg frequently used the pleasing bubble-raft model of a metal. In the most ambitious aim of crystal structure analysis, the elucidation of protein chemistry, Bragg overcame some initial difficulties, provided financial backing for Perutz's work on haemoglobin, and in 1954 set up at the Royal Institution an independent team of workers on protein problems.

Bragg, like his father, was an excellent lecturer and efficient organiser. After World War II he helped to organise the International Union of Crystallography, of which he became the first president. He was concerned with science education and gave lectures for children at the Royal Institution to introduce them to the beauty and excitement of scientific discovery.

Charles Glover Barkla

1877–1944

Awarded the 1917 Nobel Prize for physics for his discovery of the secondary x-radiation characteristic of elements.

Charles Barkla found, at Cambridge, that x-rays were scattered by gases in an amount proportional to the density and therefore to the molecular weight. He deduced that the more massive the atom, the more electrons it contained, a move toward the concept of atomic number. In 1904 Barkla established that x-rays were transverse waves, by showing their polarisation. Electrons impinging upon the anode of a x-ray tube are abruptly decelerated and the radiation they emit in a plane perpendicular to their motion should have a stronger electric field perpendicular to that plane than in it. Barkla showed that the x-ray beam was indeed thus partially polarised.

Barkla was the first to show that when x-rays are absorbed by matter there is secondary radiation of two kinds. One consists of x-rays scattered unchanged in quality; the other is a 'fluorescent radiation' characteristic of the scattering substance and accompanied by selective absorption of the primary beam. Barkla soon found two types of the characteristic rays: a more penetrating set which he called K radiation, and a less penetrating set which he called L radiation. For elements listed according to their positions in the periodic table, the characteristic x-rays they produced were more and more penetrating; their frequencies increased. H G J Moseley explored such measurements to establish the meaning of *atomic number*: the number of electrons moving about the nucleus of a neutral atom or the number of protons in the nucleus. Moseley probably would have shared the 1917 Nobel Prize but for his wartime death at Gallipoli. The origin of K and L radiation was later accounted for as being due to transitions of the innermost electrons in the atom model used by Sommerfeld and Bohr to explain the emission of visible light.

Charles Barkla was born in Widnes, Lancashire, the son of John Martin Barkla, a former secretary of the Atlas Chemical Company, and Sarah (Glover) Barkla, who was of a local family of watch manufacturers. At University College, Liverpool, Barkla obtained honours in mathematics, specialised in experimental physics under Sir Oliver Lodge, received his BSc in 1898 and his MSc in 1899. After 18 months at Trinity College he moved to King's College, Cambridge, in order to sing in its famous chapel choir—the chapel was filled for his baritone solos. After appointments at Liverpool and at King's College, London, in 1913 Barkla was appointed professor of natural philosophy at the University of Edinburgh, where he remained for the rest of his life.

In 1907 Barkla married Mary Esther, daughter of John Cowell, the receiver-general of the Isle of Man. They had three sons and a daughter, and enjoyed living in a rural setting at Braidwood. Barkla was a tall, solid man with delicate hands. He had a charming manner, a fondness for children, and was a faithful supporter of the Methodist Church.

In his experience with students in three universities, Barkla earned a reputation for the wide range of his knowledge of physics and his judgment as an eminently fair and discriminating examiner. But, oddly, in his later years he seemed to fade out of physics. He tended to cite only his own work and entered a professional seclusion. Not a strong theorist, Barkla asserted in his 1916 Bakerian lecture: 'Absorption is *not* in quanta of primary radiation,' and he repeated himself verbatim in his Nobel lecture in 1920. After 1916, Barkla committed himself to the pursuit of a will-o'-the-wisp which he called the 'J-phenomenon.'

Barkla did join in one controversy in which he was outclassed, by W H Bragg. In 1907, Bragg published an attempt to interpret the known facts about x-rays, including Barkla's information on polarisation, on the hypothesis that the rays were corpuscular. For a crucial experiment, Barkla investigated angular distribution of the scattered radiation with respect to the direction of the primary beam. From the equation he derived for intensity, and his comprehensive experimental data, Barkla was able to conclude that x-rays were indeed electromagnetic radiation and interact with matter in accordance with the Maxwell–Lorentz theory.

Max Karl
Ernst Ludwig
Planck

1858–1947

Awarded (in 1919) the 1918 Nobel Prize for physics for his contributions to the development of physics by his discovery of the element of action [quantum theory].

The impact of Planck's quantum theory has been such that physics before his time is now called classical physics. Although he did not in his writings make unusual claims for his innovation, his son Erwin recalled that in 1900, during a walk in the *Grünewald,* his father told him: 'Today I have made a discovery which is as important as Newton's discovery.'

Beginning in about 1896 Planck became interested in finding the correct theoretical expression for the radiation from a black body. He applied Boltzmann's equation from the theory of gases (relating entropy and probability) to a set of resonators, the energy of which, he hypothesised, occurred only in *discrete multiples of* ε. From Wien's displacement law he reasoned that the entropy was a function of E/v (energy/frequency). He was then led (1900) to the famous relation between a quantum of energy and the frequency, and to the introduction of the constant h named after him: $E = hv$.

The resulting Planck radiation law, unlike Wien's, fitted all the experimental data, especially those of Rubens and Kurlbaum, on black-body radiation. But Planck's contemporaries were mostly unconvinced or indifferent and Planck, who was temperamentally conservative, continued to try to wrest an acceptable radiation law from purely classical thermodynamics. Einstein spotlighted attention on Planck's work when he used the concept of quanta in his explanation of the photoelectric effect, in 1905. Next the quantum concept was exploited in the Rutherford–Bohr model of the atom. The fact that it took 25 years of experimental and theoretical work to build the quantum theory is one measure of the quality of Planck's contribution.

Max Planck was born in 1858 in Kiel, Prussia, the son of Johann Julius Wilhelm von Planck, a professor of law, and Emma Patzig Planck. The family moved to Munich in 1867. Planck studied at the University of Munich in 1874–77, and received his PhD at the University of Berlin in 1879 under Helmoltz and Kirchhoff. He served on the faculties at Munich and Kiel and in 1889 became Kirchhoff's successor at the University of Berlin where he remained until his retirement in 1926.

By his first marriage in 1887 Planck had a son and two daughters. From a second marriage in 1911 he had one son.

Planck's early research was in thermodynamics (*Swinburne and Entropy* was one paper, published in 1903), followed by work in mechanics, optical and electrical problems, and the radiation of heat which led to the quantum theory. He determined the charge on the electron to within two per cent error in 1900, and evaluated the 'Boltzmann' constant. He published some 215 research papers and seven books, including *The Philosophy of Physics* (1959).

In celebration of Planck's eightieth birthday one of the minor planets was 'given' to him and named 'Planckiana.' He was an enfeebled but pleased guest at the Royal Society's Newton Celebrations in 1946.

Planck came from an old family of lawyers and public servants. His way of life was deeply rooted in tradition and he was proud of Germany. He resisted the idea of a 'German (Aryan) physics.' He was a friend of Einstein, and they frequently played chamber music together. Eventually Nazi sycophants penetrated the administration of the German Academy of Sciences and Planck resigned his office.

Planck bore with fortitude many misfortunes: his elder son was killed in action before Verdun in 1916; his twin daughters both died in childbirth, and his gifted younger son Erwin, a secretary of state in an earlier German government, was executed in 1945 for alleged complicity in a plan to overthrow the Nazi regime. While on a lecture tour, Planck witnessed the wartime destruction of Kassel and was buried for hours in an air-raid shelter. As a final loss, his own home and invaluable library were destroyed in an air-raid on Berlin. He took shelter in a wood until recognised by members of the American Army. His last days were spent in the home of his grand-niece in Göttingen.

Planck's grave in Göttingen's Stadtfriedhof is marked by a simple rectangular stone which bears only his name and at the foot: $h = 6,62 \cdot 10^{-27}$ erg·sec.

Johannes Stark

1874–1957

Awarded the 1919 Nobel Prize for physics for his discovery of the Doppler effect in canal rays and of the splitting of spectral lines in an electric field.

Canal rays are positively charged ions produced during the conduction of electricity in gases driven to the cathode by the applied potential difference and allowed to pass through holes (canals) in the cathode. Stark looked for a shift in frequency of the light radiated by these fast-moving particles. He said he found it 'almost effortlessly' in the hydrogen lines. Stark tried to make this optical Doppler effect, found in 1905, a proof of Einstein's theory of special relativity—and a proof of the quantum hypothesis as well (1907). Curiously, after 1913 he turned vehemently against both the quantum theory and the theory of relativity.

In the other part of his award-winning research Stark succeeded where others had failed in producing a splitting of spectral lines in an electric field (as Zeeman had demonstrated for a magnetic field). Stark placed a third electrode behind the perforated cathode and only a few millimetres from it, and applied a field of 20 000 V/cm between the two. He then observed (1913) a splitting of spectral lines when examined with a spectrometer at right angles to the ray. The Stark effect was incorporated into quantum mechanics by Paul Epstein in 1916, and was shown to be consistent with wave mechanics by Schrödinger in 1926.

Johannes Stark was born in 1874 in Schickenhof, Bavaria,

the son of a farmer. He attended *gymnasia* in Bayreuth and Regensburg and in 1897 received a doctorate at the University of Munich. In 1898 he became an assistant there in the Physical Institute. He was a *privatdozent* at the University of Göttingen in 1900 and professor extraordinary at the technical high schools at Hanover (1906) and Aachen (1909). In 1917 he went as a professor to the University of Greifswald and in 1920 to Würzburg, as successor to Wien. Stark quarrelled with almost all his colleagues except Lenard, whose denunication of 'Jewish, dogmatic physics' Stark supported.

Stark, as a partisan of Hitler, was appointed president of the Physikalische-Technische Reichsanstalt (PTR) in 1933, and president of the re-named Deutsche Forschungsgemeinschaft in 1934. From this powerful position, Stark intensified his fight against modern theoretical physics, especially against von Laue, Sommerfeld, Heisenberg and Einstein. Struggles within the hierarchy forced Stark to retire from both presidencies at the end of 1936; he subsequently went to live on his estate of Eppenstatt, near Traunstein, Bavaria.

Charles-Edouard Guillaume

1861–1938

Awarded the 1920 Nobel Prize for physics for his discovery of the anomalies of nickel–steel alloys and their importance in the physics of precision.

Charles-Edouard Guillaume was born in 1861 in Fleurier, Switzerland, a town famous for clockmaking, and where his father was a watchmaker. He first studied at home and then at the Federal Polytechnic School in Zürich where he obtained his doctor's degree at the age of 21 with a dissertation on electrolytic capacitors.

In 1883 Guillaume entered the recently founded International Bureau of Weights and Measures at Sèvres, near Paris. The first work he undertook there was in achieving accuracy in the use of mercury-in-glass thermometers. Guillaume also worked on the development of international standards for the metre, the kilogram and the litre. In 1890 a search was begun to find an inexpensive substitute for the platinum–iridium alloy used to make the standard metre bars. Guillaume's systematic investigation of nickel–steel alloys resulted in his discovery of Invar, a 35·6 per cent nickel alloy which had a coefficient of expansion far lower than any previously known for a metal; and Elinvar, a nickel–chromium–steel alloy whose elasticity remained constant over a wide range of temperatures. In addition to the uses originally planned for them, these alloys were of great practical value in the construction of temperature-compensated watches. Invar measuring bars were also used for geodetic surveying purposes.

In 1888 Guillaume married A M Taufflieb, and they had

three children.

Between 1886 and 1900, Guillaume published a total of 80 scientific papers. Guillaume was a participant in the Metrical Convention of 1902, and in 1905 he was promoted to director of the International Bureau of Weights and Measures. In this position, Guillaume was able to carry out research programmes which covered the complete range of the Bureau's interests.

Other areas of science also interested Guillaume; one unusual paper he wrote was concerned with those physical processes which are analogous to physiological ones, thus constituting an elementary form of life. As director of the Bureau, Guillaume was noted for his courtesy and tact, as well as his ardent advocacy of the metric system.

Albert Einstein

1879–1955

Awarded the 1921 Nobel Prize for physics for his attainments in mathematical physics and especially for his discovery of the law of the photoelectric effect.

Albert Einstein was born of Jewish parents, Hermann and Pauline (Koch) Einstein, an accomplished pianist, at Ulm an der Donau, Germany, in 1879. In 1885 the family moved to Munich were Einstein's father operated a small electrical and engineering firm, which was financially unsuccessful. His younger sister Maja remembered Albert as being hot tempered until he was seven when he started school. He did not thrive on the regimented educational system, but his uncle Jakob aroused his interest with mathematical puzzles. Albert did not talk until he was three years old. Einstein has described his lifelong habit of thinking in concepts and diagrams: 'I rarely think in words at all. A thought comes and I may try to express it in words afterward.'

On his second attempt, after attending a school in Aarau for a year, Einstein was admitted to the Swiss Federal Polytechnic School in Zürich, 1895–1900. In 1901 he married Mileva Marec, a mathematician; they had two children, Albert and Eduard. In 1902 he became a technical assistant at the Patent Office in Berne. Einstein received his PhD from the University of Zürich in 1905.

In a landmark year, 1905, Einstein published three papers in the *Annalen der Physik*. One explained the photoelectric effect by adopting Planck's idea that energy is quantised. When light falls on a metal and its photons have sufficient energy, electrons will be ejected. They will have a kinetic energy, E_k, which is the difference between the energy received from a photon, hf, and the work w required to escape from the attraction of the positive charges left behind: $E_k = hf - w$. A second paper derived the equation to explain Brownian motion and showed that it could be used to determine the sizes of molecules.

The third paper was on Einstein's special theory of relativity. In it he took the leap which others had only thought about. The concept of relativity, that observers in different unaccelerated frames of reference would write similar equations to express the laws of nature, had occurred to others, notably Poincaré. Also, Lorentz had shown that to accommodate optical measurements (the Michelson–Morley experiment) the intuitive (Newtonian) equations for converting from one reference frame to another moving with velocity v relative to the first had to be modified by the inclusion of a factor $\sqrt{1 - v^2/c^2}$, where c is the speed of light. Einstein proceeded from a hypothesis that (contrary to 'common sense') the speed of light is the same (c, in a vacuum) for any observer, regardless of his state of motion. From this approach he derived the equations previously suggested by Lorentz for translating the position coordinates, x, y, z, and he also showed that the *time t* of an event depends on its position and reference frame. To retain the validity of the law of conservation of momentum, Einstein was led to the conclusion that mass m and energy E are interchangeable: $E = mc^2$. So in 1905 the expectation was laid that in a nuclear reaction enormous energy might be released from the mass 'lost'.

In 1909 Einstein left the Patent Office to become professor extraordinary at the University of Zürich. In 1913 he became first director of the new Kaiser Wilhelm Physical Institute in Berlin. Shortly after his arrival in Berlin, Einstein separated from his wife Mileva, who returned to Switzerland with their two sons. Later, in 1917, he married his cousin Elsa, who died in 1936. In 1921 Einstein accompanied Chaim Weizmann to the United States to encourage support for the establishment of a Jewish national homeland in Palestine and the founding of a Hebrew university.

Einstein was professor of physics at the University of Berlin, 1914–33. In the 1920s he lectured in Europe, the US, and the Far East. He was a visiting lecturer in England and the US in 1930–33, when conditions within Germany made it inadvisable for him to return. In 1933 he was appointed for life as a member of the Institute for Advanced Study in Princeton. He became a US citizen in 1940.

The 1916 general theory of relativity was Einstein's theory of gravity of which Newton's classic theory is only a special case. An eclipse of the Sun on 29 March 1919 provided an opportunity to test one prediction of the general theory: that rays of starlight passing near the Sun's mass would be slightly bent by the gravitational field. Einstein, who once remarked that discordant results from a single experiment could overthrow a theory, felt confident in this case: 'Now I am fully satisfied and I no longer doubt the correctness of the whole system whether the observation of the eclipse succeeds or not. The sense of the thing is too evident.' His relativity theory did survive the eclipse test, and all subsequent tests.

From 1953 on, with only partial success, Einstein sought to generalise still further, to embrace in a unified field theory an explanation of all the types of force encountered in physics. Einstein also contributed to less esoteric theoretical problems, such as specific heats, gas theory, radiation laws, duration of excited states, photochemical reactions, and nuclear physics. It is perhaps surprising to note that while Einstein published some 250 papers on theoretical physics, his publications on other subjects number even more.

Of the town in which he spent the last 22 years of his life, Einstein wrote: 'Princeton is a wonderful little spot, a quaint and ceremonious village of puny demi-gods on stilts. Yet by ignoring certain special conventions, I have been able to create for myself an atmosphere conducive to study and free from distractions.' During the years at Princeton, Einstein became increasingly isolated from the mainstream of research in physics, but of course he remained a beloved sage. He continued to use his influence for charitable causes, for pacifism, world government and humanitarianism. But this remark, made in 1930, admits an aloofness: 'My passionate sense of social justice and social responsibility has always contrasted oddly with my pronounced lack of need for direct contact with other human beings and human communities. I am truly a 'lone traveller' and have never belonged to any country, my home, my friends, or even my immediate family with my whole heart. In the face of all these ties, I have never lost a sense of distance and a need for solitude—feelings that increase with the years.'

Niels Hendrik David Bohr

1885–1962

Awarded the 1922 Nobel Prize for physics for his study of the structure of atoms and of the radiation which emanates from them.

Niels Bohr was a son of Christian Bohr, a professor of physiology at the University of Copenhagen, and Ellen Adler Bohr. Niels distinguished himself at the same university as a soccer player and physics student, winning a gold medal (for science) in 1907 and earning his MS in 1909 and his PhD in 1911. When he was 24, Bohr wrote his first scientific paper, on the determination of surface tension from vibrations of water drops in a jet. Later he used a vibrating droplet as his model for nuclear excitations (1937) and for nuclear fission (1939). A grant from the Carlsberg Foundation enabled Bohr to study at J J Thomson's Cavendish Laboratory at Cambridge University, and in 1912 at Rutherford's laboratory in Manchester.

Bohr married Margrethe Norlund in 1912, and they had six children. For much of his career, Bohr was professor of theoretical physics at the University of Copenhagen (1916–62) and director of the Institute of Theoretical Physics (1920–62).

The first reasonably successful attempt to use spectroscopic data to discover the internal structure of atoms was made by Bohr in 1913. He sought to combine Rutherford's notion of a nuclear atom with the quantum theory suggested by Planck in order to explain how atoms absorb and emit radiant energy. Bohr attributed to the simplest atom, hydrogen, definite, quantised energy levels. He postulated that its electron radiated energy only when it dropped from one allowed level to a lower energy level. The atom can absorb energy only in quanta, hf, which correspond to energy differences between allowed levels. (Bohr's assertion that an electron radiates no energy as long as it revolves in a particular orbit contradicts the classical view that an accelerated charge must radiate. This difficulty was removed when de Broglie showed that an electron can be regarded as a waveform and Schrödinger replaced the picture of the electron moving in a circular orbit by a 'standing wave' formed about the nucleus.)

Combining the new quantum concepts with old Newtonian mechanics and conservation of energy, Bohr was able to arrive at orbital energies which accounted for the line spectrum (definite frequencies) emitted by hydrogen atoms when excited by electrical or other means to energies higher than the ground state. Bohr was unable to devise satisfactory models for atoms more complicated than hydrogen and hydrogen-like ions (e.g. He^+), but he rightly predicted that in complex atoms electrons must exist in 'shells' and that the electron content of the outermost shell determines the chemical properties of the atoms of a particular element. Bohr's start, plus wave mechanics and Pauli's exclusion principle, clarified the meaning of the periodic table of the elements.

Two principles are associated with Bohr's name. The 'correspondence principle' (1916) says that the quantum mechanical model of the atom must join smoothly with classical concepts when dimensions become large. The 'principle of complementarity' says that evidence relating to atomic systems obtained under different experimental conditions cannot be comprehended necessarily by a single model; the wave model of the electron is complementary to the particle model.

Bohr visited the US in 1939 bringing news that Hahn and Meitner believed that fission of uranium atoms had been observed when bombarded with neutrons, releasing energy. He developed a model for the fission mechanism in which the atom behaved as a deformable drop of liquid; he predicted that fission occurred most often in the isotope uranium-235. Bohr and his family escaped from occupied Denmark in 1943, going first to Sweden, then to England, and then to the US. There he and his son Aage, known as 'Mr Nicholas Baker and Jim Baker,' gave 'invaluable aid' as advisers at the Los Alamos Atomic Laboratories.

On his return to Copenhagen in 1945, Bohr concerned himself with developing peaceful uses for atomic energy. He was chairman of the Danish Atomic Energy Commission and he was a leader in the first Atoms for Peace Conference in Geneva in 1955. He was a founding member of CERN, the European Centre for Nuclear Research. Bohr also became interested in molecular biology. His last (incomplete) paper was prepared for the opening of an institute of genetics in Cologne. Bohr had a philosophical concern about the function of language as a means of communication. On occasion he revised as many as nine sets of proofs before releasing a paper for publication.

The Institute of Theoretical Physics (now the Niels Bohr Institute) attracted to Copenhagen as visitors many of the moulders of quantum mechanics and twentieth-century physics. One, Einstein, said: 'What is so marvellously attractive about Bohr as a scientific thinker is . . . his intuitive grasp of hidden things combined with such a strong critical sense.' Fellows and alumni of the Institute expressed their affection for Bohr by issuing at five-year intervals, on his birthday of 7 October, a *Journal of Jocular Physics*, containing many reminiscences. John Cockcroft wrote in an obituary: 'We shall remember him above all for his humanity and his great friendliness to, and encouragement of, young scientists.'

Robert Andrews Millikan

1868–1953

Awarded the 1923 Nobel Prize for physics for his work on the elementary electric charge and on the photoelectric effect.

In the work cited above, Millikan established beyond all reasonable doubt and with precise measurements theories which were already generally accepted. To establish the electron as the fundamental unit of charge, Millikan, in 1911, sprayed a mist of oil droplets between the horizontal plates of a capacitor. He then followed the course of a single electrically charged drop falling through air under the influence of gravity and the pull of the charged plate above. Occasionally the drop would pick up an ion (which Millikan provided in the chamber by exposing it to an x-ray tube or radioactive source). When the charge on the drop thus changed, the effect of the charged plate above was abruptly strengthened and the speed of the drop changed. By adjusting the voltage of the capacitor, Millikan could balance the downward gravitational force on the drop by an upward electrical force, holding the drop stationary. From such observations as the voltage, the density of the oil, and the free-fall speed of the drop, Millikan could calculate the electric charge on the drop. This he found was always an integral multiple of $e = 1 \cdot 60 \times 10^{-19}$ coulomb, nature's unit of charge.

In the years 1912–15, Millikan used complex precision equipment and specimens under high vacuum to test the relation suggested by Einstein in 1905 for the photoelectric effect. Millikan measured the minimum voltage V_s needed to stop electrons ejected from a metal by illumination of frequency f. He verified Einstein's relation,

$E_k = V_s\,e = hf - w$, and made the first direct photoelectric evaluation of Planck's constant h.

Robert Millikan was born in Morrison, Illinois, the second son of a Congregational minister, Silas Franklin Millikan, and Mary Jane Andrews Millikan, a former dean of women at Olivet College. In high school Millikan did well in mathematics but gave little attention to science. At Oberlin College in 1886, Millikan was appointed assistant to the gymnasium director. Largely on the basis of self-preparation, beginning in his junior year, Millikan taught physics at Oberlin, received his BA in 1891, remained there as a tutor, and earned his MA in 1893. Oberlin professors secured for Millikan a newly created fellowship at Columbia University where, as the only physics graduate student, he obtained his PhD in 1895. He then studied at Göttingen and Berlin.

From 1896 to 1921 Millikan was a member of the physics faculty at the University of Chicago, earning a national reputation as an outstanding educator, experimentalist and organiser. His early contribution was to develop physics instruction which used laboratory experiences and quizzes more than lectures. He wrote textbooks at four levels starting with preparatory school physics. So Millikan's first 14 years at Chicago produced few research papers. Then came his oil-drop and photoelectric experiments in 1911, and these were followed in 1920–23 by hot-spark vacuum spectroscopy which bridged the gap between x-rays and ultraviolet light, and led to to such concepts as the 'stripped atom' and 'spinning electron.'

During World War I, Millikan headed the Signal Corps Science and Research Division, where he worked on anti-submarine and meteorological devices. His development of balloons to carry propaganda a thousand miles led to his investigation of cosmic rays.

In 1921, Millikan became director of the Norman Bridge Laboratory and chairman of the executive council of the then small California Institute of Technology, where he continued to work even after his retirement in 1945. To Millikan is given much of the credit for the present high standing of CalTech.

For his study of cosmic rays (which he named), Millikan and his assistants sank apparatus to the bottom of lakes and carried equipment up the highest North American mountains, climbed the Bolivian Andes in 1926 to eliminate the effect of the Milky Way, visited Tasmania in 1939, and then India. Millikan maintained for years that cosmic rays were electromagnetic radiation, like gamma rays, only more energetic. He found a religious significance in the belief that cosmic rays were the 'birth-cry' of matter being created at the boundaries of the Universe: 'The Creator is still on the job.' He clung to the wave nature of cosmic rays even when Compton and others had made it almost certain that cosmic rays were particles, mostly extremely energetic protons.

Millikan married Greta Irvin Blanchard in 1902, and they had three sons. Carl Anderson, a student and colleague of Millikan, and himself a Nobel Prize winner, has paid tribute to Millikan as intrepid, endowed with broad and deep views, an animating educator, one interested in the affairs of his country, and one having a graciously affable manner.

Karl Manne Georg Siegbahn

1886–1978

Awarded the 1924 Nobel Prize for physics for his discoveries and research in x-ray spectroscopy.

Their relative simplicity and the close similarities between the x-ray spectra of the different elements convinced Siegbahn that these radiations originated inside the atom and had no direct connection with the complicated light spectra and chemical properties governed by the outer electron structure. Beginning in 1914, Siegbahn turned from his earlier research in electricity and magnetism and set out to learn 'the x-ray language,' first by measuring up and analysing the wave systems emitted by the atoms of the 92 elements.'

With characteristic Swedish thoroughness, Siegbahn achieved an accuracy of one second of arc with his spectrometer (giving wavelengths accurate to one part in 100 000), while others were satisfied with minutes of arc. His entire measuring system was situated in a vacuum; he improved the design of vacuum pumps, particularly the molecular pump. The x-ray tubes he designed, requiring shorter exposures, were adopted by others.

Siegbahn verified the existence of Barkla's K and L radiation (for which he had only the evidence of absorption measurements) and discovered another series of lines, called M radiation. The high resolution of Siegbahn's spectrometer showed that the K lines discovered by Moseley were doublets; in the L series (in some 50 elements) Siegbahn found 28 lines and for the M series 24. Siegbahn's work supported the view of Bohr and others that the electrons in atoms were arranged in 'shells.' The series of x-rays labelled K, L, M, . . ., Q, in order of increasing wavelength, correspond to radiation emitted when an electron further from the nucleus drops into a vacancy in the innermost K shell, or shells L, M, . . ., at increasing distances from the nucleus. Siegbahn's book *Spektroskopie der Röntgenstrahlen* (1924) was long the standard reference work.

In 1924 Siegbahn succeeded in demonstrating the refraction of x-rays by a prism, an effect which had been looked for since Röntgen's time in support of the view that x-rays were short-wavelength electromagnetic radiation.

Manne Siegbahn was born at Örebro in southern Sweden, the son of Georg and Emma Sofia Mathilda (Zetterberg) Siegbahn. His father was a railway station master. Siegbahn entered the University of Lund in 1906 and obtained his doctor's degree there in 1916. During the summer terms of 1908 and 1909 he studied at the universities of Göttingen and Munich. After serving as assistant to J R Rydberg, Siegbahn became professor of physics at Lund (1914–23). He was then appointed as professor at the University of Uppsala (1923–37), and at the Royal Swedish Academy of Sciences in Stockholm (1937–64). From 1939 to 1964 Siegbahn directed the Nobel Institute of Physics and he served as a member of the International Committee for Weights and Measures.

James Franck

1882–1964

Shared the 1925 Nobel Prize for physics with Gustav Hertz for their discovery of the laws governing the impact of an electron on an atom.

Franck's scientific activity lasted over some 60 years, starting in about 1900 when the foundations of atomic physics and quantum theory were being laid, and extending to a time when these endeavours reached sophistication. Franck's work started with a thesis on ion mobilities in gases, and he proceeded from this to discover the ionisation potential as a characteristic property of every element. His study of the fluorescence of diatomic vapours led to his discovery of the general rule for vibrational energy distribution in molecular spectra, which with a wave-mechanical interpretation, became known as the Franck–Condon principle.

In a famous experiment Franck and Hertz showed that electrons could deliver energy to a mercury atom (in an inelastic collision) only if they had a kinetic energy exceeding 4·9 eV, and that the mercury atom took up exactly this quantum of energy and thereby was caused to emit light of its resonance line, 2537 Å. This was the first direct proof of the quantum nature of energy transfer postulated by Niels Bohr, and of the connection of the quantum of energy ΔE absorbed with the frequency v of the light emitted: $v = \Delta E/h$.

In his study of fluorescence quenching and sensitised photochemical processes in solutions, Franck found chlorophyll especially intriguing. So in his later years he stepped into a new field: the photochemical processes occurring in living plants, the study of CO_2

assimilation, the source of all life on Earth.

James Franck was born in 1882 in Hamburg, Germany, the son of Jacob and Rebecca (Drucker) Franck. He studied chemistry at the University of Heidelberg, and then physics at the University of Berlin, where he received his PhD in 1906. During World War I Franck served in the German Army and was decorated with the Iron Cross.

In 1921, Franck became professor of experimental physics and director of the Zweite Physikalische Institut in Göttingen, where R Pohl occupied the other chair as director of the Erste Physikalische Institut, located in the same building. Max Born had accepted the chair of theoretical physics on the condition that a chair and department be established for Franck. For the next twelve years these friends found common interests in research and attracted to Göttingen many students and colleagues including Bohr, Heisenberg, Heitler, Hund, Pauli, Weiskopf and Wigner. Franck allowed his students extreme academic freedom. He once remarked: 'I was lucky that I was not a student at an American university. I would have been entirely unable to take all the examinations.'

In 1933, after Hitler came to power, Franck resigned his professorship and published a courageous statement of protest against the new racial laws. After spending more than a year in Copenhagen, in 1935 Franck accepted a professorship at the Johns Hopkins University in Baltimore. In 1938 he was appointed professor of physical chemistry at the University of Chicago where the Samuel Fels Fund established a laboratory for research into photosynthesis. Franck directed this institute until his retirement in 1949, although he continued to work there long afterwards.

During World War II Franck worked on the atomic bomb project. He strenuously opposed using the bomb against Japan and favoured a demonstration before representatives of the United Nations in the hope that this would lead to a ban of the bomb instead of its use. In a petition to the Secretary of War (the Franck Report, 1945), Franck and others accurately forecast the nuclear stalemate that would follow failure to ban the bomb. Soon after the war, Franck predicted that the military and industrial growth of China would soon be felt as a serious threat by Russia. This pressure, combined with the ageing of a revolutionary society, he thought, would cause Russia to tone down its revolutionary fervour and come to terms with the Western powers.

At the end of the war, Franck returned to his research at Chicago. His first wife Ingrid Josephson had died after a long illness in 1942, and in 1946 he married Hertha Sponer, a professor of physics at Duke University. The German Physical Society awarded Franck its highest honour, the Max Planck medal, in 1953, and Göttingen made him an honorary citizen. He died there on a tour of Germany to visit old friends in 1964.

In honouring Franck on his seventieth birthday, Peter

Pringsheim wrote that his experimental methods were characterised by a great simplicity in the apparatus he used. The same applied in certain respects to his theoretical reasoning: very little mathematics, if any; a good deal of common sense and straight logic, and—most of all—an indefatigable intensity. Colleagues recalled Franck's obsession with science and his kindness and generosity.

Gustav Ludwig Hertz

1887–1975

Shared the 1925 Nobel Prize for physics with James Franck for their discovery of the laws governing the collision of an electron and an atom.

Gustav Hertz, a nephew of Heinrich Hertz, is best known for a famous experiment with James Franck that demonstrated that discrete energies were required for the emission of spectral lines by atoms excited by impinging electrons. This pioneering work (1914) provided decisive support for Bohr's quantised model of the atom.

Hertz was born in Hamburg, Germany, the son of Gustav and Auguste Arning Hertz. He studied at the University of Munich and in 1911 obtained his doctor's degree at Berlin, with a thesis on infrared absorption. He was severely wounded in the war and when he returned to Berlin in 1917 the only available position was as an unpaid *Privatdozent* at the University. From 1920 to 1925 Hertz worked in the laboratory of the Philips Company in Holland, one of the first industrial laboratories to support basic research. There he began his important experiments on the separation of isotopes by diffusion cascade, starting with neon.

In 1925 Hertz was offered a professorship at the University in Halle and in 1928 he moved to the Technische Hochschule in Berlin–Charlottenburg. Since he was of Jewish descent, Hertz was forced to leave that position in 1934, after Hitler came to power, but he remained in Germany and became director of Research Laboratory II of the Siemens Corporation.

After the fall of Berlin in 1945, Hertz was the leading member of a group of physicists who went to work in the Soviet Union.

He had told friends when he visited the United States in 1939 that he believed that physics in the US was too advanced to use his skills effectively. But he thought he could make a valuable contribution to the progress of physics in the USSR and he hoped especially that it would be possible for him and his family to integrate into Russian life. They were disappointed. They were segregated from society in a laboratory complex in Sukhumi on the Black Sea coast where some 200 Russian and German scientists conducted research in atomic energy, radar and supersonics. When the German scientists returned from the Soviet Union at the end of their ten-year contract, Hertz became a professor and director of the Physics Institute, University of Leipzig, 1955–61. Upon retirement, he moved to East Berlin.

Gustav Hertz married Ellen Dihlmann in 1919; they had two children, Helmuth and Johannes. Following the death of his first wife in 1941, Hertz married Charlotte Jollasse in 1943. Hertz was an excellent photographer and recorded colleagues and events over his long career.

Jean Baptiste Perrin

1870–1942

Awarded the 1926 Noble Prize for physics for his work on discontinuity in the structure of matter, and in particular for his discovery of the equilibrium of sedimentation.

Jean Perrin was born in Lille, France. He and his two sisters were raised in modest circumstances by his mother after his father died of wounds received in the Franco–Prussian War. Perrin attended the Ecole Normale Supérieure, or training college for teachers, in Paris, and he was himself a teacher of physics there from 1894 to 1897, when he obtained his doctorate. Soon after, he married Henriette Duportal; they had a daughter, Aline, and a son, François. Perrin then became a lecturer in physical chemistry at the Sorbonne. He was appointed professor there in 1910 and held that post for the next 30 years, except for the period 1914–18, when he served as an officer in the Engineers.

Perrin's earliest experiments were planned to determine the nature of cathode rays and the mechanism of conduction in gases produced by x-rays and radioactive substances. Perrin directed a narrow beam of cathode rays across the diameter of an evacuated flask. A small cylindrical metal cup was fixed at the far side, off this axis. When, by means of a magnetic field, Perrin diverted the beam into the cylinder it acquired a substantial negative charge. Both this charge and the direction of the field required to bend their path showed that cathode rays were negatively charged particles, and not a form of wave radiation, as many European physicists had thought. These experiments prepared the way for J J Thomson's determination in 1897 of the charge/mass ratio of these particles (electrons).

The work for which Perrin is best known is his investigation of Brownian motion, the erratic movements performed by microscopic particles in suspension in a fluid, now interpreted as being caused by the continuous, irregular bombardment of the particles by the molecules of the surrounding medium. Perrin thought that colloidally suspended particles undergoing Brownian motion would distribute themselves vertically in a definite way at equilibrium. By counting small particles of gum resin suspended in water, Perrin found that their number decreased exponentially with increasing height. He proved that this variation follows from kinetic theory and that from it he could calculate a value for Avogadro's number. Since the size of a water molecule appeared in the equation for the vertical distribution of the Brownian motion particles, for the first time the sizes of atoms and molecules could be calculated from actual observations. As Henri Poincaré wrote: 'The brilliant determination of the number of atoms [in a mole] made by Perrin has completed the triumph of atomism . . . The atom of the chemists is now a reality.'

Perrin's book *Les Atomes* (1913) dealt with discoveries made in molecular physics during the active period following the discovery of Röntgen rays and radioactivity. Widely read and translated, this book sold 30 000 copies before the 1936 edition was printed. In another book, *Grains de Matière et de Lumière* (1935), Perrin gave a vivid account of the theories of radiation and several problems which agitated physicists. As under-secretary of state for scientific research, Perrin sought to popularise science, particularly among young people. This led to the *Palace of Discovery* at the 1937 International Exhibition.

As an army officer in World War I, Perrin worked on military equipment such as detection devices for submarines. In the late 1930s he was primarily responsible for establishment of the Centre National de la Recherche Scientifique. An active anti-Fascist, Perrin left France in 1938 for the United States, where his son was teaching at Columbia University. In his seventies, Perrin used his influence to support the de Gaulle movement. He did not live to see his country liberated, but died in New York in 1942. After the war, his remains were returned to France and buried in the Pantheon.

Perrin was a widely liked man, lively and original in conversation. He took great interest in young people engaged in research and held parties for them each week in his laboratory for general discussions. He had more confidence in experimental investigations than in mathematical theories. Once another professor who was advancing a certain theory importuned Perrin to accept it, pleading, 'At least you must admit that there is something in it.' Perrin responded: 'My dear . . ., it would be difficult to prepare a theory that was entirely false.'

Arthur Holly Compton

1892–1962

For the discovery of the Compton effect, Compton shared the 1927 Nobel Prize for physics with Charles Wilson.

Arthur Compton, the son of a Presbyterian minister, graduated in 1913 from the College of Wooster where his father was dean and professor of philosophy. As a student he earned his letters in football, baseball and basketball, and graduated with highest honours. It was his intention to become an engineer, but his brother Karl (who became president of MIT) recommended that he should obtain more theoretical training in physics, at Princeton. There he received his MA in 1914 and his PhD in 1916.

He then taught for a year at the University of Minnesota and for two years worked for the Westinghouse Corporation and the Signal Corps on the development of aeroplane instruments. In 1919 Compton went as a national research fellow to Cambridge where he studied with Rutherford, and on his return to the US in 1920, he became head of the physics department at Washington University in St Louis. From 1923 to 1945 he was associated with the University of Chicago, but returned to Washington University, as chancellor (1945–53), and then as professor of natural history (1953–61).

In 1916 Compton married Betty Charity McCloskey; they had two sons, Arthur Allen and John Joseph.

As a college senior, Compton built apparatus for determining the Earth's rotation; he obtained a value within five per cent of the accepted value. His first major discovery (in about 1923) was the measurement (with a crystal spectrometer) and interpretation of the wavelength change which occurs when x-rays are scattered, especially by materials of low atomic number—the 'Compton effect.' He showed that x-rays were scattered by the loosely bound electrons in the material, in accordance with the principles of conservation of energy and momentum, as if the ray consisted of a stream of photons, each having energy $h\nu$ and momentum $h\nu/c$. Planck and Einstein had already assigned the energy $h\nu$ to a photon. Compton's experiment provided the first clear demonstration that x-ray photons carried quantised amounts of momentum.

During the next few years, coincidence methods of measurement were developed by Compton and A W Simon in Chicago, and independently by Walther Bothe and Hans Geiger in Germany. These experiments showed that individual scattered x-ray photons and recoil electrons appeared at the same instant. This finding was contrary to some speculations being developed by Bohr, Kramers and Slater in an attempt to reconcile quantum views with the electromagnetic theory's view of continuous waves.

In Sweden, Stenström had suggested that the index of refraction for x-rays was less than unity; Compton confirmed this (1922) by showing that a monochromatic x-ray beam could be totally reflected from glass and silver mirrors if the glancing angle was very small (a few minutes of arc). He also showed that a ruled grating should produce diffraction of x-rays if the glancing angle was less than the critical angle for total reflection; in 1925 he succeeded in measuring x-ray wavelengths by this method.

In about 1930 Compton turned to the investigation of cosmic rays, particularly their variation in intensity with latitude and altitude. From data he collected from around the world, Compton concluded that the rays did not originate in the Solar System or even in the Milky Way, but in remote space beyond. From a correlation of cosmic ray intensities with geomagnetic latitude, Compton concluded that the rays were primarily high-energy charged particles, mostly protons, being deflected by the Earth's magnetic field—and not electromagnetic radiation, a view tenaciously held by Millikan.

Compton's involvement in the atomic bomb effort has been recorded in his book *Atomic Quest*. In November 1941 Compton, as chairman, presented the report of the National Academy of Sciences committee organised to review the military potentialities of atomic energy This report, a masterpiece of scientific and technological prevision, as much as any other consideration precipitated the vast uranium project effort, started by the US in 1942. Compton took active direction of the group, 'cover-name' Metallurgical Laboratory of the University of Chicago, which concentrated on the development of controlled uranium fission reactors for the production of plutonium. Within a year the first reactor was in operation at Chicago.

After the war, Compton became chancellor of Washington University in St Louis, and from 1945 to 1953 worked with great vigour to revitalise the university and move it toward greatness. In 1953 he requested relief from administrative duties so that he could return to teaching and devote himself to problems of the social impact of science and technology and to relieving international tensions. In the first chapter of *Atomic Quest*, Compton approvingly gives a quotation ascribed to Pythagoras: 'Seek therefore to find of what and how the world is made, so that you may learn a better way of life.' Shortly before his death, Compton had begun a series of semi-public lectures on 'Science and Human Responsibility.'

Charles Thomson Rees Wilson

1869–1959

Shared the 1927 Nobel Prize for physics with Arthur Compton for his discovery of a method of rendering discernible the paths of electrically charged particles by the condensation of vapour.

In 1894 Wilson spent a few weeks in the observatory on Ben Nevis, a Scottish peak, the highest in Great Britain. 'The wonderful optical phenomena shown when the sun shone on the clouds . . . greatly excited my interest and made me wish to imitate them in the laboratory,' he wrote.

At the Cavendish Laboratory in 1895 Wilson began his investigation of cloud formation in an apparatus to condense water vapour in dust-free air. He allowed moist air to expand within a glass vessel. Expansion lowered the temperature of the air so that it could not retain all of its moisture; the excess condensed into droplets, provided nuclei were present. Dust particles encouraged drops to form immediately, so Wilson carefully removed dust from his apparatus. He then found that condensation occurred on ions, produced when an x-ray tube irradiated the expansion chamber. Negative ions acted as nuclei at an expansion ratio of 1·25 (fourfold supersaturation); positive ions became nuclei at 1·31 (sixfold supersaturation). The vapour pressure of a spherical drop is greater than that of a plane surface and in inverse ratio to its radius, so if a minute drop forms, it may re-evaporate immediately. A nucleus provides the larger radius needed for the persistence of a drop. If a drop carries an electrical charge, it acts contrary to the surface tension and tends to enlarge the drop.

A 'hair-raising' experience during a thunderstorm at the summit of Carn Mor Dearg diverted Wilson's interest to a study of the Earth's electrical field and thunderstorms. He developed the basic knowledge of atmospheric electricity (1895–1900). Noting that even well insulated electroscopes showed a residual leakage, the same in daylight and darkness, Wilson made a prophetic remark: 'Experiments were now carried out to test whether the production of ions in air could be explained as being due to radiation from sources . . . outside our atmosphere . . .' Victor Hess tested this hypothesis in 1911 by taking an electroscope up in a balloon, finding that the conductivity of air increases with altitude. To explain this effect he postulated the existence of 'cosmic radiation.'

In 1910 Wilson resumed his work on the expansion chamber, making provision for photographing the tracks (vapour trails) left by charged particles. When the chamber was subjected to a magnetic field the nature of the curved path showed whether the charge was positive or negative and how massive the particle was. The cloud chamber became an invaluable tool in the study of cosmic rays, especially in refined models devised by Patrick Blackett. Their tracks indicate collisions of particles with other particles and provide information about events taking place during and after the collision. J J Thomson wrote: 'It is to Wilson that we owe the creation of a method which has been of inestimable value to the progress of science.'

Charles Wilson was born in 1869 in Glencorse, near Edinburgh, Scotland, the youngest of the eight children of a sheep farmer, John Wilson, and his second wife, Annie Clark Harper Wilson. His father died when Charles was four, and his mother then moved to Manchester. At the age of 15, Wilson entered Owens College, Manchester; he registered as a medical student but took a BSc degree when he was 18. In 1888 he entered Sidney Sussex College, Cambridge, with a scholarship, undertook special studies of physics and chemistry, and graduated in 1892. Wilson carried out his research on the expansion chamber, initiated with the encouragement of J J Thomson, for three years as a Clerk Maxwell student. Then his research on atmospheric electricity was sponsored by the Meteorological Office.

In 1900 Wilson was appointed a university lecturer in physics; from then until 1918 he supervised the advanced physics teaching at the Cavendish Laboratory. He liked to give his students minor research problems to solve in the laboratory, rather than carry out textbook experiments. From 1925 until his retirement in 1934, Wilson was Jacksonian Professor of natural philosophy at Cambridge.

When he was 39, Wilson married Jessie Fraser Dick; they had a son and two daughters. On retirement, he returned to Scotland where he spent 23 active years; he continued mountain climbing until he was well into his eighties. At 86 he took delight, whenever occasion offered, in flying on the weather flights over the Outer Isles as an honorary member of the meteorology department of the University of Edinburgh. In 1956, at the age of 87, Wilson, the oldest fellow of the Royal Society, presented to the Society his last paper, *A Theory of Thundercloud Electricity*, a 20-page paper of closely reasoned statements of current value. P M S Blackett wrote of Wilson, 'Of the great scientists of this age, he was perhaps the most gentle and serene, and the most indifferent to prestige and honour: his absorption in his work arose from his intense love of the natural world and from his delight in its beauties.'

Sir Owen Willans Richardson

1879–1959

Awarded (in 1929) the 1928 Nobel Prize for physics for his work on thermionic phenomena and especially for discovery of the law which bears his name.

Before the physical atom and the concept of the electron had been widely accepted, Edison had detected an electric current across the vacuum in a bulb containing a heated filament and collector. This phenomenon had been used by Fleming to devise a rectifier and by de Forest to construct a diode, although it was Richardson who worked out the theory of electron and ion emission, and made possible the rapid development of radio, telephony, television and x-ray technology.

Intuitively Richardson felt that both negative and positive charges emanated directly from heated solid filaments themselves, rather than from chemical interactions of neighbouring gas molecules with hot bodies. He applied kinetic theory to the simple hypothesis that freely moving electrons in the interior of a hot conductor escape when they reach the surface provided that their kinetic energy is great enough to overcome the attraction of the positive charges in the material.

Richardson's law expresses the dependence of the saturation current i on the temperature T of the filament: $i = AT^2 \exp(-w/kT)$, where A is a universal constant, w is the electronic workfunction of the metal, and k is Boltzmann's constant. Richardson persevered in his experimental checks, improving on the hand pumps then used to obtain a vacuum, and on vacuum clean-up techniques, and welcoming the advert of ductile tungsten (1913). Some 15 years of Richardson's early career were invested in the painstaking study of thermionics (a term he coined), culminating in his book *The Emission of Electricity from Hot Bodies* (1910). He was pleased that his basic equation of thermionic emission (re-interpreted as the Richardson–Dushman equation above) survived the quantum mechanical revolution of the 1920s.

Owen Richardson was born in 1879 in Dewsbury, Yorkshire, the only son of Charlotte Maria and Joshua Henry Richardson, who sold industrial tools. Owen's precocity brought him, at the age of 12, a scholarship to Batley Grammar School, where he won many contests and a scholarship to Trinity College, Cambridge, in 1897. At the Cavendish Laboratory he encountered such scholars as J J Thomson, Ernest Rutherford, C T R Wilson, Paul Langevin and H A Wilson. He obtained a first in the tripos for physics, chemistry and botany, and in 1900 received his BA from Cambridge (MA in 1904) and his BSc from the University of London. He remained at the Cavendish Laboratory until 1906, starting his work on thermionics and collaborating with H A Wilson and H O Jones on studies in physical and organic chemistry.

In 1906 Richardson married Lillian Maud Wilson, the sister of H A Wilson, and they then moved to Princeton University where he was appointed professor of physics. Their two sons and one daughter were born during their seven-year stay in the United States. *The Electron Theory of Matter* (1914), a model of a not-too-concentrated presentation and a classic text for a generation of students, was developed from lectures Richardson gave at Princeton for graduate students, among whom were Robert H Goddard and the brothers Arthur H and Karl T Compton.

Richardson was lured to return to England as Wheatstone Professor of physics at King's College, University of London, in 1913. During World War I he engaged in military research in telecommunications but also managed to publish a few papers on spectroscopy, on tests of Bohr's theory of the atom, and on Einstein's interpretation of the photoelectric effect. During the 1920s and 1930s Richardson published about three papers each year, all meticulous and following the thread of his chief interest: the connection between physics and chemistry. In 1939 Richardson was knighted. During World War II, he concentrated on radar, sonar, electronic testing instruments, magnetrons and klystrons.

As president of the Physical Society and its honorary foreign secretary, Richardson had occasion to entertain many distinguished visitors. They found his wife a most gracious hostess in a beautiful home with the finest English period furniture and a collection of paintings by Dutch and other masters fit for a national gallery.

When Richardson retired from the University of London in 1944 he bought a farm a few miles from his country home near Alton, Hampshire. There he and his wife enjoyed gardening and ran a dairy farm until her death the following year. In 1948 Richardson married

Henrietta M G Rupp, a distinguished physicist and an authority on luminescence in solids.

Sir Owen was a quiet and kindly man of few, well chosen words. He had a keen sense of humour and was proud of his Yorkshire origins. In physics he contributed to the understanding of an extraordinary range of problems of current interest. His library contained 2700 books on the atom; his bookplate carried a simple device, the sign for infinity, ∞. He encouraged his students in dexterity, patience and faith in following hunches—cautiously.

Louis-Victor
Pierre Raymond,
Prince de Broglie

1892–1960

Awarded the 1929 Nobel Prize for physics for his discovery of the wave nature of electrons.

A year before the explanation of the Compton effect, which settled the existence of light quanta, de Broglie in 1922 wrote an article in which he derived Wien's radiation law without using the electromagnetic theory. In it he said: 'The hypothesis of quanta of light is adopted.' He treated photons as particles or 'atoms of light' with mass hv/c^2, and momentum hv/c. This interest in the properties of quanta led de Broglie to search for a theory that would unify wave and particle aspects. Suddenly, in the summer of 1923, de Broglie said, the idea occurred to him to generalise the wave–particle duality to include material particles, particularly electrons, as well. He presented these ideas in two short articles in *Comptes Rendus* and a note in *Nature*. He elaborated them in his 1924 doctoral thesis at the Sorbonne, which was published as a paper of over 100 pages in the *Annales de Physique* in 1925.

De Broglie assumed that a particle, an electron for example, had associated with it a system of 'matter waves' having slightly different velocities of propagation. At regular intervals along the path of propagation the waves would combine to form a wave-crest; the crest would disappear at one point and appear an instant later at another point. The velocity of the crest, the 'group velocity,' is quite different from the velocities of the waves which combine to form it. De Broglie identified the group velocity with the velocity of the electron. This distance between successive crests is the de Broglie wavelength of the 'matter wave.' It is calculated from $\lambda = h/mv$, where h is Planck's constant and mv is the momentum of the particle.

For an object such as a thrown baseball (large mv) the wavelength so calculated is so fantastically small as to defy detection, but for an electron moving at 100 cm/s, λ is about 0·07 cm. A crystal lattice with comparable atomic spacing might serve to detect de Broglie waves through interference. Indeed, in 1927 Davisson and Germer working with slow (59 eV) electrons, and G P Thomson working with fast electrons, showed that a beam of electrons having a common velocity exhibits diffraction (a wave property) when impinging on a crystal lattice, and that λ calculated from the energy and angle of deviation definitely agrees with the value of λ predicted by the de Broglie equation.

Louis de Broglie was born in 1892 in Dieppe, France, the son of Duc Victor and Pauline d'Armaille Broglie. The de Broglie family, of Piedmontese origin, had served French kings in war and diplomacy for hundreds of years, and in 1740 King Louis XIV made a member of the family a *Duc*, a hereditary title which could only be held by the head of the family. The son of the first duke aided the Austrians in the Seven Years War and was rewarded with the title *Prinz*, to be carried by all members of the family. With the death of his older brother Maurice, who maintained a private research centre for x-rays, in 1960, Louis de Broglie became concurrently a French duke and a German prince.

De Broglie studied at the Lycée Janson de Sailly in Paris, and obtained a degree in history from the Sorbonne in 1909. He said he was brought to science 'by philosophy, by generalisations, and by the books of Henri Poincaré.' He obtained a *licence* in science in 1913 from the Faculté des Sciences, Paris. Throughout World War I de Broglie served in the French Engineers, spending much of this period working at the wireless station on the Eiffel Tower.

At the age of 32, after he had already published some two dozen papers on electron, atom and x-ray problems, de Broglie received his doctorate with a thesis which was to be the starting point for his later work on wave mechanics. Not entirely satisfied with the probability amplitude interpretation Schrödinger and others had placed on the wave equation, de Broglie continued to seek a causal interpretation of wave mechanics. De Broglie taught at the University of Paris and at the Henri Poincaré Institute. He was the author of more than 20 books, in addition to his many research papers.

Maurice and Louis de Broglie were named counsellors to the French High Commission of Atomic Energy in 1945. They were deeply interested in the peaceful development of atomic energy and in strengthening the bonds between science and industry. As permanent secretary of the Academy of Science, de Broglie urged that body to consider the harmful effects of thermonuclear explosions.

Sir Chandrasekhara Venkata Raman

1888–1970

Awarded the 1930 Nobel Prize for physics for his work on the scattering of light and for the discovery of the Raman effect.

After Compton's discovery of the Compton effect for x-rays, Heisenberg predicted (1925) that a similar effect ought to be found for visible light. Raman had already been investigating light scattering and had come to the same conclusion. When monochromatic light is directed through a transparent substance, some of the light is scattered. The spectrum of the scattered light contains, in addition to light of the original wavelength, weaker lines which differ from this by constant amounts. These now-called Raman lines are due to the loss or gain of energy experienced by the photons as a result of their interaction with the vibrating molecules of the substance through which they pass. The Raman effect, first described in the *Indian Journal of Physics* in 1928, is therefore valuable in the study of molecular energy levels.

Venkata Raman was born in 1888 in Trichinopoly, Madras Presidency, a descendant of a long line of Indian landholders. He was educated at the Hindu College, Vishakapatam, where his father taught mathematics and physics, and at the Presidency College, Madras. While still an undergraduate, he started investigations in acoustics and optics and published his first paper in the *Philosophical Magazine* at the age of 18.

There were then no opportunities or incentives for a young Indian to enter a career in science, and so Raman worked for ten years in the Indian Finance Department, most of the time in Calcutta. He continued his research and during this period published no fewer than 30 papers. When the Palit Professorship was endowed at the University of Calcutta and was offered to Raman, he accepted it, at some financial sacrifice. He held this post for 16 years, and with collaborators such as M Saha and S N Bose he helped make Calcutta a centre for scientific research. There significant contributions were made to the fields of vibration and sound, musical instruments, ultrasonics, diffraction, meteorological and colloid optics, photoelectricity, x-ray diffraction, magnetism, dielectrics and Raman spectroscopy.

Starting in 1930 Raman divided his time between training future leaders of science and investigations into the science of crystallography which he believed '. . . will ultimately have repercussions in the whole scientific world.' He gave a substantial part of his $40 000 Nobel Prize for the purchase of diamonds for laboratory investigation. He thought that there must be two and possibly four types of diamond based on tetrahedral and octahedral symmetry. He showed that the luminescence of a diamond excited by ultraviolet light is not due to impurities or defects, as had previously been believed, but is a characteristic of the diamond itself.

In 1933 Raman became director of the Indian Institute of Science at Bangalore, where he instituted work on the diffraction of light by ultrasonic waves, Brillouin scattering in liquids, and light scattering by colloids. In 1947 Raman founded an institute of his own, near the offices of the Indian Academy of Science, which he had also founded in 1935. Raman was the first Asian to win a Nobel Prize, and through his achievements in physics and his fostering of Indian science, he became a national hero. A proud man of strong presence, he represented India at numerous international meetings. He was fluent in American slang and prided himself on being a humorist.

Sir Venkata's wife was Lokasundrammal Raman; they married in 1907 and had two children, Chandrasekhara and Radhakrishnan.

In addition to research already mentioned, Raman was interested in the vibration of musical instruments and the physiology of vision. He studied flowers spectroscopically, loved roses, and maintained a large rose garden. He was cremated there when he died at the aged of 82.

Werner Karl Heisenberg

1901–1976

Awarded (in 1933) the 1932 Nobel Prize for physics for his establishment of quantum mechanics whose application has led, among other things, to the discovery of the allotropic forms of hydrogen.

Werner Heisenberg was born in 1901 in Duisberg, Germany, the son of Annie Wecklein and August Heisenberg, who became a university professor of history. Werner studied theoretical physics under Arnold Sommerfeld at the University of Munich and received his PhD there in 1923. He then advanced from assistant to lecturer, successively, under Max Born at Göttingen and under Niels Bohr at Copenhagen, 1924–26. He then returned to Germany as professor of theoretical physics at the University of Leipzig, 1927–41. From 1941 to 1945 he was director of the Max Planck Institute and professor at the University of Berlin, and after 1958 he held a similar dual appointment in Munich.

Heisenberg felt that the Bohr theory had not received better confirmation from experiment because it was based on things not directly observable, such as the picture of electrons moving in orbits. In 1927, making use of matrix algebra, Heisenberg developed a system called matrix mechanics. This consisted of an array of quantities which when appropriately manipulated gave the observed frequencies and intensities of spectral lines. Schrödinger's wave mechanics, announced only months later, was shown by von Neumann to be equivalent to Heisenberg's approach.

Heisenberg applied his matrix mechanics to explain alternations of strong and weak lines in the spectrum of molecular hydrogen.

He concluded that two forms existed: one orthohydrogen, in which the spins of the two separate hydrogen nuclei (protons) are in the same direction, and another, parahydrogen, in which they are in opposite directions.

Philosophically, the most engaging consequence of Heisenberg's work is his principle of uncertainty (*Unbestimmtheit*). If we accept the view that a particle is represented by ('guided by') a de Broglie wave packet, then according to Heisenberg it is impossible to make an exact and simultaneous determination of both the position x and the momentum mv of any body. The smaller we pin down the uncertainty in one, say Δx, the larger the uncertainty, $\Delta(mv)$, will be in the other. The product of these is related to Planck's constant, h: $\Delta x \Delta(mv) \geqslant h/4\pi$. The very act of 'looking at' an electron, by scattering photons off it, changes the electron's momentum. The uncertainty principle disturbed people because it weakened the law of cause and effect. Many had believed, like Laplace, that the entire history of the Universe, past and future, could in principle be calculated *if the position and velocity of every particle in it were known for any one instant in time.* The uncertainty principle says this premise is impossible. Einstein found Heisenberg's replacement of complete predictability by a statistical probability uncomfortable; they had numerous discussions.

In 1932 Heisenberg pointed out that an atomic nucleus consisting of protons and neutrons was more satisfactory than one consisting (as had previously been assumed) of protons and electrons. He held that the nucleons would be held in the nucleus by means of 'exchange forces'—a wave-mechanical concept later elucidated by Yukawa.

During World War II, Heisenberg was the man most feared by US atomic bomb experts as they raced to perfect that weapon. The facts are not clear, but perhaps Germany's interest in developing, under Heisenberg's leadership, atomic energy for industrial purposes was not diverted into a weapons programme because of the higher priority assigned by the government to planes and flying bombs.

After the war, Heisenberg criticised Chancellor Konrad Adenauer for failing to provide a larger budget for the construction of a nuclear reactor. As a protest, Heisenberg declined to be a member of the West German delegation to the UN International Conference on Peaceful Uses of Atomic Energy held in Geneva in August 1955. He did represent West Germany as a delegate to the UNESCO conferences to plan a European atomic research centre. In his autobiography *Physics and Beyond*, Heisenberg wrote on the moral and philosophical implications of scientific discovery.

Heisenberg married Elisabeth Schumacher in 1937; they had three sons and four daughters. The whole family frequently gathered to play chamber music.

Paul Adrien Maurice Dirac

1902–

Shared the 1933 Nobel Prize for physics with Erwin Schrödinger for the discovery of new and productive forms of atomic theory.

Unlike de Broglie's pioneer work, Schrödinger's wave mechanics had been worked out only in the non-relativistic form. Schrödinger was aware that a relativistic treatment brought out finer details but that they were in disagreement with experiment. In 1928 Dirac gave the wave theory a fascinating new direction; his new wave equation automatically accounted for the so-called spin properties which, as a special hypothesis, Goudsmit and Uhlenbeck had ascribed to the electron in 1925 to account for the doublet nature of terms in the alkali spectra. Dirac also obtained correct values for the fine structure of the hydrogen lines, in which the de Broglie–Schrödinger theory had failed.

Dirac also predicted the existence of a *positive* counterpart of the electron—a prediction verified in 1932 when Anderson discovered the positron in cosmic radiation. 'We begin,' said Dirac, 'with the equation connecting the kinetic energy W and momentum p . . . of a particle in relativistic mechanics: $W^2/c^2 - p^2 - m^2c^2 = 0$ . . . One sees that it allows the kinetic energy W to be either a positive quantity greater than mc^2, or a negative quantity less than $-mc^2$.' To give meaning to these negative-energy states, Dirac made use of the exclusion principle of Pauli: there can be only one electron in any state of motion. He then made the bizarre assumption that in the world as we know it, nearly all the states of negative energy for electrons are occupied and that a uniform filling of all the negative-energy states is completely unobservable by us. But, '. . . any unoccupied negative-energy state, being a departure from uniformity, is observable and is just a positron.' In this view the positron is just a mirror image of the electron, having exactly the same mass and opposite charge.

From Dirac's theoretical picture, one should expect an ordinary electron with positive energy, to be able to drop into a 'hole' in the otherwise uniformly filled negative-energy states and fill up this hole, the kinetic energy being liberated in the form of electromagnetic radiation. This would be a process in which an electron and a positron annihilate each other. The converse process, the creation of an electron and a positron from electromagnetic radiation, should also be possible. Both of Dirac's predictions were later confirmed by experiments. Dirac's theories marked the start of the investigation into antiparticles and antimatter.

Paul Dirac was born in 1902 in Bristol, England, the son of a Swiss father, Charles Adrien Ladislas Dirac, and an English mother, Florence Hana Dirac. He was educated at the Merchant Venturers' School in Bristol, and obtained his BSc degree in electrical engineering at the University of Bristol in 1921. He remained there to study mathematics for a further two years and then went to St John's College, Cambridge, as a research student in mathematics. He began work on the new quantum mechanics as soon as it was introduced by Heisenberg in 1925. In 1926 he obtained his PhD degree at Cambridge, and later married Margit Wigner.

Travel attracted Dirac; he studied at various foreign universities. In 1929, after spending five months in America, he went round the world, visiting Japan, together with Heisenberg, and then returning to England across Siberia. Dirac was Lucasian Professor of mathematics at Cambridge from 1932 to 1969.

Dirac was a visiting lecturer at several American universities: Wisconsin, Michigan, Princeton and Miami; he was a member of the Institute for Advanced Study, Princeton, in 1934–35. His 1969 lectures at the University of Miami were published as *Spinors in Hilbert Space* (1974), a highly mathematical updating of his earlier *Principles of Quantum Mechanics* (1930). While at Florida State University, Dirac published his 'large numbers' hypothesis of cosmology, which asserts that '. . . all the large dimensionless numbers occurring in nature are connected with the present epoch, expressed in atomic units, and thus vary with time. It requires that the gravitational constant G in atomic units shall vary.'

Erwin Schrödinger

1887–1961

Shared the 1933 Nobel Prize for physics with Paul Dirac for their discovery of new and productive forms of atomic theory.

Schrödinger was profoundly influenced by de Broglie's work on waves associated with the motion of free particles (1923–24) and he set about trying to apply this concept to bound particles, to improve on the Bohr model of the atom. In Schrödinger's atom an electron can be in any orbit in which its matter wave fits in a whole number of wavelengths. This picture of a standing wave replaces that of an electron in accelerated, circular motion; so long as the electron remains in orbit it need not radiate light, and there is no violation of Maxwell's equations.

Initially Schrödinger took into account relativistic mechanics for the motion of the electron and he was disappointed when his results did not agree with observations. The discrepancy was due solely to his not taking into account the spin of the electron, which was not recognised until 1925 by Goudsmit and Uhlenbeck. However, Schrödinger noticed that if he treated the electron non-relativistically his method gave results in agreement with observations in the non-relativistic approximation. So it was in this form that he first published his work in 1926.

Schrödinger's wave equation is the key relationship in a mathematical fabric which was one of the most surprising and important of the sudden advances that have occurred in the development of physics. Dirac and Born made notable contributions to the development of this wave mechanics. It was later shown that Heisenberg's matrix mechanics (1925) was equivalent to wave mechanics. To many, Schrö-dinger's representation was psychologically more attractive because it offered a sort of picture of the atom, although more abstract than Bohr's.

Erwin Schrödinger was born in 1887 in Vienna, Austria. He was taught at home until he was eleven, and his father encouraged his interest in nature with a microscope and other equipment. At the University of Vienna, where he received his PhD in 1910, Schrödinger was much influenced by Fritz Hasenöhrl, a professor of theoretical physics who was killed during World War I. Schrödinger himself served as an artillery officer. In 1920 he married Annemarie Bertel and he became assistant to Max Wien in Vienna. He was extraordinary profes-sor at Stuttgart, professor of physics at Zürich for six years, and then succeeded Max Planck as professor of theoretical physics at Berlin.

With the rise of Nazism, in 1933 Schrödinger accepted an invitation to be guest professor at Magdalen College, Oxford, and in the same year he received the Nobel Prize. In 1936 he was offered a situation at Graz, and although he was aware of the uncertain position of Austria, his desire to return to his native country outweighed caution and he accepted. With the German annexation of Austria in 1938, Schrödinger escaped to Italy, and then to the United States. Following a short stay at Princeton, Schrödinger became director of the School of Theoretical Physics, Institute for Advanced Studies in Dublin, and was joined there by Dirac. In 1956 he returned to the University of Vienna. For a time he represented Austria in the International Atomic Energy Agency.

In addition to his pioneering work in wave mechanics, Schrödinger published research papers on specific heats of solids, statistical thermodynamics, atomic spectra, radium, space and time, theory of colour, science and the human temperament, as well as a collection of poems and a treatise on the physical aspects of the living cell. He did not like the generally accepted dual description of atomic physics in terms of waves and particles, and tried to set up a theory in terms of waves only. Like Einstein, he sought to unify gravitation and electromagnetism.

According to Dirac, Schrödinger was unconventional. 'When he went to the Solvay conferences in Brussels, he would walk from the station to the hotel where the delegates stayed, carrying all his luggage in a rucksack and looking so like a tramp that it needed a great deal of argument at the reception desk before he could claim a room.'

Sir James Chadwick

1891–1974

Awarded the 1935 Nobel Prize for physics for his discovery of the neutron.

In the period 1930–32 Bothe and the Joliot-Curies found that when certain light elements such as beryllium were bombarded with alpha particles, some sort of radiation occurred which showed its presence by ejecting protons from paraffin. They did not reach a satisfactory identification for this radiation, but Chadwick repeated the experiments and in 1932 suggested a consistent interpretation in terms of the *neutron*, a neutral particle of approximately the mass of a proton, whose existence had been intuitively foreseen by Rutherford. Chadwick proposed that alpha particles knocked neutrons out of the nuclei of beryllium atoms and that these neutrons in turn knocked protons out of paraffin (rich in hydrogen atoms). Energy measurements confirmed Chadwick's suggestion; using data on different targets he was able to calculate the mass of the neutron.

Unaffected by electric charges, the neutron can slip into a nucleus; it proved to be the most useful particle for initiating nuclear reactions. An important type, nuclear fission, was discovered by Hahn and Meitner in 1938. The concept of an atomic nucleus built of protons and neutrons (as suggested by Heisenberg) explained why, when the elements are arranged in order of increasing mass, the atomic mass (the sum of proton and neutron masses) increases more rapidly than the atomic number (the number of protons). Further, different isotopes of a particular element all contain the same number of protons (and hence

101

have the same number of peripheral electrons and the same chemical properties); they differ in mass by having a different number of neutrons.

James Chadwick was born in Manchester, in 1891. He attended Manchester Grammar School, entered the University of Manchester in 1908, and graduated from the Honours School of Physics in 1911. He continued work at the university on radioactivity under Rutherford from 1911 to 1913 when he received his MSc. He then received an 1851 Exhibition Scholarship which required its holder to carry out research in a laboratory new to him. Unfortunately, Chadwick chose to work with Geiger at the Physikalische-Technische Reichsanstalt in Berlin. When the German preparations for war became apparent, Chadwick delayed leaving Germany, under conflicting advice from friends, and was interned (1914–18), quartered in stables of a racecourse at Ruhleben near Spandau—initially six men in a cubicle intended for two horses. Conditions improved somewhat, and with money from England and kind help from Planck, Nernst and Meitner, Chadwick was even able to do some physics. In the camp, Chadwick met C D Ellis, an engineer, and converted him to his 'science society.' Later the co-authors of the renowned *Radiations from Radioactive Substances* (1930) were Rutherford, Chadwick and Ellis.

In 1919 Chadwick was awarded the Wollaston Studentship at Gonville and Caius College, Cambridge; his research there was chiefly on the artificial disintegration of elements by bombardment with alpha particles. He was elected fellow of the college in 1921, and was appointed assistant director of the Cavendish Laboratory in 1923. He held the appointment of Lyon Jones Professor of physics at the University of Liverpool, 1935–48.

Chadwick headed the delegation of British technical experts to the US in 1943 and actively engaged in experiments which led to development of the atomic bomb. The sometimes threatened British participation in this nuclear energy development was maintained largely by Chadwick's deep knowledge of nuclear physics and of German physics, together with his personal sincerity and integrity. But it cost him frequently prostrating pain and anxiety.

In 1946 Chadwick returned to Britain, exhausted. After the war he devoted himself to three rather distinct efforts: nuclear energy development in Britain, pure research in nuclear and particle physics in the universities, and more specific matters at Liverpool and Cambridge. Chadwick believed that fundamental research in nuclear physics should be pursued at universities; he objected to Cockcroft's establishment for such research at Harwell. When Chadwick left Liverpool to become master of Gonville and Caius College (1948), he was faced with problems in finance as well as physics. He was able to increase the number of fellows, from 33 to 47, by encouraging bequests and by putting some endowment in an equity portfolio which he managed successfully. Uncomfortable with divergent views about university policy, Chadwick resigned his post of master in 1958 and retired to a cottage in North Wales.

Chadwick had married Aileen Stewart-Brown of Liverpool in 1925, and they had twin daughters. In 1969 he and Lady Chadwick returned to live in Cambridge to be near their daughters. In the last years of his long life, the anxieties of two war periods and post-war transitions gave way to serenity and many honours.

Victor Franz Hess

1883–1964

For his discovery of cosmic radiation, Hess shared the 1936 Nobel Prize for physics with Carl Anderson.

Victor Hess was born in 1883 at Schloss Waldstein, near Graz, Austria, the son of forester Vincens and Seraphine Grossbauer Hess. He studied at Graz University and the University of Vienna, obtaining his PhD from Graz in 1906. He remained there for advanced work until 1908 and then joined the new Institute for Radium Research at the University of Vienna. In the period 1919–38 Hess was professor of physics at the Universities of Vienna, Graz and Innsbruck. While on leave of absence, he was director of the Research Laboratory of the US Radium Corporation and consulting physicist to the Bureau of Mines, Washington, DC.

Following the Nazi occupation of Austria, Hess was dismissed from his professorship because of his strict Roman Catholicism. He became professor of physics at Fordham University in New York in 1938, and remained there until he retired with emeritus status in 1956. He became a US citizen in 1944. Hess had married Mary Bertha Warner in 1920, and after her death in 1955, he married Elizabeth M Hoenke.

When Hess joined the radium research laboratory in Vienna, he found workers concerned with locating the source of background radiation that showed up as ionisations in the air, even within containers that were shielded. Some thought that contamination by radioactive materials was the cause. In 1910 Theodor Wulf, while performing experiments at the Eiffel Tower, noted that the ionisation in the air at a height of 300 m above a gamma-ray source was greater than that at a horizontal distance of 300 m. He suggested the possibility of extraterrestrial origins for such radiation and that this hypothesis might be confirmed by balloon experiments.

With the aid of the Austrian Aeroclub, in 1911 Hess made ten daring balloon ascents to collect ionisation data up to a height of 5350 m. His striking results showed that ionisation decreases from the Earth to a height of some 150 m, but thereafter increases markedly with increasing altitude. Since radiation at all levels was the same night or day, it could not result from the direct rays of the Sun. Hess's discovery of what Millikan had named *cosmic rays* was important not only for what information they might give concerning astrophysical processes and the history of the Universe, but also important as an especially concentrated form of energy. In cosmic-ray research, Anderson discovered the positron and Powell discovered the pi-meson. Tantalising results from cosmic-ray research led to the construction of high-energy particle accelerators for laboratories, as sources more convenient and controllable than cosmic rays.

In continuing his work with radium, Hess (with R W Lawson) determined the rate of emission of alpha particles from a gram of radium (the basis for the unit of radioactivity, the *curie*). In his work on cosmic rays, he conducted experiments on the tower of the Empire State Building in New York, on voyages to South America, and in the Pacific. He further concerned himself with radiation safety for workers, having himself suffered a thumb amputation in 1934 as a result of an accident with radioactive material. For his Nobel lecture he chose a title expressive of his curiosity: 'Unsolved Problems in Physics.'

Carl David Anderson

1905–

Shared the 1936 Nobel Prize for physics with Victor Hess for his discovery of the positron.

The 1932 discovery of the positron, said by the Royal Society of London to be 'one of the most momentous of the century,' was wholly accidental, Anderson has said. In 1928 Dirac announced results of his study of the requirements of a combination of quantum and relativity theories. An experimenter working in any well equipped laboratory, had he taken the Dirac theory at face value, 'could have discovered the positron in a single afternoon.' But the Dirac theory included so many novel and seemingly unphysical ideas that most experimenters did not accept it wholeheartedly until *after* the existence of the positron had been established by experiment.

      The original aim of the experiments that led to the discovery of the positron was to measure directly the energy spectrum of secondary electrons produced by incoming cosmic radiation which, at that time (1930), was thought to consist of a beam of photons or gamma-rays of several hundred millions of electron volts energy. The apparatus planned by Anderson and Millikan consisted of a cloud chamber operated in a strong magnetic field. Some of the tracks observed seemed to suggest that they were left by cosmic-ray particles unexpectedly moving upwards. A lead plate was inserted across the centre of the chamber to ascertain the direction in which the low-velocity particles were travelling. Soon photographs were obtained of paths of particles travelling in the same general direction but deflected in the opposite direction by the magnetic field, indicating that the particles had charges of opposite sign. The thickness of the path and magnitude of curvature ruled out the proton. The observations were consistent with Dirac's prediction of the existence of an electron carrying a positive charge (positron), and represented the first example of a particle consisting of antimatter. It is now generally believed that all particles have their corresponding antiparticles: antiproton, antineutron, etc.

Anderson's discovery of the muon, unlike that of the positron, was not sudden and unexpected. Anderson and Neddermeyer had conducted a two-year study of cosmic-ray particles arranged to follow certain clues and to resolve certain paradoxes. Beginning in 1935 they obtained experimental evidence suggesting the existence of positive and negative particles of unit charge but of a mass intermediate between that of a proton and an electron. Yukawa's suggestion of the particle now called a pi-meson, to explain nuclear forces, was published in a Japanese journal before the experiments on the muon, but was unknown to the American experimenters. For a short while it was thought that experiment had confirmed theory, but then the two particles turned out to be different. The discovery of the somewhat oddball muon has been followed by the discovery of an embarrassingly large number of 'elementary' particles. This of course undermined the concept of 'elementary particle,' and led Oppenheimer to define: 'An elementary particle is something so simple that one knows nothing whatever about it.'

Carl Anderson was born in New York City in 1905, the only child of Carl David and Emma Adolfina (Ajaxson) Anderson. He was educated in Los Angeles, where he trained as a high-jumper, and completed his undergraduate studies at the California Institute of Technology in three years and received a BS in physics and engineering in 1927. He was Coffin Research Fellow 1927–28, and Teaching Fellow at CalTech 1928–30. He obtained his PhD in 1930 and continued on the faculty at CalTech, where he became professor of physics in 1939.

Anderson worked with the Defense Research Committee and the Office of Scientific Research and Development from 1941 to 1945, during which time he was connected with the CalTech Artillery Rocket Project and was responsible for the adaptation of suitable military aircraft to fire rockets for various tactical uses. He spent a month on the beachhead in Normandy in June 1944 to observe and assist in the use of aircraft rockets under active combat conditions. After the end of the war he requested and received the use of a B-29 aircraft for carrying cloud chambers to high altitudes for further studies of cosmic rays.

In 1950 working on White Mountain, California, with R B Leighton of CalTech he found many cases of the decay of the so-called V-particles, thus confirming for the first time the discovery of these particles made two years previously by Rochester and Butler in England.

Carl and Lorraine Elvira Anderson, married in 1946, have

two sons, Marshall David Lee and David Andrew Keith. Anderson has listed his recreations as tennis, mountains, deserts and music.

Clinton Joseph Davisson

1881–1958

Shared the 1937 Nobel Prize for physics with G P Thomson for their experimental discovery of the diffraction of electrons by crystals.

The famous Davisson and Germer experiment, which confirmed de Broglie's hypothesis that moving particles were guided by 'matter waves,' was a result of a patent suit. The momentous suit was concerned with the basic patent for the three-element vacuum tube, invented by Lee de Forest. His patent had been bought by the Western Electric Company in the expectation that its use could improve long-distance telephone calls. De Forest's tube used an oxide-coated platinum filament as its source of electrons. At the General Electric Company, Langmuir soon devised a three-element vacuum tube with a tungsten filament. The company applied for a basic patent, contending that the tungsten-filament tube was a true high-vacuum tube, whereas the de Forest tube depended for its operation upon air left in the tube which caused emission of electrons from the oxide coating of the filament by bombardment with positive ions.

During this law suit, which dragged through the courts for about a decade, the laboratories of the Western Electric Company (which later became Bell Telephone Laboratories) undertook measurement of the magnitude of the emission of electrons from oxide-coated platinum when bombarded with positive ions. With the assistance of L H Germer, Davisson proved that the source of the electrons from oxide-coated platinum was not the bombarding ions. Eventually, the US Supreme Court disallowed the Langmuir claim and awarded the patent to Western Electric.

In the same apparatus in which emission of electrons under ion bombardment was measured, it was possible, by changing a few potentials on some of the electrodes, to measure electron emission under *electron* bombardment. Davisson and C H Kunsman found that although most of the electrons emitted under electron bombardment were of very low energy, a few had the full energy of the primary electrons! Davisson realised that these must be primary electrons deflected through large angles. He visualised exploring the potentials within atoms using electrons in experiments of the Rutherford alpha particle scattering type to explore the outer regions of atoms.

In 1925 while Davisson was investigating the scattering of electrons from nickel, his target was heavily oxidised by an accidental explosion of a liquid-air bottle. He cleaned the target by prolonged heating, and then observed that the distribution angle of the secondary electrons had completely changed; it now showed a strong dependence on crystal direction. He attributed this change to the fact that prior to the accident the target had consisted of many tiny crystals but the heating had converted it to several large crystals. The investigation was continued by bombarding targets of single crystals; it was found that the scattering had a maximum at a particular angle.

In the summer of 1926, on a visit to England, Davisson learned about de Broglie's hypothesis that an electron possesses a wave nature and has a wavelength $\lambda = h/mv$. Discussion at Oxford persuaded Davisson that his experimental results were due to *diffraction* of electrons by the crystal lattice and confirmed de Broglie's hypothesis. This interpretation of earlier Davisson and Kunsman experiments had been suggested a year earlier by Walter Elsasser who had carried out experiments to confirm his point, but without success. When Davisson returned from England, he and Germer obtained data, in January 1927, on electron beams resulting from diffraction by a single crystal of nickel, in good agreement with de Broglie's predictions.

Clinton Joseph Davisson was born in 1881 in Bloomington, Illinois. His father, Joseph, was a contract painter; his mother, Mary Calvert Davisson, was a schoolteacher. Davisson graduated from Bloomington High School in 1902 and entered the University of Chicago, where he came under the influence of R A Millikan. Unable for financial reasons to continue at the university the following year, he found employment with a telephone company in Bloomington. In 1904 Davisson was appointed assistant at Purdue University, and from 1905 to 1910 he was part-time physics instructor at Princeton University. There, as his duties permitted, he studied under E P Adams, James Jeans and Owen Richardson. By attending summer sessions, he received his BS degree from Chicago in 1908, and then his PhD from Princeton in 1911. His thesis, under Richardson, was *On the Thermal Emission of Positive Ions from Alkaline Earth Salts*.

In 1911, Davisson married Charlotte Sara Richardson, a sister of Professor Richardson. They had three sons and a daughter.

During 1911–17 Davisson was an instructor at the Carnegie Institute of Technology, Pittsburgh. When he was refused enlistment in the US Army in 1917, he accepted wartime employment in the Engineering Department of the Western Electric Company. Investigations which led to the discovery of electron diffraction were begun in 1919 and continued until 1929. In 1930–37 Davisson studied the theory of electron optics and applied this theory to engineering problems. During World War II he worked on the theory of electronic devices and on problems of crystal physics. After his retirement from Bell Laboratories in 1946, Davisson was a visiting professor of physics at the University of Virginia until 1954.

Sir George Paget Thomson

1892–1975

Shared the 1937 Nobel Prize for physics with C J Davisson for the experimental discovery of the interference phenomena in crystals irradiated by electrons.

George Paget Thomson was the only son of the dean of British physicists, Sir Joseph John Thomson. He was born in Cambridge and attended the Perse School and university there. He followed his father in physics; like him he received a Nobel Prize and the honour of knighthood. Like his father, he became master of a Cambridge College, and he died, as his father did, in his eighty-fourth year.

After a brilliant college career in which he took first class honours in both the mathematics and natural science tripos in 1913, Thomson was elected to a fellowship at Corpus Christi College and was appointed to the teaching staff in 1914. At the outbreak of World War I he was commissioned in the Royal West Surrey Regiment and served a year in France. In 1915 he was attached to the Royal Flying Corps to work on problems of aircraft stability. In 1918 Thomson was a member of the British War Mission to the US.

On his return to Cambridge in 1919, Thomson investigated the isotopic constitution of the alkali metals, analysing the anode rays by J J Thomson's parabola method. At the age of 30, Thomson was appointed professor of natural philosophy at the University of Aberdeen, where (in 1927) he and Alexander Reid were the first to observe that a pattern of circular fringes resulted when they passed a beam of electrons through a thin metal foil, in a vacuum. Although not undertaken for that purpose, Thomson's demonstration of electron interference in a foil (and the interference observed by Davisson and Germer for electrons reflected from a nickel crystal) provided proof for de Broglie's theory associating wave systems with moving particles. Further, once Thomson had established their diffraction characteristics, electrons became ideal tools to probe surface properties; too penetrating x-rays can explore only the depths.

In 1924, Thomson married Kathleen Buchanan, daughter of the principal of Aberdeen University. They had two sons and two daughters. Mrs Thomson died in 1941.

Thomson moved to the University of London in 1930, where a group had been studying slow-neutron reactions. Later Thomson was appointed chairman of the Maud Committee to examine the possible relevance of the fission phenomenon to the war effort. In July 1941 the committee reported that a superbomb could be made with isotopically separated uranium-235. The main burden of coordinating British scientific efforts in the US bomb project passed to James Chadwick, and Thomson became head of the British Scientific Office in Canada. He returned to Britain in 1943 to serve as science adviser to the Air Ministry.

Thomson supported the US plan for a world atomic energy authority and favoured, under proper control, utmost international cooperation to develop atomic energy for peaceful purposes. He described President Truman's decision in 1947 to release radioactive isotopes to other countries as 'one of the greatest contributions made in the last generation to the progress of biology and medicine.'

In 1952 Thomson left the University of London to become master of Corpus Christi College. At a farewell dinner held at Imperial College, Thomson was presented with a watchmaker's lathe suitable for the miniature model-making which was his favourite hobby. After he retired in 1962, Thomson wrote *The Inspiration of Science* (1961) and *J J Thomson and the Cavendish Laboratory in His Day* (1965).

Enrico Fermi

1901–1954

Awarded the 1938 Nobel Prize for physics for the discovery of new radioactive elements produced by neutron irradiation, and for the discovery of nuclear reactions induced by slow neutrons.

Enrico Fermi was born in Rome, the son of Alberto Fermi, a railway employee, and Ida de Gattis Fermi, in 1901. With several papers already published, he received his doctor's degree, with a dissertation on x-rays, at the University of Pisa in 1922, a few months before Mussolini seized power in Italy. Soon afterwards he went to the universities of Göttingen and Leiden where he worked for some months with Professors Born and Ehrenfest. While a lecturer at the University of Florence (1924–26), Fermi made his first important contribution to theoretical physics, earning worldwide attention. Accepting Pauli's exclusion principle, that no more than one electron can occupy a given quantum state in an atom, Fermi developed what became known as the Fermi–Dirac statistics, the statistical law followed by anti-symmetrical particles, later called fermions.

In 1927 Fermi became professor of theoretical physics at the University of Rome and over some twelve years he worked on the theory of the Raman effect, hyperfine structure, the latitude effect of cosmic rays, the concept of virtual quanta and statistics—he was a versatile physicist. In 1933 Fermi accounted for the beta-decay type of radioactivity whereby a neutron changes into a proton with the creation of an electron and a neutral particle called a neutrino. Following the Joliot-Curie discovery in 1934 of artificial radioactivity induced by alpha particles, Fermi concluded that transmutations could be produced more effectively by bombarding nuclei with neutrons since they would not be repulsed by the electric field of the atom. In this way in a few months he discovered more than 40 new artificial radioactive isotopes. Fermi and his co-workers (Amaldi, Rasetti, Pontecorvo and Segrè, known as the 'School of Rome') discovered the enhancement of activity induced by neutrons which had been slowed down in passing through water or paraffin. Slow neutrons enter a nucleus in the same way a slow golf ball will fall into the cup while a fast one rolls by. For these discoveries Fermi received the 1938 Nobel Prize.

Fermi in 1928 had married Laura Capon, daughter of an admiral in the Italian Navy; they had two children, Nella and Giulio. The Fermi family had decided to leave Fascist, anti-Semitic Italy, and so from the Nobel ceremony in Stockholm they sailed directly to New York where Fermi joined the physics faculty of Columbia University. A few days after his arrival, he learned that Hahn and Strassmann in Berlin had guessed the true nature of mysterious phenomena which Fermi had observed in 1934 but had not fully understood. They had determined that when uranium was bombarded with neutrons, the nucleus might split into two almost equal parts and release some 230 MeV of energy. Further, it became apparent that if this fission process released neutrons, a chain-reacting system could be set up releasing enormous amounts of energy.

The Hahn and Strassmann work was quickly confirmed at Columbia, so Fermi and Szilard induced Einstein to write his historic letter to President Roosevelt urging the development of a nuclear weapon before the Axis powers succeeded in doing so. This led to the Manhattan Project and ultimately to the production of the first atomic bomb, at a cost of some \$2 billion. Fermi's group at the University of Chicago achieved the first controlled self-sustaining nuclear reaction, using graphite in their reactor ('pile') to moderate the energy of fission-produced neutrons, on 2 December 1942. Arthur Compton telephoned the news of this success to James Conant at Harvard with the cryptic message: 'The Italian navigator has reached the New World.' Technically an enemy alien during this work, Fermi became naturalised US citizen in 1945. Although Fermi approved of the use of the fission bomb over Japan in August 1945, he like Oppenheimer opposed the development of the even more deadly H-bomb (or fusion bomb).

In 1946 Fermi returned to the University of Chicago's Institute for Nuclear Studies. Thereafter his studies were concentrated on the nature of nuclear particles, especially mesons. He served on the general advisory committee of the Atomic Energy Commission and as a consultant in the design of the synchro-cyclotron at the University of Chicago. He found it necessary to engage in political action to free nuclear research from military censorship and to defend Robert Oppenheimer, former director of the Los Alamos Laboratory, against charges that he was a security risk and was disloyal in opposing the development of thermonuclear weapons.

Students from various countries found Fermi an inspiring teacher and a warm person. He was noted for his vivacious character, love of outdoor sports, the clarity of his lectures, and his construction of apparatus not for beauty, but with simplicity to get the needed information.

Ernest Orlando Lawrence

1901–1958

Awarded the 1939 Nobel Prize for physics for his invention and development of the cyclotron, and for the results obtained with the aid of it, especially with regard to artificially radioactive elements.

Ernest Orlando Lawrence, the elder of two sons of Carl Gustavus and Gunda Regina Lawrence, was born in 1901 in Canton, South Dakota, where his father was superintendent of schools. He received his AB degree in 1922 from the University of South Dakota and his MA from the University of Minnesota. There he came under the influence of W F G Swann, an authority on cosmic rays. After studying for a year at the University of Chicago, Lawrence went to Yale where Swann had accepted a professorship. Working under him, Lawrence obtained his PhD in 1925, his thesis being on the photoelectric effect in potassium vapour.

In 1928 Lawrence joined the University of California at Berkeley and a year later he started to develop what was to become a key device in nuclear physics—the cyclotron. (Lawrence considered this name laboratory slang and preferred the more dignified term 'magnetic resonance accelerator'.) In this device protons travelled in circular paths between the flat poles of a large electromagnet. In those paths, in vacuum, the protons travelled back and forth across a gap between two D-shaped electrodes. An alternating voltage was applied to the D's so that each proton received two 'kicks' of energy in each revolution. As the protons travelled faster and faster they followed a sort of spiral path, coming closer to the rim of the instrument and finally passing through a

117

slit to bombard a target.

Because the radius of the cyclotron, together with the strength of the magnetic field, determined the maximum energy the protons could reach, Lawrence and his colleagues built successively larger models, at rapidly increasing costs. Lawrence was not only an imaginative physicist but also a spectacular fund-raiser. In 1941 Lawrence announced 'the first man-made cosmic ray'—a beam of 96 MeV carbon ions. In the same year Lawrence was one of six top-ranking scientists appointed to evaluate the importance of the uranium atomic energy programme. After the attack on Pearl Harbor, all-out work on the uranium fission bomb was undertaken, with Lawrence, Arthur Compton and Harold Urey as programme chiefs. Lawrence had already started work on his large magnet to separate the chemically identical isotopes U-235 and U-238. The day before Pearl Harbor he reported that he had been able to deposit in one hour one microgram of U-235 largely purified from U-238. Six Lawrence cyclotrons were eventually used in pilot plant operations leading in 1942 to General Groves' authorisation of the building of the $350 million Oak Ridge project to obtain weapons-quality U-235, the first for incorporation in the 'atomic pile' built in Chicago by Fermi to study the neutron-induced fission reaction.

Following the war, Lawrence continued to expand his research at Berkeley. The Lawrence Radiation Laboratory was responsible for many discoveries. A host of new radioisotopes were investigated, among them tritium, radiocarbon-14, uranium-233 and plutonium. About a dozen synthetic elements were produced, and the first laboratory production of mesons and antiparticles took place there.

Much of Lawrence's work was of immediate value to the well-being of mankind. He and his brother John, formerly at the Yale School of Medicine, applied radiation in the study of problems in biology and medicine and developed the clinical use of neutrons in cancer therapy. Radioiodine proved useful in the diagnosis and treatment of hyperthyroidism. Radioisotopes of many elements important in the human body were used as tracers in the study of the blood and nutrition.

Lawrence married Mary Kimberly Blumer, daughter of the emeritus dean of the Yale School of Medicine, in 1932. They had two sons and four daughters.

Lawrence lived his life at a tremendous pace and was always an inspiring leader. In 1958 he went to Geneva as a US delegate at a meeting of Western and Soviet bloc scientists to discuss nuclear test detection methods. During those talks he became ill and returned to California, where he died a month later.

Otto Stern

1888–1969

Awarded the 1943 Nobel Prize for physics for his contributions to the development of the molecular ray method and his discovery of the magnetic moment of the proton.

Otto Stern was born in 1888 in Sohrau, Germany (now Zory, Poland), the oldest of five children of Oskar Stern, a prosperous grain merchant, and Eugenie (Rosenthal) Stern. He was given the means to travel and explore several fields before deciding on a career. Thus he attended lectures on theoretical physics by Arnold Sommerfeld and on experimental physics by Otto Lummer and Ernst Pringsheim. The reading of works by Boltzmann, Clausius and Nernst on thermodynamics appears to have influenced Stern to specialise in physical chemistry at Breslau University, where he obtained his doctor's degree in 1912.

Stern later described himself as an 'experimenting theoretician.' His scientific activity was chiefly theoretical from 1912 to 1919 and experimental from 1919 to 1945. On the theoretical side he was influenced by Einstein whom he joined as a post-doctoral associate in Prague and with whom he moved to Zürich in 1913; by Ehrenfest and von Laue in Zürich; and to a lesser degree by Max Born with whom he began to work in Frankfurt in 1919, after he returned from military service. During this period Stern published several papers on problems in statistical mechanics.

The experimental work for which Stern is famous developed from the observation that atoms or molecules introduced into a high-vacuum chamber travel in straight paths, forming beams of particles that in some respects are similar to light beams. His first application of this method in 1919 used beams of silver atoms and verified the values for molecular velocities in a gas which had been calculated theoretically around 1850. In 1920, while a *Privatdozent* at Frankfurt, Stern asked his colleague Walther Gerlach to join him in an experiment to prove the reality of space quantisation and to measure the magnetic moment of the proton. Sommerfeld had predicted that certain atoms—for example, those of hydrogen, the alkali metals or silver—should possess a magnetic moment $M = eh/4\pi mc$, and that if placed in a magnetic field they should be able to assume only *two* orientations, with the axis and magnetic moment either parallel or opposed to the direction of the magnetic field. Stern recognised that a molecular-beam experiment could give a clear choice between classical and quantum theory. If the classical theory were correct a narrow beam of silver atoms should merely be broadened when passed through a non-homogeneous magnetic field; but if the spatial quantisation theory were correct, the beam should be split into two separate beams. The reality of space quantisation was proven in the Stern–Gerlach experiment; the five papers reporting this work established Stern's reputation worldwide.

Stern's first professional appointment was as associate professor of theoretical physics at the University of Rostock, in 1921. In 1923 he became professor of physical chemistry and director of the laboratory in the University of Hamburg where he set out to organise an influential laboratory for molecular-beam research. At Hamburg, there was close collaboration between Stern and Pauli, in both experiment and theory. Frequent visits by Niels Bohr and Paul Ehrenfest and others helped maintain a high level of achievement. Stern reinforced the de Broglie hypothesis (1923–4) of the wave nature of particles by extending experimental verification from electrons to atoms and molecules. Stern's determination of the magnetic moment of the proton led to a surprising value two or three times that predicted by Dirac.

With the advent of Nazi power in 1933, Stern's work at Hamburg came to an abrupt end. He and a colleague, I Estermann, accepted posts at Carnegie Institute of Technology in Pittsburgh where they began to build a molecular-beam laboratory. Stern was made research professor of physics, but his work received meagre support during the depression years and the momentum of the Hamburg laboratory was never regained. In 1946 Stern left Pittsburgh for Berkeley, California, going into premature retirement while his powers were still great.

Isidor Rabi, who first met Stern in 1927 in Hamburg, has written: 'It was there, from Stern and Pauli, that I learned what physics should be . . . The new thing, which was not strong in the then provincial United States, was the development of taste, insight, and standards . . . in the choice of researches, and a feeling for what is good and what is not so good . . . This quality of taste Stern had to the highest degree . . . he never devoted himself to a minor problem . . . Stern was always close to the basic problems of physics as they evolved.' Stern valued experiment, ' not only for the direct result but also for style, the "Witz," the clever and ingenious strategem or invention . . .' Earlier Stern had said that from his lifelong friendship with Einstein he had learned evaluation of physical problems and what questions to ask.

Rabi has described Stern as one of the anti-stuffy generation of German professors who observed with amusement the pomposity of their predecessors. A bachelor, he lived alone; but he could also be excellent company. His eccentricities included a little hypochondria and a love of luxurious hotels, good food and first-class railway accommodation. Stern was a devotee of the cinema and it was in a theatre that he was stricken by a heart attack at the age of 81.

Isidor Isaac Rabi

1898–

Awarded the 1944 Nobel Prize for physics for his resonance method for recording the magnetic properties of atomic nuclei.

The magnetic moment of the atomic nucleus is an important property in finding the nature of the nuclear forces and the appropriate nuclear model. Building on experiments performed by Stern on molecular beams, Rabi arranged to deviate a beam in a strong non-uniform magnetic field and then by a second such field to refocus the beam on a detector. In a weak uniform field between the two magnets Rabi put an oscillator which would provide an additional weak alternating magnetic field, like a radio transmitter. He could control the frequency of this oscillator very accurately. When, say, a sodium atom entered the weak-field region it was in one of eight possible states determined by the orientation quantisation of its angular momentum. Now, by tuning the oscillator Rabi could cause the oscillations to jump from one such state to another. Whenever this happened, the alignment of the atom was disturbed and that beam missed being focused on the detector. Thus by determining the frequency at which the beam stopped focusing, Rabi had a direct measure of the energy required to cause the spin to jump, and this was proportional to the magnetic moment. Nuclear magnetic resonance (NMR) experiments have led to additional Nobel Prize awards and a veritable industry in several areas of investigation—with an accuracy of measurement of a few parts in a billion.

Isidor Isaac Rabi was born in 1898 in Rymanov, Austria, the son of David Rabi, a tailor, and Janet (Teig) Rabi. In 1899 his family took him to New York, where he received his early education. He obtained a BChem degree at Cornell University in 1919. After three years in non-scientific work, he attended the graduate schools at Cornell University and at Columbia University where he received his PhD in 1927. In 1926 Rabi married Helen Newmark; they have two daughters.

Aided by fellowships, Rabi spent two months with Sommerfeld in Munich, two months with Born in Copenhagen, a year with Pauli and Stern in Hamburg, two months with Heisenberg in Leipzig, and six months with Pauli in Zürich. Then, with his money running low, Rabi received a welcome telegram from Columbia University offering him a position and a salary of $3000, 'beyond the dreams of avarice.' While visiting Columbia, Heisenberg had recommended Rabi.

An exception to the publish-or-perish rule, with little initial publication, Rabi rose rapidly through the academic ranks: 1929 lecturer, 1930 assistant professor, 1931 associate professor, 1945–49 chairman of the physics department, 1951–64 Higgins Professor, and 1964–67 university professor. Rabi attributed his early promotions to Dean Pegram's confidence in him and to the fact that 'I was the life of the place. Students were flocking around me and I was close to other physicists who were well known.'

When Rabi went to the University of Göttingen in 1927 he had found that the library held the American *Physical Review* to be of such little current value that, to save postage, it had accumulated issues shipped once a year to be put on its shelves. In the late 1920s influential American scientists who had studied in Europe—such as Condon, Oppenheimer and Rabi in physics—came home with a determination to bring excellence to US science. Ten years later, the *Physical Review* was the leading physics journal in the world (Rabi was on its editorial board during two periods). It was during this time that the exciting and fruitful ideas of quantum physics were brought to America.

The bust of Rabi placed in Pupin Laboratory in 1974 honours the man who virtually created Columbia University's prestigious physics department twice, first in the 1930s, and again following World War II when university physicists were dispersed in war programmes. During the war, Rabi was one of the many from various branches of physics who volunteered to expand the capabilities of radar (so ably pioneered by the British) at the MIT Radiation Laboratory. He also served at Los Alamos, '. . . not on the payroll, just as Oppenheimer's adviser.'

Jeremy Bernstein, theoretical physicist and science writer, in a profile written for the *New Yorker* (1975) gave a fascinating review of Rabi's facilitating influence in a golden age of physics, together with evaluations and anecdotes relating to his wide circle of professional associates. He quoted Rabi as saying, 'The Nobel Prize puts a winner on a sort of pedestal . . . So unless you are very competitive you aren't likely to function with the same vigour afterward . . . The Nobel Prize did not help me in my scientific development but enhanced my activity of a more public nature.' Among many such important activities have been Rabi's service in arms control, UNESCO, the foundation of CERN, his instigation of the International Conference on Peaceful Uses of Atomic Energy (1955), and his concept of a special scientific advisory service for the President of the United States.

Rabi thinks that 'Only by the fusion of science and the humanities can we hope to reach the wisdom appropriate to our day and generation.' Questioned about the ageing of physicists he remarked, 'Physicists are the Peter Pans of the human race. They never grow up, they keep their curiosity.'

Wolfgang Pauli

1900–1958

Awarded the 1945 Nobel Prize for physics for the discovery of the exclusion principle, also called the Pauli principle.

Wolfgang Pauli was born in 1900 in Vienna, Austria, the son of Wolfgang Joseph Pauli, a physician who later became professor of biochemistry at the University of Vienna, and Bertha (Schutz) Pauli. He received his PhD from the University of Munich in 1921. Pauli's mentor, Arnold Sommerfeld, invited him to write the article on relativity for the *Mathematical Encyclopaedia*. This article also appeared as a small book in 1922 which Einstein reviewed with admiration for 'the psychological appreciation of the development of ideas, the sureness of the mathematical deduction, the deep physical insight, the mastery of clear systematic exposition, the familiarity with the literature, and the trustworthiness of the critical faculty' exhibited by Pauli. Einstein, Schrödinger and several other physicists wrestled with the problem of a unified field theory of gravitation and electromagnetism late in their careers; one of the first papers Pauli published was on this subject.

In 1924 Pauli enunciated his 'exclusion principle' with which much of the then existing knowledge of atomic structure fell into order: no two electrons in an atom can be in the same quantum state. In 1925 Pauli wrote that a new quantum theory property of the electron, which he called a 'two-valuedness not describable classically,' was indispensable to an understanding of the anomalous Zeeman effect. Goudsmit and Uhlenbeck identified this fourth quantum number with an angular momentum (spin) of the electron. The exclusion principle could then be stated: no two electrons in an atom can have the same set of four quantum numbers. In this form, Pauli's principle led to an understanding of the formation of electron shells in an atom and the periodicity of chemical properties observed when the elements are arranged in order of increasing atomic number.

After post-doctoral work with Bohr in Copenhagen in 1922–23, Pauli became a *Privatdozent* at the University of Hamburg, 1923–28. However, his name is chiefly associated with Zürich where he was professor of theoretical physics at the Federal Institute of Technology for some 25 years. Pauli was at the Institute for Advanced Study in Princeton in 1935, again during the war years, and in 1946 he became a US citizen.

Other research papers by Pauli dealt with the relation of quantum spin and the appropriate distribution statistics for elementary particles, paramagnetic properties of gases and of metals (leading to the quantum mechanical theory of electrons in metals), extension of wave mechanics from one to a large number of particles, explanation of the meson, and the nuclear binding force. To explain the beta-decay of radioactive nuclei, Pauli in 1931 postulated the existence of a new subatomic particle; it was named the *neutrino* by Fermi in 1932, and was detected in 1956.

Pauli was noted for his wit, spirit and sharp criticism. Writing to a colleague, Ehrenfest said: 'You have Pauli—that scourge of God—there among you in Hamburg!' To which Pauli, who was fond of telling this story, delighted in adding: 'He seems prepared to ascribe my critique to a divine mandate!' James Franck once advised Pauli to suppress his barbs lest those 'who know how to assess your talent regret that this gift happened to fall on you.' Physicists at Hamburg believed in a legend called the 'Pauli effect': the mysterious breakdown of apparatus caused by Pauli's mere presence in a laboratory.

Through personal discussions and letters Pauli exerted a stimulating influence on many physicists. He believed that the 'advance of physics . . . cannot be forced by planning in a grand scale . . . further development can take place only in an atmosphere of free investigation and unhampered exchange of scientific results between nations . . .' (Princeton, 1945).

Percy Williams Bridgman

1882–1961

Awarded the 1946 Nobel Prize for physics for the invention of apparatus for attaining very high pressures, and for the discoveries which he made by means of this apparatus in the field of high-pressure physics.

Attainment of high pressures first became a concern in the liquefaction of gases, chiefly by L P Cailletet and E H Amagat. In the late 1880s Amagat had succeeded in attaining a pressure of 3000 atm (about 3000 kg/cm²). Bridgman was at first interested in studying the influence of high pressures on certain optical phenomena. Ultimately his apparatus increased Amagat's limit approximately 140-fold, but only after Bridgman designed packing with such geometry that it became tighter the higher the pressure, designed a method for giving external support to the pressure vessel in such a way that the support increased with the increase in internal pressure, and found materials such as carbaloy sufficiently strong for the piston and chamber. Novel methods also had to be found to measure such variables as pressure, temperature and viscosity within that chamber.

In *The Physics of High Pressure* (1931) Bridgman described his measurement of compressibilities, viscosities, polymorphic transitions, and other properties of many compounds and elements. He found, for example, that except for water, viscosities increased tremendously with increasing pressure (a factor of importance in lubricating bearings). He found a new form of phosphorus by heating and increasing pressure. Ordinary ice became unstable above 2000 atm and was replaced by new crystalline forms; one produced above 40 000 atm was so-called hot ice with a melting point about 200 °C. Synthetic diamonds were created in 1955 by a team at the General Electric Company where Bridgman was a consultant. To the geologist, Bridgman offered a means of duplicating pressures corresponding to those at a depth of several hundred miles below the Earth's surface. During World War II Bridgman measured the compressibility of uranium and plutonium for the Manhattan Project and studied the plastic flow of steel under high pressure as related to the strengthening of armour plate.

Percy Williams Bridgman was born in 1882 in Cambridge, Massachusetts, the son of Raymond Landon Bridgman, a newspaper reporter and author, and Mary Ann Maria (Williams) Bridgman. Bridgman's scientific life was entirely associated with Harvard University. He earned his AB and AM degrees there, and his PhD in 1908. He joined the Harvard faculty and remained a member until his retirement as Higgins Professor Emeritus in 1954—and even after continued research at the Jefferson Physical Laboratory.

A skilled experimentalist, Bridgman was also interested in the philosophy of science. In *Dimensional Analysis* (1922) he presented a method for arriving at the form of a physics equation one might not be able to derive rigorously, from the dimensions (in terms of mass, length, time, etc) of the relevant quantities. In *The Logic of Modern Physics* (1927) and *The Nature of Physical Theory* (1936), Bridgman advocated operational analysis and operationalism. The problem in methodology to which he addressed himself was that of relating the realm of observations (data) with the realm of conceptions (thought). Among Bridgman's other books are *Reflections of a Physicist* (1956) and *A Sophisticate's Primer of Relativity* (1962).

Bridgman was married to Olive Ware in 1912, and they had two children, Jane and Robert Ware. When almost 80, with a long and influential career behind him, and incurably ill, Bridgman died, a suicide, at his summer home in Randolph, New Hampshire.

Sir Edward Victor Appleton

1892–1965

Awarded the 1947 Nobel Prize for physics for his work on the physical properties of the upper atmosphere, and especially for his discovery of the so-called Appleton layer.

Born in Bradford, Yorkshire, Edward Appleton attended the Hanson School there. An early ambition was to become a professional cricketer, but a scholarship enabled him to go to St John's College, Cambridge. His studies under J J Thomson and Ernest Rutherford were cut short by the war. As a captain in the Royal Engineers, Appleton was concerned with the propagation and fading of radio signals. In 1902 Oliver Heaviside and A E Kennelly had independently suggested that an electrified layer in the upper atmosphere acts to reflect electromagnetic waves and accounts for Marconi's success (1901) in transmitting wireless signals around the curved surface of the Earth. Appleton tested this hypothesis in 1924 by arranging with the BBC to vary the frequency of the transmitter in Bournemouth while the strength of the received signal was recorded at Cambridge. He looked for a strengthening of the signal when the waves travelling directly, along the Earth, interfered constructively with those bounced off the layers of charged particles postulated by Heaviside and Kennelly. From this information he concluded that the Kennelly–Heaviside layer (E layer) was some 60 miles high.

Typically, at dawn the Kennelly–Heaviside layer broke up and signal fading was no longer very noticeable, although there was still some reflection from an F layer higher up. By 1926 Appleton determined that this, later named the Appleton layer, was about 150 miles high.

Appleton initiated the study of the ionosphere, the charged layers above the stratosphere, and the manner in which they are altered by the position of the Sun and by sunspot activity. With Hartree, he established the magneto-ionic theory of the ionosphere in 1927–32. This lifelong interest led to Appleton's work with the International Scientific Radio Union, of which he was president from 1938 to 1954. He also led in proposing international collaboration in the second International Polar Year (1932–33) and in the International Geophysical Year (1957–58). A practical consequence was 'ionospheric forecasting,' whereby it would be possible to forecast several months ahead the most suitable frequencies for use at any time of day in any part of the world for radio transmissions of any distance.

In another method for measuring the height of reflecting layers, Appleton used a transmitter which sent out radio energy in short bursts and detected, with a receiver and oscilloscope, the time for the reflected signal to return. This technique became the radiolocator or radar system of aircraft detection, developed by Robert Watson-Watt and researchers who had worked with Appleton.

From 1924 to 1936 Appleton was Wheatstone Professor of experimental physics at King's College, University of London; and from 1936 to 1939 he was Jacksonian Professor of natural philosophy at the University of Cambridge.

For ten years during World War II, Appleton was secretary of the Department of Scientific and Industrial Research. He was responsible for many laboratories, including some aspects of atomic energy research. He also studied methods of civilian defence, dehydration, fuel economy, high explosives and building design. At the end of the war Appleton was appointed to two government committees on science, one to study atomic energy, and the other to plan the development of British scientific manpower and resources over the next ten years. Appleton had an earnest concern for the international control of atomic weapons and the development of peaceful uses of atomic energy, as carried out at the research centre he helped to establish at Harwell. Appointed as principal and vice-chancellor of the University of Edinburgh in 1949, Appleton had the administrative responsibility for the large building programme in the George Square area, and the development of new patterns of education for the increased intake of students.

Appleton was described as having 'the sturdy figure and balanced mind characteristic of Yorkshiremen.' Eminent as a researcher, administrator and university professor, he was an inspiring leader and wise counsellor to many younger physicists. In 1915 Appleton married Jessie Longson, daughter of a clergyman; they had two daughters, Margery and Rosalind. After the death of his first wife, Appleton was married to Helen Allison in 1965.

Baron Patrick Maynard Stuart Blackett

1897–1974

Awarded the 1948 Nobel Prize for physics for his improvement of the Wilson cloud chamber method and for the resulting discoveries in the field of nuclear physics and cosmic rays.

Baron Blackett of Chelsea was born in London in 1897. Trained at two naval colleges, Osborne and Dartmouth, he saw action in the Battle of the Falkland Islands in 1914 and the Battle of Jutland in 1916. In 1919 Lieutenant Blackett resigned from the Navy and entered Magdalene College, Cambridge, where he studied physics under Rutherford, who had just succeeded J J Thomson as Cavendish Professor. Blackett received his BA degree there in 1921, and later his MA. Continuing his research, in 1924 he obtained cloud chamber photographs proving an experiment first conducted by Rutherford in 1919: the transmutation of nitrogen into oxygen-17 through bombardment with alpha particles. In the same year Blackett married Constanza Bayon; they had two children, Giovanna and Nicholas. During the next year he worked at Göttingen with James Franck.

Blackett returned to Cambridge in 1925 and with G P S Occhialini adapted the Wilson cloud chamber to make cosmic rays take their own pictures. The chamber was placed between two Geiger counters, so that any cosmic-ray particle that passed through both counters had to pass through the cloud chamber. Blackett arranged circuits so that a coincidence of signals from the two counters triggered the expansion of the cloud chamber and produced a photographic record. This was much more economical than the procedure used earlier, which had been to photograph at random in the hope of finding interesting events. The cloud chamber was placed in a magnetic field so that information about the charge and momentum of a particle could be obtained from the curvature of its path.

In 1933 Blackett and Occhialini confirmed Anderson's discovery of the positron announced a few months earlier. As many as 23 particles were found on a single photograph diverging from a region over the chamber. Blackett and Occhialini named this phenomenon 'cosmic-ray showers' of positive and negative electrons, which they related to Dirac's theory of the electron.

In 1933 Blackett became professor of physics at Birkbeck College, University of London. He continued his cosmic-ray research, at one time studying their penetration in a laboratory set up in Holborn Underground station about 100 feet below street level. In 1937 Blackett succeeded W L Bragg as Langworthy Professor of physics at the University of Manchester.

Early in World War II Blackett joined the instrument section of the Royal Aircraft Establishment, and in 1940 was made science adviser to General Sir Frederick Pile. Blackett urged an analytical approach to tactical and strategic problems of defence. His team of pioneers of operational research effected economies in military resources (reducing, for example, the rounds of ammunition required to bring down an enemy plane from 20 000 to 4000); their research also had great influence on post-war science and world affairs. For his application of scientific methods in submarine warfare, Blackett received the US Medal for Merit. He also initiated work on a new bomb-sight for the Royal Air Force, served as a member of the Atomic Advisory Committee, and in 1948 visited India to advise Nehru on defence.

After the war, Blackett vehemently advanced his opinion that nuclear weapons were incapable of determining the outcome of warfare. He was a prominent member of the British Association of Scientific Workers (described as leftist) and he wrote political articles and the books *Military and Political Consequences of Atomic Energy* (1948), *Atomic Weapons and East–West Relations* (1956), and *Studies of War* (1962).

A different, fascinating area of Blackett's research was his development of a general theory linking the magnetic properties of the Earth, Sun and stars. His hypothesis was that magnetism is a property of rotating bodies. He derived an equation relating magnetism to mass, size, rate of spin, and Newton's gravitational constant—which fit numerical data for the Earth, the Sun and the star 78 Virginius.

A tall, dark-haired man, Blackett was as charming as he was distinguished. He was described as vigorous, vehement and emphatic. He was exceptionally good at inspiring research students. Blackett always saw beyond the immediate future, and few men have achieved so much in so many different enterprises.

Hideki Yukawa

1907–

Awarded the 1949 Nobel Prize for physics for his prediction of the existence of mesons on the basis of theoretical work on nuclear forces.

Hideki Yukawa's prediction of the existence of the meson was an exploit of theory comparable to Dirac's prediction of the positron. Yukawa wished to account for the nuclear force which binds neutrons to protons and other neutrons in the atomic nucleus. He recognised, with Wigner, that this force must have a very short range (about 10^{-13} cm) in order to account for the rapid increase in the binding energy from the deuteron to the alpha particle. In 1935 while at Osaka University, Yukawa postulated that the nuclear forces were related to exchanges of a then unknown particle in the same way that electromagnetic forces in an atom are related to the emission and absorption of light (quanta). Using Planck's constant from quantum theory, Einstein's relation $E = mc^2$, and the assumed range of the nuclear force, Yukawa estimated the mass of the particle sought to be about 200 m_e, where m_e is the mass of the electron. Since its mass lies between that of an electron and that of a proton, the name *meson* was later suggested for the particle; *yukon* in honour of its predictor was considered but abandoned because of possible confusion.

Yukawa's prediction seemed to find gratifying experimental support when Anderson and Neddermeyer found particles of mass about 200 m_e in cosmic rays, but it was soon found that these particles, now called mu-mesons, had nothing to do with nuclear forces. In 1947 a heavier pi-meson with mass about 285 m_e was found which interacts strongly with nucleons, that is, is responsible for at least a part of the nuclear force. Yukawa's pi-meson decays into mu-mesons and neutrons.

Hideki Yukawa was born in Tokyo in 1907, the son of Takuji Ogawa, who later became professor of geology at Kyoto University, and Koyuki Ogawa. In the family were three other sons who became university professors and two daughters who married professors. Hideki and Sumiko Yukawa were married in 1932; they have two sons, Harumi and Takaaki.

Yukawa received an MS degree from Kyoto University in 1929 and a DS from Osaka University in 1938. Between 1932 and 1938 he was a lecturer at Kyoto University and assistant professor at Osaka University. From 1939 he was professor of theoretical physics at Kyoto University. Yukawa planned to contribute a part of his $30 000 Nobel Prize toward a new Institute of Theoretical Physics at Kyoto.

Yukawa has said that his decision to enter theoretical physics was influenced greatly by his professors—K Tamaki at Kyoto and Y Nishina at Tokyo—and partly by his inability 'to master the art of making simple glass laboratory equipment.'

In 1949 Robert Oppenheimer invited Yukawa to join the group of nuclear physicists working at the Institute for Advanced Study at Princeton. When he left to become visiting professor at Columbia University, Oppenheimer said, 'Dr Yukawa's anticipation of the meson is one of the few really fructifying ideas in the last decade . . . He was deeply loved by all his colleagues in his year here, both as a scientist and as a man.'

Cecil Frank Powell

1903–1969

Awarded the 1950 Nobel Prize for physics for his development of the photographic method of studying nuclear processes and his discoveries regarding measurements made with this method.

Cecil Frank Powell showed that discoveries of fundamental importance could still be made with the simplest apparatus—in this case photographic plates and microscopes. From 1935 to 1945 Powell and his colleagues at Bristol developed techniques for using photographic emulsions to detect, by their tracks, individual nuclear particles and to study low-energy nuclear reactions. Powell established the reliability and usefulness of the nuclear emulsion technique as quite the equal of counters or of the Wilson cloud chamber.

By 1947 Powell was using improved versions of these emulsions to study nuclear physics in cosmic rays at energies much higher than those attainable in any laboratory accelerators. To record the tracks of incoming particles, Powell sent nuclear plates aloft in hydrogen-filled polyethylene balloons 20 metres in diameter which could give level flight at 90 000 feet for many hours. At first these were launched from the sports field of the University of Bristol. Powell's 'balloonantics' excited first curiosity, but then anger, in particular the wrath of British Railways on the occasion when a balloon came down in the path of an express on the Bristol–Bath line.

During 1951–57 Powell took his balloon-flying operations to Sardinia and the Po Valley, and received welcome help from the Italian Navy. By 1952 some 24 universities were cooperating in the launching,

135

tracking and recovery of balloons and analysis of the photographs. These experiences in sharing through international cooperation in exciting research at modest cost were valuable in the later setting up and running of the CERN organisation, in which Powell played such a large part. Powell's 'scanning girls' played an indispensable role in identifying important nuclear events; they were a step toward today's even more automated data factories.

Powell's discovery in 1947 of the pion (pi-meson) produced in nuclear reactions in cosmic rays, may justify calling him the father of particle physics. It is the pion which is related to Yukawa's 1935 prediction of a quantum associated with the nuclear field. Powell and his colleagues explored the decay modes of heavy mesons (kaons), the charge spectrum of primary cosmic rays, and first observed pair creation by energetic electrons. At the 1953 Rochester Conference, Leprince-Ringuet of the Ecole Polytechnique paid tribute to the richness and variety of this work saying that in Europe, 'Bristol est le soleil.'

Cecil Frank Powell was born in Tonbridge, Kent, in 1903, the son of Frank Powell, a gunsmith, and Elizabeth Caroline Bisacre. Powell emulated his self-reliant father and his Uncle Horace in liking to do what he could with his own hands. His mother was deeply concerned in securing educational opportunities for him; because his spelling was poor, she gave him daily dictation. Powell won a scholarship at the age of eleven to Judd School, Tonbridge, and from there he won a scholarship to Cambridge, where he graduated with first class honours in the natural science tripos. As a post-graduate student, Powell worked in the Cavendish Laboratory under C T R Wilson and Rutherford until he gained his PhD in 1927, and then moved to the University of Bristol.

In 1932 Powell married Isobel Therese Artner, daughter of an Austrian father and Scottish mother. She gave close support to every aspect of his research and social life; they had two daughters. In 1936, as seismologist on a Royal Society expedition to Montserrat, Powell was able to offer assurances that the volcanic activity there would not lead to an eruption similar to that of Mont Peleé in 1903. He returned to Bristol the next year and in 1948 was appointed Melville Wills Professor of physics.

As accelerators and bubble chambers superseded cosmic rays and nuclear emulsions, Powell turned toward the formation of scientific policies and the social responsibilities of scientists. On arms control Powell believed that it must 'embrace people with conflicting opinions on almost all other issues, but who can be united on this.' Powell participated in the conference on science and world affairs first held at Pugwash, Nova Scotia, in 1957 and as he chaired later meetings showed a gift for keeping people with seemingly irreconcilable views working together.

Sir John Douglas Cockcroft

1897–1967

Shared the 1951 Nobel Prize for physics with E T S Walton for their pioneering work on the transmutation of atomic nuclei by artificially accelerated atomic particles.

In 1919 Rutherford discovered how to change one element into another by bombardment with alpha particles from a radium source. However, only a few nuclear transmutations could be produced by these natural projectiles, and at first it seemed that the enormous energies required might not be attainable for artificially accelerated particles. In a timely visit to the Cavendish Laboratory in 1928, Gamow discussed with Cockcroft calculations which showed that if one attributes wave properties to the bombarding particles one finds that they have a small but significant probability of tunnelling through the potential barrier around a nucleus when the particles have a relatively modest amount of energy: 3×10^5 electron volts for protons targeted on boron nuclei.

With Rutherford's support, Cockcroft designed and built apparatus for accelerating protons. He had the advantage of a background in electrical engineering and experience in designing the generator and electromagnets for Kapitza's low-temperature experiments. Cockcroft was joined by Walton, whose experiments with primitive forms of betatrons and linear accelerators had not borne fruit. Together they arranged a high-voltage transformer, voltage-doubling circuits and rectifying tubes in a four-stage system to apply up to 600 000 volts to the evacuated glass tube down which the protons were accelerated. When these protons were directed onto a lithium target, the experimenters at once observed, with a zinc sulphide screen, bright scintillations obviously due to particle emission from the lithium. Rutherford, when called to see them, enthusiastically pronounced them 'the most beautiful sight in the world.' Proof that alpha particles were indeed being knocked from the lithium was obtained by measuring their range (energy) and by photographing in an expansion chamber the tracks of the two alpha particles moving off in opposite directions in the reaction

$$_3^7\text{Li} + {}_1^1\text{H} \rightarrow {}_2^4\text{He} + {}_2^4\text{He} + 17 \cdot 2 \times 10^6 \text{ eV}.$$

Publication of this discovery attracted worldwide attention and ushered in the new era of nuclear physics. It gave impetus to the development of the cyclotron and other methods of accelerating particles to high energies to obtain further information about nuclear structure and properties.

The Cockcroft family settled in Todmorden, Lancashire, in the fifteenth century and were continuously involved in the weaving industry of the Calder Valley. John Cockcroft, the eldest of five sons, was sent to the Todmorden Grammar School in 1909 where physics and mathematics were well taught. He received a scholarship to the University of Manchester in 1914 chiefly to study mathematics under Horace Lamb, and he was fortunate to be able to attend lectures by Rutherford. By 1915 Cockcroft was a signaller in the Royal Field Artillery.

After his release from the army in 1918, Cockcroft studied electrical engineering at the University of Manchester, and in 1920 became a college apprentice at the Metropolitan Vickers Electrical Company. For research performed for that company at Trafford Park he received the MSc Tech degree in 1922. He went on to St John's College, Cambridge in 1922, distinguishing himself in part two of the mathematics tripos and obtaining a BA in 1924. After this exceptionally long period of training (seven years excluding the war years), Cockcroft was granted scholarships and was accepted by Rutherford as a research student in the Cavendish Laboratory.

Following their initial experiment on producing nuclear transformation by proton bombardment, Cockcroft and Walton used deuterons, obtained from heavy water supplied by G N Lewis at Berkeley, to bombard lithium, boron and carbon. In 1934 they showed that radioactive nuclei were produced from boron and carbon exposed to protons and deuterons in their machines.

Early in his Cambridge career, Cockcroft adopted a very systematic approach to his work. He carried a small black loose-leaf book in which he noted in microscopic writing every commitment and all information he felt important. He was economical in his use of words and time. He was genial and approachable, yet made firm, impartial and prompt decisions. Cockcroft wrote few scientific papers from 1935 onwards, but rather he devoted himself increasingly to the organising and administration of research. Wherever he was and in whatever project he was engaged, he gathered together a team of able men and worked indefatigably to provide them with the conditions and equipment needed.

In 1939 Cockcroft accepted the wartime position of assistant director of scientific research in the Ministry of Supply and worked on the development of a radar defence system. In August 1940 he went to the United States as a member of the Tizard mission to negotiate scientific and technological exchanges of military importance. On his return, he took the position of head of the Air Defence Research and Development Establishment at Christchurch. In 1944 he investigated possible applications of nuclear fission as head of the Canadian Atomic Energy Project and director of the Montreal and Chalk River laboratories. Returning to England again in 1946, Cockcroft became director of the new Atomic Energy Research Establishment at Harwell where different types of reactors were evaluated. He stimulated nuclear developments from basic research to power reactors. Rutherford had thought that the idea that nuclear energy would ever become a practical source of power was 'all moonshine.' Cockcroft was confident that it would.

In 1959 Cockcroft led in the establishment of the Rutherford High-Energy Laboratory which he called 'a British Brookhaven,' at Chilton, near Harwell, and he obtained approval to build there the 7 GeV proton synchrotron, NIMROD. He also did much to promote science through international organisations such as CERN. From 1961–65 he was chancellor of the Australian National University in Canberra. At his death in 1967 at the age of 70, Cockcroft held the positions of president of the University of Manchester College of Science and Technology, master of Churchill College, Cambridge, and president of the Pugwash Conferences on science and world affairs.

Ernest Thomas Sinton Walton

1903–

Shared the 1951 Nobel Prize for physics with J D Cockcroft for their pioneering work on the transmutation of atomic nuclei by artificially accelerated atomic particles.

Working in Rutherford's laboratory in Cambridge in 1932, Cockcroft and Walton performed experiments now acknowledged as a landmark in the history of science, in at least four respects: they were the first to make nuclear changes by means wholly under the control of man; they released enormous amounts of nuclear energy per reaction; they provided the first major proof that, as Einstein had theorised, mass and energy are interchangeable; and they confirmed the estimate made by Gamow of the proportion of projectiles that would sneak into the nuclear interior in spite of the repulsion of the electric charges. The high-voltage accelerating equipment with which the name 'Cockcroft–Walton' has become associated was designed in response to Rutherford's call for 'a million volts in a soapbox' which one could use to impart to protons sufficient energy to disintegrate nuclei bombarded by the protons.

      In 1929, Cockcroft and Walton developed a voltage-multiplier circuit with which by 1932 they sent hydrogen ions down an evacuated tube with energy of about 600 000 electron volts and current of about 5 microamperes. The original apparatus may be seen in the Science Museum, South Kensington, London. The impact of these high-velocity ions on targets of light elements, notably lithium and boron, produced a copious yield of alpha particles. These were detected by scintillation screens and the measured energies showed that the alpha particles came from nuclear transmutations. Each proton of average energy which entered a nucleus liberated about 60 times the energy lost, but for each such event the energy of 1000 million other protons is lost. Hence the process is not an efficient source of energy. However, the work of Cockcroft and Walton stimulated many theoretical and technical developments and influenced the whole course of nuclear physics.

Ernest Walton was born in Dungarvan, County Waterford, Ireland, in 1903. His father John Arthur Walton was a Methodist minister whose ministry required him to move from place to place every few years, and his mother Anna Elizabeth (Sinton) Walton was from Ulster; her family had lived in the same house in County Armagh for at least 200 years.

Walton was educated at various academies and at Trinity College, University of Dublin, where he received his BA degree in 1926, MSc in 1928, and MA in 1934. As an overseas research scholar, he received his PhD from Cambridge University in 1931. He remained there as Clerk Maxwell Scholar until 1934 when he returned to Trinity College, Dublin, first as fellow, and in 1946 as Erasmus Smith's Professor of natural and experimental philosophy.

At the Cavendish Laboratory, Walton found himself on a team which Rutherford 'drove, or rather led, to the point of exhaustion.' Walton's first investigation was the possibility of accelerating electrons by spinning them in a circular electrical field surrounding a changing magnetic field (1929). This work led toward the development of the betatron by Wideroe and Kerst. In addition to his major interest in nuclear physics, Walton published papers on hydrodynamics and on microwaves.

Walton has taken an active part in committees concerned with advanced studies, government, the church, industrial research and standards, scientific academies, and the Royal City of Dublin Hospital. He has been described as 'quiet, undemonstrative, little given to talk.' In 1934 he married Freda Wilson, a former pupil of the Methodist College, Belfast. They have two sons and two daughters: Alan, Marian, Philip and Jean.

Felix Bloch

1905–

Shared the 1952 Nobel Prize for physics with Edward Purcell for their development of new methods for the precise measurement of nuclear magnetism and for discoveries in connection therewith.

At the age of 23 Bloch published a famous paper which provided the modern picture of the structure of metals and insulators and became fundamental to much contemporary work on semiconductor devices. While still in his twenties, Bloch conducted work in atomic physics of such originality and diversity that there are at least five laws and concepts to which his name is attached: Bloch wavefunctions, Bloch spin waves, Bloch wall, Bloch equations, the Bloch $T^{3/2}$ law, etc. His work is marked by intense examination of each problem from all points of view; he wrote no 'quickie' papers. One notes a close interplay of science and technology in his work and his career-long concern with magnetism.

The work for which Bloch received his Nobel Prize was inspired by Pauli's interpretation (1924) that the hyperfine structure of spectral lines results from the fact that atomic nuclei possess an intrinsic angular momentum (spin) and parallel to it a magnetic moment. The energy of interaction of this magnetic moment with the magnetic field produced by the atomic electrons depends on the angle between them and leads to the observed small splitting of the energy levels.

'The idea that a neutral elementary particle, the neutron, should possess an intrinsic magnetic moment had a particular fascination to me,' said Bloch. It could not be explained by the spinning charge picture Dirac had offered for the magnetic moment of the electron.

Believing that it was important to have a direct experimental proof of the existence of a magnetic moment of the free neutron, Bloch pointed out (1936) that the scattering of neutrons in iron could provide such proof: the strongly inhomogeneous magnetic field in the neighbourhood of each iron atom should result in the polarisation of the scattered neutron beam. This was demonstrated in 1937 by a group at Columbia University.

In 1946 Bloch described his method, called *nuclear induction,* and formulated in 'Bloch's equations,' of measuring nuclear magnetic moments with great precision. Bloch visualised the resultant magnetic moment of the nuclei to precess under conditions of resonance with the AC field at a finite angle around the DC field; he interpreted the observed signal as the voltage, a Faraday-induced EMF. The nuclei became tiny radio transmitters whose emission Bloch received. The display on an oscilloscope screen showed, by the direction of the streak, whether nuclei were rotating with or against the field. It was the method of detection which distinguished Bloch's experiments from those of Purcell and Rabi. In a deeper sense, the thinking of Purcell and Bloch are really equivalent; it only so happened that the phase relation in their first experiments differed by 90 degrees so as to display the same phenomenon under the two aspects of 'absorption' and 'emission' (or better, 'dispersion').

Felix Bloch was born in Zürich in 1905, the son of Gustav Bloch, a wholesale grain dealer, and Agnes (Mayer) Bloch. At the Federal Institute of Technology in 1924–27 Bloch changed his programme from engineering to physics, and attended, among others, courses taught by Debye, Scherrer, Weyl and Schrödinger. He continued his studies with Heisenberg at Leipzig, where he received his PhD degree in 1928, with a dissertation developing the theory of metallic conduction. Fellowships held in following years gave him the opportunity to work with Pauli, Kramers, Heisenberg, Bohr and Fermi.

In 1934 Bloch emigrated to Stanford University, California, where he started as associate professor of physics, became full professor in 1936 and Max H Stein Professor of physics from 1963 until his retirement in 1971. While continuing his theoretical studies, he also became interested in experimental physics. In 1940, with Luis Alvarez, he was the first to determine the magnetic moment of the neutron. War research at Stanford University, at the Los Alamos Laboratory, and at Harvard University occupied the years 1942–45. After his return to Stanford in 1945, Bloch collaborated with Hansen and Packard in the development of the new method of nuclear induction. This has proved to be an increasingly useful tool in physics and in organic chemistry.

In 1954 representatives of twelve nations unanimously approved the appointment of Bloch as director of the new European Nuclear Research Centre (CERN) at Geneva.

Bloch is an energetic man who enjoys skiing and mountain climbing. Indoors, he enjoys playing the piano. He was married to

Lore C Misch, also a physicist, in 1940, and they have three sons, George, Daniel and Frank, and a daughter, Ruth.

As a university professor, Bloch is widely respected not only for his clear lectures on topics of research interest, but also for his many years of teaching physics to freshmen and sophomore students at Stanford. He once told an interviewer: 'Teaching undergraduates is gratifying—and by no means easy. It means putting complex ideas into their very simplest form. Sometimes this forces one to clarify his own ideas—not a bad thing.'

Edward Mills Purcell

1912–

Shared the 1952 Nobel Prize for physics with Felix Bloch for the development of new methods to measure nuclear magnetism exactly and for discoveries made with the aid of these methods.

'To see the world for a moment as something rich and strange is the private reward of many a discovery,' observed Purcell in his Nobel lecture. He said that he remembered during the winter of his first experiments on nuclear resonance (1945), 'looking on the snow with new eyes. There the snow lay around my doorstep—great heaps of protons quietly precessing in the Earth's magnetic field.'

As a group leader in the wartime Radiation Laboratory at MIT, Purcell became associated with Rabi and others from Columbia University where 'the whole field of nuclear moments and resonance had just been broken open.' Returning to Harvard, Purcell used skills acquired in building airborne radar to probe the behaviour of the proton and electron in the hydrogen atom. Both spin like tops and act as magnets. The relationship between these two tiny magnets can change only in certain ways, with absorption or emission of precise amounts of energy.

To measure those energy transfers, Purcell made atomic nuclei dance in rhythm with a radio wave. The atoms were placed inside the core of a high-frequency coil, this was placed in the field of a strong magnet, and the magnet aligned the tiny nuclear magnets. Then Purcell changed their orientation by subjecting them to radio waves. By noting the frequency that permitted the atoms to absorb energy he found the energy for nuclear realignment, and hence the magnetic moment, with a precision exceeding almost all other measurements in physics.

Each kind of atom and its isotopes has a sharply defined characteristic nuclear frequency which can be identified by the method of nuclear magnetic resonance in solid, liquid or gaseous substances and without the sample being affected in any perceptible way by the analysis.

In 1951 Purcell and Harold Ewen built a radio telescope with which they detected the radiation coming from hydrogen clouds in space. In random encounters of hydrogen atoms, occasionally the spins of proton and electron are flipped from parallel to antiparallel orientation and radiation is emitted at a wavelength of 21 cm. Purcell's discovery gave radio astronomers a frequency to use (1420·4 megahertz) in measuring the motion of hydrogen clouds in the Milky Way.

Edward Purcell was born in Taylorville, Illinois, in 1912, the son of Edward A and Mary Elizabeth (Mills) Purcell. Although he graduated from Purdue University in electrical engineering, his interest had already turned to physics. Encouraged by Lark-Horovitz, he took part in research in electron diffraction while an undergraduate.

After a year at the Technische Hochschule at Karlsruhe in Germany, Purcell continued his graduate work at Harvard University in 1934, where he received the PhD degree in 1938. After serving two years as an instructor at Harvard, he joined the Radiation Laboratory at MIT and became head of the fundamental development group concerned with exploration of new frequency bands and the development of new microwave techniques.

Purcell became professor of physics at Harvard in 1949, and since 1974 has been Gerhard Gade University Professor. Purcell served with distinction on the President's Science Advisory Committee (1957–60), and on the scientific advisory board of the US Air Force. He was a member of the committee which planned the Physical Science Study Committee (PSSC) programme. Thousands of students saw him as lecturer in two films on inertia and inertial mass. He was active in the production of the Berkeley physics course, for which he wrote a textbook on electricity and magnetism.

Purcell is not overly concerned with practical applications of his work, but he likes to stimulate the interest of students. To one he suggested reflecting an electron beam from a diffraction grating. They found it gave off monochromatic light, somewhat analogous to the tone one hears when running a stick along a picket fence.

Purcell married Beth C Busser in 1937; they have two sons, Dennis and Frank.

Frits Zernike

1888–1966

Awarded the 1953 Nobel Prize for physics for his demonstration of the phase-contrast method, especially for his invention of the phase-contrast microscope.

A microscopist often fails to see all the details he would like to have revealed in a specimen. Techniques of staining and the use of polarised light may be helpful, but they are not complete answers to the problem of revealing more detailed structure. In a microscope image there are variations in light wave amplitude (intensity) and in phase; the eye responds only to the former. In a brilliant analysis Zernike proved, unexpectedly, that invisible effects due to changes in phase can be transformed into visible equivalent changes in amplitude.

A phase-contrast microscope, invented by Zernike, makes visible differences in phase or optical path in transparent or reflecting specimens. A perfectly transparent object does not absorb light, the intensity is unaltered, and such an object is invisible in an ordinary microscope. But light that passes through the transparent object is slowed down. These delays, described as phase changes or differences in optical paths, are made detectable by the eye in Zernike's microscope.

To separate the direct light from that diffracted by the object, a diaphragm, such as an annulus, is placed at the front focal plane of the condenser. Parallel rays from each point of the focal plane pass through the specimen and are brought to focus at the rear focal plane of the objective lens. An image of the annulus will be seen there formed by the incident light when the eyepiece is removed. Also, when a specimen is present, some light is diffracted by it and fills the whole of the back lens of the objective pair. A phase plate is inserted between the two components of the objective. This can be a disc with an annular groove which coincides with the image of the diaphragm.

All direct light now passes through the groove in the phase plate; diffracted light passes mostly outside the groove. The plate thus introduces a phase difference between the direct and the diffracted light. If the phase plate is made to retard the incident wave by a quarter of a wavelength, the crests and troughs of the two waves will coincide, giving a resultant of large amplitude; the refractile details will appear light.

Especially in biological material there exist many objects which under a conventional microscope appear to have no structure because they are quite transparent, even though they do have structure related to changes in thickness or in refractivity. A similar situation may occur for metallurgical specimens where light reflected from tiny areas of different heights differs in phase but not amplitude. Zernike's method brought hitherto invisible detail in transparent objects or on metal surfaces into vivid contrast.

Zernike not only gave the theoretical treatment, but he also constructed the first phase microscopes. When he demonstrated one at the Zeiss Works in Jena in 1932 a senior scientist told him: 'If this had any practical value, we would ourselves have invented it long ago.' However, after his unenthusiastic reception, Zeiss did develop phase-contrast objectives and accessories, which were marketed in 1942. At the end of the war the US military authorities 'liberated' two Zeiss phase-contrast microscopes found in Jena. American and British manufacturers woke from their apathy and competed in its manufacture.

Frits Zernike was born in Amsterdam in 1888. His father, Carl F A Zernike, was headmaster of a primary school and author of textbooks in mathematics; his mother Antje Dieperink was also a teacher of mathematics. During his school years, Zernike performed endless experiments, enjoyed colour photography, and built a miniature observatory equipped with the clockwork of an old record player which enabled him to take pictures of a comet. With his parents he also indulged in solving arduous mathematical problems. At 19 he won a gold medal for his answer to a mathematics problem posed by the science faculty of the University of Groningen.

Zernike's doctoral thesis on *Critical Opalescence* (University of Amsterdam, 1915) is still quoted in textbooks of thermodynamics and statistical mechanics. In 1913 the astronomer J C Kapteyn invited Zernike to become his assistant at the University of Groningen, where he held various academic positions until his retirement at the age of 70.

Zernike was a 'classical' physicist in the best sense of the word, quite unperturbed by the 'modern' excitements with which most

Nobel Prizes have been concerned. His ideal appears to have been Lord Rayleigh, and in many respects he resembled him. His interest in establishing the limits of precision in measurements led to the development of the Zernike galvanometer. He studied how to make the most accurate measurements possible in the face of deflections imparted by the impact of molecules in their normal Brownian motion. Statistical mechanics, thermodynamics and chemistry were lifelong interests. As a boy, Zernike synthesised ether required for his photographic experiments; his continued interest in chemistry led him to publish papers on the phase rule and the thermodynamics of alloys.

Even before his development of the phase-contrast microscope, Zernike used the phase contrast method to detect precisely the surfaces of concave mirrors. The equations he developed for expressing these errors are now known as 'Zernike polynomials.' His theory of 'partial coherence' began a new branch of wave optics.

Zernike married twice: his first wife, Dora van Bommel von Vloten, died in 1944 (they had one son); and in 1954 he married Mrs L Koperberg-Bannders. Zernike was witty and at times caustic; he was a lucid lecturer with an admirable command of English. He was earnest and methodical, and his judgments were well considered; he shunned polemics.

Max Born

1882–1970

Awarded, with Walther Bothe, the 1954 Nobel Prize for physics for his fundamental work in quantum mechanics and especially for his statistical interpretation of the wavefunction.

The Rutherford–Bohr planetary model of the atom and Bohr's hypothesis concerning energy levels of the electron in which Planck's concept of quanta was associated with atomic spectra were used to interpret subsequent data but with indifferent success. At this period of transition from classical to modern physical theory, around 1923, Wolfgang Pauli and Werner Heisenberg were Born's assistants at the University of Göttingen. In his 1924 thesis in Paris, Louis de Broglie suggested that the electron was associated with a group of waves. In his 'uncertainty principle,' Heisenberg demonstrated that the laws of classical mechanics could not be applied to subatomic particles because their position and velocity could not be known simultaneously.

Born took up the problem at this point, and formulated a system in which de Broglie's electron wave became a wave of probability for the presence of the electron. The Born–Heisenberg–Jordan matrix mechanics has a different mathematical formulation from the wave mechanics developed by Schrödinger. Dirac showed that the two systems could be blended into one, the quantum mechanics to which the name is applied today.

Early in his career, Born's interests centred about lattice dynamics, the theory of how atoms in solids stick together and vibrate. Born and T von Karman published a paper on the vibrational spectra of crystals in 1912, even before von Laue finally demonstrated the lattice structure of crystals. Born returned to the study of crystal theory several times; his last book on crystals was written in 1954.

Interested in unifying quantum mechanics and relativity, Born proposed in his reciprocity theorem (1938) that the fundamental laws of physics are invariant in a change from position to momentum representation. After his retirement, he continued to work toward the sort of unified field theory that Einstein and Infeld had sought.

Max Born was born in Breslau (now Wroclaw), Poland, in 1882, the son of a physician, Gustav Born, and Margarette (Kaufmann) Born, who died when Max was four. Grandmother Kaufmann was influential in his early life. Born studied at the universities of Breslau, Berlin, Heidelberg, Zürich and Cambridge, and took his PhD at the University of Göttingen in 1907, where he remained as *Privatdozent* until 1915. After teaching in Berlin and Frankfurt, Born returned to Göttingen to head the physics department which, under his administration, became a centre of theoretical physics rivalled only by the Niels Bohr Institute in Copenhagen.

Born rated his first lectures as disastrous, but as a teacher he became noted for his clarity, informality, and warm concern for his students at a time when a typical German professor would not even shake hands with a student.

Hitler's policies forced Born to leave Germany in 1933, and he taught at Cambridge University. He lectured for a year at the Institute of Science at Bangalore under circumstances which led to an estrangement with Raman. There followed 17 years of enjoyable work as Tait Professor of natural philosophy at the University of Edinburgh. In 1953, Born retired to Bad Pyrmont, a spa near Göttingen.

Born continued his father's concern over the degradation of war. In *My Life* he recounted light-heartedly how as a pacifist, a Jew, and one afflicted with chronic asthma and bronchitis, he was nevertheless required to serve three times in the German Army. Later Born took a public stand against the development of nuclear weapons and all warlike applications of scientific knowledge. He was a founder of the Pugwash movement. Among Born's more than 300 papers and 20 books was the charming semi-popular *The Restless Universe*.

In 1913 Born married Hedwig Ehrenberg; they had three children. He joined the Lutheran Church, and his hobbies included hiking and music—Born and Heisenberg played concerts on two pianos.

Born did not share Einstein's repugnance for the probability interpretation of physical laws; the Born–Einstein letters were translated and published by Irene Born in 1971. Born wrote: 'I believe that ideas such as absolute certitude, absolute exactness, final truth, etc, are figments of the imagination which should not be admissible in any field of science. On the other hand, any assertion of probability is either right or wrong from the standpoint of the theory on which it is based. This *loosening of thinking* seems to me to be the greatest blessing which modern science has given us. For the belief in a single truth and in being the possessor thereof is the root cause of all evil in the world.'

After 'bridging nineteenth and twenty-first century physics,' Born died at the age of 87. In Göttingen his tombstone bears the equation he considered his main single contribution to science: $pq - qp = h/2\pi i$.

Walther Wilhelm Georg Bothe

1891–1957

Shared the 1954 Nobel Prize for physics with Max Born for the coincidence method and his discoveries made therewith.

Walther Bothe, who began his career as a theoretical physicist, received his Nobel award for an experimental technique. A Geiger counter has the property of transmitting an electric current when a charged particle, such as an electron or an alpha particle, passes through it. A counter can also be contrived to respond to photons. Bothe's innovation in 1924 was to use two counter tubes in such a manner that they would register only when ionising collisions occurred in both simultaneously. Bothe used the coincidence method to decide whether the conservation laws for energy and momentum were valid for every collision between a photon and an electron (as Einstein and Compton had assumed), or whether these rules were valid only as a statistical average (as Bohr and his collaborators had inferred). Bothe and Geiger examined individual Compton collisions, using counters to study coincidences between the scattered x-ray and the recoil electron. They concluded that the conservation rules were valid for every individual collision.

The coincidence method has been widely used in the study of cosmic radiation. To explore the directional effect, a telescope to detect radiation within a narrow cone can be devised by placing a number of coincidence counters along a common axis. Absorption of cosmic rays into various materials can be determined by placing a layer of the material between counters and noting the reduction in the number of coincidences.

Walther Bothe was born at Oranienburg, near Berlin, in 1891, the son of a merchant. From 1908 to 1912 Bothe studied at the University of Berlin where in 1914 he obtained his doctorate under Max Planck for a study of the molecular theory of reflection, refraction and dispersion. During World War I Bothe was taken prisoner and spent a year in Siberia, where he continued his mathematical studies and learned the Russian language. He was sent back to Germany in 1920 when he married Barbara Below of Moscow and accepted Hans Geiger's invitation to work in the radioactivity laboratory at the Physikalische-Technische Reichsanstalt. In his Nobel lecture, Bothe acknowledged Geiger's guiding influence on his career. He recalled Geiger's desire to keep scientific work within economic bounds, adding 'I think the main lesson which I have learnt from Geiger is to select from a large number of possible and perhaps useful experiments that which appears the most urgent at the moment, and to do this experiment with the simplest apparatus, i.e., clearly arranged and variable apparatus.'

In 1932 Bothe succeeded Philipp Lenard as director of the Institute of Physics at the University of Heidelberg, becoming in 1934 director of the Institute of Physics at the Max Planck Institute for Medical Research at Heidelberg. In 1930 Bothe and Becker bombarded beryllium-9 with alpha particles derived from polonium and detected a highly penetrating radiation coming from the beryllium. They assumed that it was gamma radiation, but after clarifying experiments on its absorption were done in France and England, Chadwick showed in 1932 that the radiation consisted of a new particle, the neutron.

At Heidelberg, after much difficulty, Bothe was able to obtain funds for building a cyclotron. During the war he had worked on uranium and neutron transport theory, becoming one of the foremost scientists of Germany's uranium project for nuclear energy. In the early 1950s he again worked on electron scattering and cosmic rays, and on beta and gamma spectra.

Bothe had a remarkable gift of concentration and he worked at great speed. In the laboratory he was a strict master, but in the evenings at home with his Russian wife he was very hospitable. Among his hobbies were music and painting. He played the piano, being especially fond of Bach and Beethoven. During his holidays he visited the mountains and did many paintings in oil and water-colours. Like Geiger, Bothe reached the end of his career in a period of physical suffering; he was unable to attend the Nobel Prize ceremonies in Stockholm.

Willis Eugene Lamb, Jr

1913–

Shared the 1955 Nobel Prize for physics with Polykarp Kusch for his discoveries concerning the spectrum of hydrogen.

When the Nobel Prizes were first awarded in 1901, physicists knew about just two objects which are now called elementary particles: the electron and the proton. In his Nobel lecture, Willis Lamb acknowledged the consternation of theorists over the deluge of other elementary particles discovered after 1930 by quoting a suggestion, 'the finder of a new elementary particle used to be rewarded by a Nobel Prize, but such a discovery now ought to be punished by a \$10 000 fine.'

The hydrogen atom, which is the union of the first known elementary particles, has been studied for many years and from its spectrum much has been learned about the electron. The series of spectral lines observed with a spectrograph of medium resolution (to an accuracy of a few tenths of an ångström unit) gave good agreement with the energy levels predicted by the Bohr theory and by the Schrödinger equation. However, by operating the light source at a very low temperature (to minimise Doppler broadening of the radiation) and using a spectrograph of higher resolution, the hydrogen spectrum is seen to have a *hyperfine structure,* inviting theoretical explanation.

According to the Dirac theory (1928), the hydrogen atom could exist in two states, called $2^2S_{1/2}$ and $2^2P_{1/2}$, both with the same energy. Lamb passed microwaves through hydrogen atoms in one state and converted them to the other state. Since microwave energy was absorbed, it was proved that the two states did not contain the same energy. The energy difference was small, but important for the theory. The deviation is 1077·77 ± 0·01 megahertz. This quantum electrodynamical effect is called the *Lamb shift*. By 'postdiction' (as opposed to prediction) theorists can now say that the source of the Lamb shift is the interaction of the electron with both the electromagnetic field and the field of negative-energy electrons which affect the electron even when the fields are in the lowest energy state.

Another important measurement which came from the same experiment was a precise value for the fine structure constant, $\alpha = e^2hc$, one of the intriguing dimensionless numbers which occur in quantum electrodynamics, the '137' which fascinated Eddington. Lamb's result was $1/\alpha = (1/137·0365) ± 0·0012$. Lamb has since continued work on experimental tests of quantum electrodynamics.

Willis Lamb Jr was born in 1913 in Los Angeles, the son of Willis Lamb, a telephone engineer, and Marie Helen (Metcalf) Lamb. He obtained his BS in 1934 and his PhD in 1938 at the University of California at Berkeley, where he studied theoretical physics under J Robert Oppenheimer. He became a physics instructor and ten years later professor of physics at Columbia University. He was a professor at Stanford University (1951–56), at Oxford University (1956–62), at Yale University (1962–74), and since 1974 at the University of Arizona.

Numerous experiences and contacts in Lamb's career seem to have combined in a serendipitous manner in his Nobel Prize-winning work. His 1938 thesis dealt with field theories of nucleons which predicted a very small discrepancy from Coulomb's law about a proton. At Columbia University, Lamb had close contact with I I Rabi and members of the molecular beam laboratory. During the war he acquired first-hand experience, in the Radiation Laboratory, of microwave radar and vacuum tube construction techniques, plus a start in the post-war field of microwave spectroscopy. In 1945, while teaching from a book by Herzberg, Lamb was challenged by reference to some unsuccessful 1932 attempts to detect absorption of short-wavelength radio waves in hydrogen. It was this cumulative interest and skill that enabled Lamb to conduct and interpret his high-precision experiments with Robert Retherford.

Lamb has felt a strong interest and responsibility in physics teaching, with students ranging from freshmen to graduate students. Indeed, when first informed of his Nobel award, he went to teach his quantum mechanics class before meeting reporters.

Lamb married Ursula Schaefer in 1939. Mrs Lamb, who has a PhD degree in history, taught at Barnard College until the Lambs went to Stanford in 1951, and is now professor of history at the University of Arizona. Tall and athletic, Lamb enjoys swimming, sailing, chess and photography.

Polykarp Kusch

1911–

Shared the 1955 Nobel Prize for physics with Willis Lamb for his precise determination of the magnetic moment of the electron.

The discoveries of Kusch and Lamb working on different projects at Columbia University involved measurements of effects which were exceedingly small, but which became the experimental cornerstones of quantum electrodynamics, the study of the relationship between matter and electromagnetic radiation. To explain data available from spectroscopy, Goudsmit and Uhlenbeck (1925) made two postulates: (a) the electron has an intrinsic angular momentum of $h/4\pi$, and (b) it has a magnetic dipole moment equal to $eh/4\pi mc$, a quantity named the Bohr magneton, μ_0. When, in 1928, Dirac formulated the relativistically invariant quantum mechanics, the Goudsmit and Uhlenbeck postulates were shown to be consequences of the Dirac quantum mechanics.

In 1947, Kusch and Foley used the principle of Rabi's molecular beam apparatus to construct exquisitely precise equipment to determine energy changes induced by high-frequency radio waves in atoms of gallium and sodium. From their results they calculated that the intrinsic magnetic moment of the electron is not exactly one Bohr magneton, but $(1 \cdot 001146 \pm 0 \cdot 000012)$ Bohr magneton. This anomalous magnetic moment for the electron was given theoretical treatment by Tomonaga, Schwinger and Feynman during 1943–48, and for it they received the Nobel Prize in 1965. In his experiment, Lamb found a new effect, not predicted by the Dirac theory. The 'Lamb shift,' too, found a place in the 1943–48 theory.

Polykarp Kusch was born in Blankenburg, Germany, in 1911, the son of John Matthias and Henrietta (van der Haas) Kusch. His father, a Lutheran missionary, took the family to the United States in 1912 where for a few years they moved from town to town in the Midwest, until they settled in Cleveland. In 1926 Kusch started working as a page for the Cleveland Public Library, where he began his voracious, lifelong hobby of reading. Kusch graduated from Case Institute of Technology in 1931 and received his MS (1933) and PhD (1936) from the University of Illinois. He taught physics at Illinois (1931–36), at the University of Minnesota (1936–37), and at Columbia University (1937–41).

During World War II, Kusch engaged in research and development on microwave generators at Westinghouse, Bell Telephone Laboratories and Columbia University. He found the experience important not only in that it gave him knowledge of microwave methods, but also in that it suggested applications of these techniques of vacuum tube technology to a whole range of problems in experimental physics.

Kusch has been increasingly concerned with problems of education, especially in educating the young to understand a civilisation strongly influenced by science and technology. While he has been wary of survey courses—'You make too many dogmatic statements'—Kusch has successfully taught courses for non-scientists at Columbia and the University of Texas. As a department chairman, vice-president, dean of faculty and provost, Kusch felt a strong concern for the creation of an environment in which learning and scholarship can flourish.

Polykarp Kusch has been married twice, and has five children. He has been described as tall, lean, looking alert, zestful and ageless. His present wife, recalling the days when she was a student in the back of a large hall, described Kusch's style and voice as 'reaching the man in the back row and grasping him by the lapels and implanting ideas by sheer voice and personality.'

John Bardeen

1908–

Shared the 1956 Nobel Prize for physics with William Shockley and Walter Brattain for their discovery of the transistor effect. Shared the 1972 Nobel Prize for physics with Leon Cooper and John Schrieffer for their theory of superconductivity known as the BCS theory.

John Bardeen was the first person to receive two Nobel Prizes in the same field. The insight which solved the 50-year old riddle of superconductivity and led to the second prize came only a few months after receipt of the first award.

In 1911 Kamerlingh Onnes discovered superconductivity, a new state in which certain metals at low temperatures (usually below 15 K) exhibit perfect diamagnetism and can maintain an electric current, once started, almost indefinitely (zero resistance). The importance of superconductivity as a problem for theory is attested in part by the number of eminent theorists attracted to its solution, including Bohr, Heisenberg, F London, Bloch, Landau and Feynman.

In about 1950, E Maxwell at the Bureau of Standards, and a group working at Rutgers University under B Serin, independently discovered that the temperature at which a metal becomes superconducting is inversely proportional to its atomic mass. When Bardeen learned of this in a telephone call from Serin, he immediately thought that electron–phonon interactions must be involved; that is, one must consider the effect the atoms in the metal lattice have on the conduction electrons. Herbert Fröhlich, then visiting Purdue University, without knowing of the isotope effect, also proposed a theory based on electron–

phonon interactions. These early attempts failed to account for superconductivity; it was not until 1957 that Bardeen, Cooper and Schrieffer developed a satisfactory explanation.

In 1956, Cooper, then a research associate at the University of Illinois, showed that in a metal two electrons with energies near the Fermi energy which weakly attracted each other would form a resonant state, a 'Cooper pair.' The next year, Bardeen, Cooper and Schrieffer, then a research student, applied Cooper's idea to many electrons and showed how a new cooperative state of all the conduction electrons may be formed. The pairs have a common momentum which is not affected by random scattering of individual electrons, so the effective electrical resistance is zero.

The BCS theory has been called one of the most important contributions to theoretical physics since the development of quantum theory. The fascinating study of superconductivity has already led to superconducting magnets and may find application in computers and in power transmission lines, since the BCS theory helps in devising alloys that become superconducting at less extreme temperatures. While Fritz London regarded a superconductor as a 'quantum structure on the macroscopic scale,' Josephson used the BCS theory to predict microscopic phenomena and to construct Josephson junctions. These led to sensitive devices for measuring electric currents, voltages and magnetic fields, and to the new international standard for the volt.

John Bardeen was born in 1908 in Madison, Wisconsin; he studied electrical engineering at the University of Wisconsin, receiving his BS in 1928, and MS in 1929. After three years of work in geophysics at the Gulf Research Laboratories, Bardeen pursued graduate studies in mathematical physics at Princeton University where his introduction to solid state physics came from Eugene Wigner. He received his PhD in 1936. After holding appointments at Harvard, the University of Minnesota, and the Naval Ordnance Laboratory, Bardeen joined a new group in solid state physics at Bell Telephone Laboratories where he, Brattain and Shockley discovered the transistor effect late in 1947. He left in 1951 to become professor of electrical engineering and of physics at the University of Illinois, where he is now Emeritus Professor. At Illinois, Bardeen helped establish research programmes on semiconductors, but in recent years his interest has been more on the theoretical aspects of low-temperature physics, including a study of helium-3 as a superfluid.

Bardeen was married to Jane Maxwell in 1938; they have a daughter and two sons. Bardeen is an avid golfer and also enjoys travel, although the latter has been mostly in connection with professional activities.

Walter Houser Brattain

1902–

Shared the 1956 Nobel Prize for physics with William Shockley and John Bardeen for their investigations on semiconductors and their discovery of the transistor effect.

A transistor (transfer resistor) is a semiconductor device that will amplify or process electrical signals. The invention of the transistor, announced in July 1948, resulted from fundamental research on semiconductors begun at Bell Telephone Laboratories in 1931–32 when Becker and Brattain started to investigate them and found that rectification was a surface property. Just before World War II it was discovered that silicon was a good semiconductor, and it was used to rectify radar signals throughout the war.

In 1946 the research was started again with Shockley the leader. He had concluded that it should be possible to control the number of charge carriers near the surface of a semiconductor by applying an electric field to the surface. Bardeen proposed a theory involving surface traps to explain the negligible results. Brattain and Gibney found they could make this work by using an electrolyte to apply a field to the surface. When Bardeen and Brattain were trying to improve the response time on a piece of germanium, they discovered instead the transistor effect. The use of this effect to produce an amplifier was demonstrated on 27 December 1947 by putting two small metal contacts only 0·005 cm apart on the germanium surface and greatly changing the power output in one contact by very small changes in the current through the other.

Among the first uses of the transistor was the tone-dialling equipment in the Bell system and the card translator for automatic routing of long-distance telephone calls. The Explorer and Vanguard satellite transmitters used transistors to relay scientific data to Earth. In 1978 the production of transistors in the United States alone reached $469 million.

The now ubiquitous transistor and the miniaturisation of circuits have revolutionised electronic devices: radios, hearing aids, data-processing equipment, tape recorders, cameras, fuel injection and ignition systems, alarms, and many sorts of measuring equipment.

Walter Brattain was born in Amoy, China, in 1902, the eldest of five children of Ross R Brattain and Ottilie (Houser) Brattain. He spent his childhood and youth in Tonasket, Washington State, where his father was a homesteader, cattle rancher and flour miller. Brattain received his BS degree from Whitman College (where both his parents had graduated) in 1924, MA from the University of Oregon in 1926, and PhD from the University of Minnesota in 1928.

After a year in the radio section of the National Bureau of Standards, Brattain joined the staff of the Bell Telephone Laboratories in 1929, where he was a research physicist until 1967. The chief field of his research has been the surface properties of solids. His main contributions have been the discovery of the photoelectric effect at the free surface of a semiconductor, the invention of the point-contact transistor with Bardeen, and work leading to a better understanding of the properties of germanium.

When informed of his Nobel award, Brattain said: 'Much of my good fortune came from being in the right place, at the right time, and having the right sort of people to work with.' The invention of the transistor is an outstanding example of the combination of research teamwork and individual achievement increasingly characteristic of progress in physics. Since 1951, multiple awards of the Nobel Prize have been more frequent than single awards.

During World War II Brattain worked for 22 months on the magnetic detection of submarines. He has also done research on piezoelectricity, frequency standards, magnetometers, infrared detection and blood clotting. Since his retirement from Bell Laboratories, Brattain has taught a course for non-science students at Whitman College and has continued research there on phospholipid bi-layers as a model for the surface of living cells.

In 1935 Brattain married Dr Keren Gilmore, a physical chemist, who died in 1957. They were parents of one son, William Gilmore Brattain. In 1958 Brattain married Emma Jane (Kirsch) Miller.

William Shockley

1910–

Shared the 1956 Nobel Prize for physics with John Bardeen and Walter Brattain for their investigations on semiconductors and their discovery of the transistor effect.

The limitations of vacuum tubes (bulkiness, short life, high power consumption, fragility and their failure to operate at radar frequencies) stimulated the post World War II search for an alternative device to rectify an alternating current and amplify a signal. In early crystal radio sets, rectification had been accomplished by a piece of galena with a 'cat's whisker' probe—a crystal diode. Shockley's 1939 experiments toward making a semiconductor device to amplify as well as rectify were interrupted by the war. He directed anti-submarine warfare research at the Columbia University division of war research in 1942–44, and served as expert consultant to the office of the Secretary of War in 1945.

At Bell Telephone Laboratories in 1945 Shockley concluded that it was possible to control the supply of movable electrons inside a semiconductor by an electric field imposed from the outside. Bardeen proposed a theory involving surface traps to explain the initial negligible results. When Bardeen and Brattain immersed a germanium diode in an electrolyte and connected it to a source of direct current, they were led to the idea that some of the current resulted from holes flowing near the surface. Replacement of the electrolyte by metal contacts led to the point contact transistor. About a month later, Shockley invented the junction transistor which avoided the troublesome metal contacts by controlling impurity distributions so as to produce a n-p-n or p-n-p

163

sandwich structure in the semiconductor. Rectification and amplification then occurred, not on the surface, but inside the crystal.

William Shockley was born in 1910 while his parents William Hillman Shockley, mining engineer, and May (Bradford) Shockley were living in London. From the age of three, he was brought up in California. He received a BS degree from the California Institute of Technology in 1932. While on a teaching fellowship he earned a PhD at the Massachusetts Institute of Technology, and then in 1936 joined the technical staff of Bell Telephone Laboratories, where he became director of the transistor physics department in 1953. He was associated with Beckman Instruments (1955–58), president of Shockley Transistor Corporation (1958–60), and director of Clevite Transistor Division (1960–63). He became Alexander M Poniatoff Professor of engineering and applied science at Stanford, and two years later rejoined Bell Laboratories as an executive consultant. He retired from both positions in 1975.

In 1965, Shockley applied his operations research skills, which had won him the Presidential Medal for Merit in World War II, to the threat of dysgenics, in his words, 'retrogressive evolution through the excessive reproduction of the genetically disadvantaged.' Public criticism and disruptions at universities, including burning him in effigy, blocked many of his presentations.

Shockley is married to the former Emmy Lanning and has three children by a marriage to his first wife, the former Jean A Bailey. Of moderate stature, five feet eight inches, with light blue eyes and friendly manner, Shockley 'looks much like anybody's grandfather.' But his conversation is meticulously ordered and challenging. He considers the portable tape recorder as perhaps his own most important application of the transistor. He records telephone calls, interviews and conversations concerning human quality problems. Shockley contends that focusing attention on the dysgenic threat may be 'of greatest benefit to mankind,' the objective that Alfred Nobel's will demanded of the contributions deserving his prizes.

Chen Ning Yang

1922–

Shared the 1957 Nobel Prize for physics with Tsung Dao Lee for their penetrating investigations of the parity laws which led to important discoveries regarding subatomic particles.

In the 1950s the famous atom-smashers such as the cosmotron at Brookhaven and the bevatron at Berkeley raised more problems than they solved. One was that some K mesons, short-lived particles knocked out of atomic nuclei, themselves broke up in a way inconsistent with a revered principle: the conservation of parity. It states that no fundamental distinction can be made between left and right; the laws of physics are the same in a right-handed system of coordinates as they are in a left-handed system.

Yang and Lee dared to question this widely held concept. For experimentalists, they suggested several decisive experiments. The first was carried out by Chien-Shiung Wu, associate professor at Columbia, who worked with a team at the National Bureau of Standards. She cooled radioactive cobalt-60 to 0·01 K to suppress the random thermal motion of the nuclei, and then applied a strong magnetic field to align the cobalt nuclei in one direction. Their disintegration continues regardless of temperature. According to the parity principle, the emitted electrons should shoot off in equal numbers in both directions along the spin axes of the aligned nuclei. Actually, far more electrons came out of the 'south' end of the nuclei, which didn't look good for parity.

A confirming experiment was performed, at Lee's suggestion, by L M Lederman and R L Garwin who caught mu-mesons streaming from the Columbia cyclotron in a block of carbon with a coil of wire wound around its perimeter. The disintegrating mesons shot their electrons predominantly in one direction (or the other, with a magnetic field applied) proving that mesons can be mirror twins and still not behave in the same way. So it is now meaningful to refer to particles as right-handed or left-handed, contrary to what the principle of parity held.

The eldest of five children, Yang was born in 1922 in Hofei, Anhwei, China, and was brought up in the atmosphere of Tsinghua University, outside Peiping, where his father was an eminent mathematician. Yang, known to his friends as Frank, married Chih-Li Tu in 1950; they have two sons, and a daughter.

Yang received his college education at the National Southwest Associated University of Kunming and his MSc degree from Tsinghua University, which moved to Kunming during the Sino–Japanese war, 1937–45. At the end of the war, on a Tsinghua fellowship, Yang entered the University of Chicago and came under the influence of Enrico Fermi. He received his PhD in 1948, and after a year as instructor at Chicago, Yang went to the Institute for Advanced Study in Princeton, where he became professor in 1955. Since 1966 Yang has been Einstein Professor of physics and director of the Institute of Theoretical Physics at the State University of New York at Stony Brook.

The quiet, modest and affable young physicist looked more like an undergraduate student in the year of his Nobel award. He is five feet ten inches tall, has brown eyes and black hair. He regards thinking as his full-time job. He has said: 'There has not been enough respect in the United States for learning and learnedness.'

Tsung Dao Lee

1926–

Shared the 1957 Nobel Prize for physics with Chen Ning Yang for their penetrating research on the laws of parity which has led to important discoveries regarding elementary particles.

Tsung Dao Lee was born in Shanghai in 1926, the third of six children. He married university student Jeannette Hui-Chin in 1950; they have two sons, James and Stephen.

In 1945 Lee moved south ahead of Japanese invaders, studied in several southern Chinese universities and met Chen Ning Yang at National Southwest Associated University. A brilliant student, Lee was awarded a Chinese government fellowship in 1946 enabling him to study at the University of Chicago where he and Yang lived in International House. He received his PhD in 1950; his thesis was entitled *The Hydrogen Content of White Dwarf Stars*. In 1950–51 Lee was a research associate and lecturer at the University of California, and from 1951 to 1953 he was a member of the Institute for Advanced Study in Princeton. The director of the Institute, J Robert Oppenheimer, stated: '. . . We saw him leave with great regret. He [is] one of the most brilliant theoretical physicists we have known. His work in statistical mechanics and in nuclear and submuclear physics has brought him worldwide renown . . . His work has shown a remarkable freshness, versatility, and style.'

Lee joined the faculty at Columbia University in 1953 and at the age of 29 earned the distinction of being the youngest full professor. In 1963 he became Enrico Fermi Professor of physics at Columbia University. His collaboration with Yang continued by visits and telephone. Lee and Yang were the first Chinese physicists to receive the Nobel Prize and Lee became the second youngest Nobel laureate (the youngest was W L Bragg).

Boyish in appearance and modest in manner, Lee has brown eyes and black hair and stands five feet seven inches tall. He claims never to have found time for hobbies, since for him, as for Yang, 'thinking is a continuous process.' However, he occasionally relaxes by reading 'whodunits.' In 1977, Lee joined Weisskopf in protesting against the political abduction of scientists in Argentina.

When Lee and Yang demonstrated an unexpected limitation in the conservation of parity principle, they were tampering with a large and important structure in physics: symmetry principles and the conservation laws they generate. 'In a certain sense,' commented Isidor Rabi in 1957, 'a rather complete theoretical structure has been shattered at the base, and we are not sure how the pieces will be put together.' However, with the abolition of parity, the Lee–Yang theories may eventually lead to the goal which eluded Einstein: a unified field theory encompassing all the laws of matter, energy and the Universe.

Pavel Alekseivich Cherenkov

1904–

Shared the 1958 Nobel Prize for physics in equal parts with Ilya Frank and Igor Tamm for their discovery and interpretation of the Cherenkov effect.

The discovery of the Cherenkov effect is an interesting example of how a relatively simple physical observation investigated in the right way can lead to a deeper understanding of matter, energy and radiation, and can provide an instrument for important new research. As a student at the Lebedev Physical Institute in Moscow in the early 1930s, Cherenkov was asked by Academician S I Vavilov to investigate what happens when radiation from a radium source penetrates and is absorbed in different fluids. Others had observed the weak bluish glow that emanated from the liquid as the radiation penetrated it. They attributed it to fluorescence, the well known phenomenon used by a radiologist when he directs x-radiations onto a fluorescent screen which then lights up.

Cherenkov, however, suspected that the glow he observed was not fluorescence. By observing radiation even in doubly distilled water he ruled out the possibility of minute impurities fluorescing. The only means available for detecting the very faint radiation at that time was the highly sensitive human eye and to increase his sensitivity Cherenkov spent an hour or more in complete darkness before each experiment. He found that the radiation was polarised along the direction of the incoming radiation and that it was the fast secondary electrons, produced by the latter, that were the primary cause of the visible radiation. He verified this by irradiating the liquids with only the electrons from a radium source.

While the papers Cherenkov published in 1934–37 established the general properties of the new radiation, the mathematical description of the effect was provided by his colleagues, Frank and Tamm (1937). The Cherenkov effect can be compared to the bow wave of a vessel that moves through the water with a speed exceeding that of the waves. In air, an analogous phenomenon occurs when the speed of a jet plane exceeds the propagation speed of sound waves. A Cherenkov 'bow wave' of ordinary light is found when a charged particle, such as an electron, traverses a medium at a speed greater than that of light *in the medium*.

An instrument based on the Cherenkov effect is capable of registering the passage of single particles. Further, the angle of the bow wave is a measure of the particle's speed. Cherenkov counters were essential in the apparatus used in 1955 in the discovery of the anti-proton, and the cosmic-ray counter on board Sputnik III was based on the Cherenkov effect.

Pavel Cherenkov was born in the Voronezh region of Russia in 1904. His father, Aleksei Cherenkov, and his mother, Mariya, were peasants. He had to work for a living while going to school and did not enter college until he was 20. After graduating from the Voronezh State University, Cherenkov studied at the Physical Institute of the Academy of Sciences in Moscow, where he received his doctorate in 1940. He has been on the staff there since 1930.

In 1946 the Soviet State Prize was awarded to Cherenkov, Vavilov, Tamm and Frank for their elucidation of the Cherenkov effect. Vavilov died in 1951, before the 1958 Nobel award for this work.

In post-war years, Cherenkov helped to plan the electron synchrotron in the laboratory of V I Veksler and he has headed research carried out with that accelerator. In addition to his distinguished work in high-energy physics, Cherenkov is noted for his skill in training young research physicists.

In 1930 Cherenkov married Marya Putinseva, daughter of a professor of Russian literature; they have a son Aleksei and a daughter Elena.

Ilya Mikhailovich Frank

1908–

Shared the 1958 Nobel Prize for physics equally with Pavel Cherenkov and Igor Tamm for their discovery and interpretation of the Cherenkov effect.

Ilya Frank was born in Leningrad in 1908, the younger of the two sons of Mikhail L Frank, a professor of mathematics, and Yelizaveta M Gratsianova, a physician. In 1937 Frank married Ella A Beilikhis, an historian, and they have one son, Alexander.

Frank graduated from the University of Moscow in 1930, where as a student of Academician S I Vavilov he had carried out research on the photoluminescence of solutions. He then moved to the State Optical Institute in Leningrad and worked in the laboratory of A H Terenin on the optical dissociation of molecules and on photochemistry, which was the subject of his DSc thesis (1935).

Since 1934 Frank has worked at the Lebedev Institute of Physics of the USSR Academy of Sciences, where he heads the nuclear physics laboratory. He has taught at the University of Moscow since 1944, and is director of the neutron laboratory at Dubna. In 1946 Frank was elected corresponding member of the USSR Academy of Sciences.

Frank collaborated with Pavel Cherenkov and Igor Tamm in research on electron radiation, and for this they were awarded the Stalin Prize in 1946. Their work on the Cherenkov effect and related problems included an investigation of the Doppler effect in a refractive medium, and on transition radiation. An important practical application of the Cherenkov effect was the development of the Cherenkov counter, a device made of a dielectric such as glass, water or clear plastic, in which when particles enter at a speed greater than the speed of light within the matter, Cherenkov radiation is produced and this can then be detected photoelectrically. Cherenkov counters were incorporated in the apparatus used in the discovery of the antiproton, and the cosmic-ray counter on board Sputnik III was based on the Cherenkov effect.

Cherenkov, Frank and Tamm were the first Russians to be awarded the Nobel Prize for physics. This honour, remarked the *New York Times* on 29 October 1958, gave 'definitive international recognition to the high quality of experimental and theoretical research being done in the Soviet Union.'

Igor Evgenievich Tamm

1895–1971

Shared the 1958 Nobel Prize for physics equally with Pavel Cherenkov and Ilya Frank for their discovery and interpretation of the Cherenkov effect.

Igor Tamm was in the vanguard of Soviet nuclear physics, as a researcher and teacher, for some 40 years. His position as a leading scientist in the Soviet Union and his international prestige gave him some freedom to criticise bureaucracy constructively. Much of his work involved uniting the Einstein theory of relativity, sometimes regarded in Russia as anti-Marxist idealism, with quantum mechanics. He revised university course materials to teach these theories, and as a teacher he urged such reforms in science training as the elimination of work programmes. As a member of the Soviet Academy of Sciences, which distributes funds and directs research activity, Tamm championed abiding by majority vote and prudent use of time, manpower and resources. When Tamm appeared on a CBS television interview in May 1963, the *Washington Post* praised his warmth and humanity, calling him 'a cultured scientist whose stature allows him a breadth of outlook and a candor of expression . . .' During that interview Tamm recommended a 'drastic change in our political thinking which starts from the point of view that no war at all is possible.' Tamm was active in the Pugwash movement.

Igor Tamm was born in Vladivostok in 1895, son of Evgenij Tamm, an engineer, and Olga (Davydova) Tamm. After he finished the secondary school in Elisabethgrad (southern Russia), Tamm spent the year 1913-14 at the University of Edinburgh, and thereafter spoke English with a Scottish accent.

Despite political crises, Tamm managed to complete his university education, receiving his PhD degree from the University of Moscow in 1918. He married Natalie Shuiskaia in 1917; the couple had two children, Irene and Eugen. In 1919 Tamm began to teach physics, first in Simpheropol and Odessa, and from 1922 in Moscow where he was associated with several universities simultaneously. In 1930–37 he was head of the physics department of the University of Moscow, and from 1934 until his death he was head of the theoretical department of the Lebedev Physical Institute of the Academy of Sciences. He was elected a corresponding member of the Academy of Sciences in 1933 and a member in 1953. He received the Order of State Prize in 1946 for his services to science.

It was in 1934 that Tamm (jointly with Frank) arrived at a correct interpretation of Cherenkov radiation, for which the three physicists received the 1958 Nobel Prize. Tamm himself thought that he had made a more important advancement with his beta-theory of nuclear forces (1934), in which forces inducing beta-decay were assumed to be the forces of nucleon–nucleon interactions, which are very small in comparison with nuclear forces. Hideki Yukawa, developing Tamm's ideas, showed that nuclear forces were due to mesons, and not to electrons and neutrinos. The later theories of nuclear forces were developed according to the same scheme as Tamm's theory but took into account the role of the pi-meson.

Tamm acknowledged a decisive influence on his activity from L Mandelstam, his professor and friend, with whom he was associated from 1920 until Mandelstam's death in 1944. One of the most important interests they shared was the meaning of the indeterminacy between time and energy in quantum mechanics.

In 1932–33 Tamm showed that, together with the known 'zone' electron states inside a crystal, there could also be states of a different type on the surface of the crystal. These 'Tamm surface levels' are evident in many phenomena, particularly in semiconductors, and lead to 'barrier' layers.

Tamm showed that although the neutron is a neutral particle, it has a magnetic moment; he correctly predicted the negative sign of this moment.

Jointly with Andrei Sakharov, Tamm initiated the USSR research on controlled thermonuclear reactions, developing in 1950 the theory of gas discharge in a powerful magnetic field.

Owen Chamberlain

1920–

Shared the 1959 Nobel Prize for physics with Emilio Segrè for their discovery of the antiproton.

When the construction of the bevatron, the large accelerator at Berkeley, was budgeted for the production of 6 BeV (10^9 eV) protons, that was not an arbitrarily chosen figure; rather it was related to the 20-year search for the antiproton. The success of the 1928 Dirac theory and Anderson's discovery of the positron (or 'anti-electron') in 1932, strengthened expectations that the proton, too, had a mirror-image particle, the antiproton, having a negative charge and an oppositely directed magnetic moment. It was expected that the creation of an antiproton would necessitate simultaneous creation of a proton or a neutron, each of rest mass equivalent to about 1 BeV. To provide the necessary high-energy collision, it was estimated that the projectile proton would have to have about 6 BeV of energy in order that 2 BeV would be available to make new particles.

Using the bevatron to fire 6·2 BeV protons at a copper target, the Chamberlain–Segrè team created antiprotons, but a great deal of experimental skill was required to detect them among the subatomic debris of protons, neutrons and mesons which made up most of the emerging beam. The expected negative charge of the antiproton could be verified by deflection in a magnetic field, but to determine its mass, at least two independent quantities had to be measured for the same particle: momentum, energy, velocity or range. Such measurements were made using magnetic arrangements and Cherenkov velocity-selecting counters some 40 feet apart. Corroboration of the existence of antiprotons was obtained in a photographic emulsion which recorded as a 'star' the explosive disintegration of an atomic nucleus hit by an antiproton.

The achievement of Chamberlain and Segrè was marked by great skill in identifying the extremely rare antiprotons in a beam which included many other particles. In the magnetically analysed beam, only one in 30 000 particles was an antiproton, and in the first apparatus only one antiproton was recorded every 15 minutes. When some 40 events were recorded which corresponded within an acceptable margin of error with the properties of the antiproton, it was regarded as 'discovered.' With similar methods, an antiparticle to the neutron was later discovered, extending the concept to neutral particles and reinforcing an aspect of symmetry among fundamental particles.

Owen Chamberlain was born in San Francisco in 1920, the son of Genevieve Lucinda (Owen) and Edward Chamberlain, a radiologist. He received his AB at Dartmouth College in 1942, and then joined the Manhattan Project where, with Emilio Segrè, he investigated nuclear cross sections and spontaneous fission of heavy elements. In 1946 Chamberlain resumed his graduate work at the University of Chicago under the guidance of Enrico Fermi, with whom he experimented on the diffraction of slow neutrons in liquids. He received his PhD in 1949.

In 1948 Chamberlain began teaching at the University of California at Berkeley where he became professor of physics in 1958. His research on proton–proton scattering and polarisation effects led to a team effort in the first triple-scattering experiment. In 1951 Chamberlain was awarded a Guggenheim Fellowship to study the physics of antinucleons at the University of Rome. Following his Nobel award, Chamberlain has studied the interaction of antiprotons with hydrogen and deuterium, the production of antineutrons from antiprotons, and the scattering of pi-mesons.

Chamberlain is tall, angular and bespectacled. He was married to Beatrice Babette Cooper in 1943; they have three daughters, Karen, Lynn and Pia, and a son Darol.

Emilio Gino Segrè

1905-

Shared the 1959 Nobel Prize for physics with Owen Chamberlain for their discovery of the antiproton.

Occasionally one notices that an equation acceptable in physics permits an interpretation contrary to common sense (previous experience). A theorist who probes such an interpretation may come up with ideas which, although initially repugnant to his contemporaries, have real value in the science. For example, take the relativistic equation relating the total energy E of a particle to its momentum p and rest mass m,

$$E^2 = p^2c^2 + m^2c^4,$$

where c is the speed of light. This equation clearly permits either positive or negative values for the energy E. In everyday life we do not encounter particles of negative energy, but in 1928 Paul Dirac announced that his combination of quantum and relativistic theories required that the very existence of a particle (electron) implies the existence of its antiparticle (positron) which has the same mass, opposite charge, and oppositely directed magnetic moment. Further, a particle may have a total energy more negative than $-mc^2$ or more positive than $+mc^2$.

After C D Anderson found the positron in 1932, the search was stimulated for other antiparticles in the expectation that nature was indeed symmetrical in this respect. Confirmation of the existence of the antiproton, which had been a tantalising prospect for 20 years, was so important to physics that the experience with nucleons and the ex-

177

perimental ingenuity which enabled Segrè and his former students Chamberlain, Wiegand and Ypsilantis to identify the antiproton in 1955 were honoured by the award of the 1959 Nobel Prize.

Emilio Segrè was born in Tivoli, Rome, in 1905, one of three sons of Giuseppe Segrè, an industrialist, and Amelia Treves Segrè. He had been interested in physics since childhood but studied engineering at the University of Rome for four years before changing to physics. Segrè received his PhD in 1928, the first such degree to be awarded under the sponsorship of Enrico Fermi.

After service in the Italian Army in 1928–29, Segrè became assistant to O M Corbino at the University of Rome. In 1930 he held a Rockefeller Foundation Fellowship to work with Otto Stern in Hamburg and with Pieter Zeeman in Amsterdam. In 1932 he was appointed assistant professor at the University of Rome where he collaborated with Fermi on neutron studies. During 1936–38, Segrè was director of the physics laboratory at the University of Palermo.

Since 1938 Segrè has been associated with the University of California at Berkeley, except for the period 1943–46 when he was a group leader in the Los Alamos Laboratory. In 1974 he was appointed professor at the University of Rome.

Segrè's early work was in atomic physics and spectroscopy. His results in the study of forbidden spectral lines, his discovery of the quadratic Zeeman effect, and his investigations on molecular beams are of permanent interest. Segrè's work in nuclear physics included participating in Fermi's pioneering neutron research, the discovery of the first artificial element technetium (and of the elements astatine and plutonium-239), and the development of a chemical method for separating nuclear isomers. He also succeeded in changing slightly the radioactive decay constant of a substance by chemical means. As higher energies became available he conducted, with Chamberlain, Wiegand and others, extensive investigations on nucleon–nucleon scattering, including polarisation.

Segrè is cosmopolitan in manner, grey-haired and grey-eyed, and about five feet six inches tall. He was married to Elfriede Spiro in 1936 (she died in 1970); they had one son, Claudio, and two daughters, Amelia and Fausta. In 1972 Segrè married Rosa Mines. Segrè has been a US citizen since 1944; for relaxation he enjoys fishing and mountain climbing.

Donald Arthur Glaser

1926–

Awarded the 1960 Nobel Prize for physics for his invention of the bubble chamber.

'What have we done about the pothooks today?' was a question Glaser read at the top of Carl Anderson's blackboard at CalTech in 1949. The new 'strange particles' discovered in cosmic rays were first called V-particles or 'pothooks' because of their unusual appearance in cloud chamber photographs. To detect and determine the properties of elementary particles more energetic than the 30 then known called for a technique which would produce records more rapidly and over longer paths than the Wilson cloud chamber, and which would also overcome the difficulty of relating correctly events associated with neutral V-particles in the Powell nuclear emulsion technique—both valuable techniques for detecting low-energy particles which had been recognised previously by Nobel Prizes.

Glaser set himself the task of devising a particle detector of high density and large volume in which tracks could be photographed and scanned at a glance and which permitted precision measurements of track geometry. He systematically investigated numerous amplifying processes that might be sensitive to minute amounts of energy dissipated along the path of a fast charged particle. The process he selected utilised the thermodynamic instability of a liquid superheated to a temperature roughly two-thirds of the way from boiling point to critical point. The sensitive state is obtained by controlled temperature and a sudden decrease in the external pressure on the liquid. He found that with diethyl ether in this state boiling was triggered by radiation from a cobalt-60 source or from cosmic rays; high-speed films showed well defined tracks before boiling erupted throughout the liquid.

Glaser has remarked: 'Before making these detailed calculations and experiments, I wanted to be sure not to overlook simple experimental possibilities, so I took some bottles of beer, ginger ale, and soda water into my laboratory, warmed them as much as I dared, and opened them with and without a radioactive source nearby. There was no apparent gross difference in the way they foamed.'

Rapid development of the bubble chamber led to the use of many liquids, including xenon which records neutral particle events, and especially liquid hydrogen near 27 K which is favoured for making interpretation of nuclear events easier. In size, bubble chambers have grown from Glaser's 3 cm^3 flasks of 1952 to hydrogen bubble chambers the size of a Volkswagen bus, costing \$2 million, with refrigerating plant and a huge magnet for deflecting particles. Even larger chambers are now operating at Fermilab in Illinois. It was once feared that bubbles forming on gaskets and scratches in a large chamber would prevent the obtaining of useful information. Fortunately even in 'dirty' chambers the desired tracks can be caught photographically before unwanted bubbles intrude.

Some bubble chamber physicists have turned toward developing automatic pattern recognition, measuring and computing machines. It is dreamed that such a machine, armed with a memory filled with knowledge of all processes now known to occur in high-energy physics will devour miles of film each day, noting the numbers and characteristics of all the processes it recognises. Only when it cannot 'understand' an event by searching its memory will it ring a bell to call a physicist who will try to understand the new event.

Donald Glaser's parents, William J Glaser, a businessman, and Lena Glaser, emigrated from Russia and settled in Cleveland where Donald was born in 1926. He attended schools in Cleveland Heights and earned his BS degree in physics and mathematics at the Case Institute of Technology. Four years later he received his PhD from the California Institute of Technology. He began his career of teaching and research in 1949 at the University of Michigan where in the autumn of 1952 he started the bubble chamber experiments.

Chancellor G Seaborg has said that he realised that Glaser was highly eligible for a Nobel Prize and enticed him to Berkeley, in 1959, just in time to get some credit for the University of California. Glaser's research has been in a wide variety of problems in high-energy physics. More recently he has followed an interest in microbiology, molecular biology and cell biology.

In 1960, shortly before going to Stockholm to receive his Nobel Prize, Glaser married Ruth Bonnie Thompson who as a graduate student programmed mathematical problems at Lawrence Radiation

Laboratory. They had two children and were divorced.

Glaser played in a symphony orchestra when he was 16, and he maintains a lively interest in music. He climbs mountains, skis, makes underwater movies and sails his sloop.

Robert Hofstadter

1915–

Shared the 1961 Nobel Prize for physics with Rudolf Mössbauer for his pioneering research in electron scattering by atomic nuclei and for the discoveries he made in this way concerning the structure of the nucleus.

Robert Hofstadter took up the study of the atom where Rutherford, Bohr and Pauli had left it. To probe the structure of the nucleus, Hofstadter used a scattering technique. First, starting in 1950, he used the Stanford linear accelerator to shoot high-energy electrons at targets which were nuclei of gold, lead, tantalum and beryllium. The electrons penetrated the nuclei and the particles comprising the nucleus deflected the electrons by their magnetic fields. A magnetic spectrometer sorted the electrons by energy and by angle of deflection from their original paths. Hofstadter was thus able to distinguish the charge distributions of nuclear particles and to obtain an idea of the structure of the nucleus.

Next, with more powerful accelerating and scattering devices, Hofstadter used electrons with energies up to 1 BeV to examine individual protons and neutrons within the atomic nucleus. He found (1957) the proton and neutron to have similar sizes and shapes, a diameter of 10^{-14} cm, and he presented the first reasonably consistent picture of nuclear structure, which was the basis for his Nobel award.

Robert Hofstadter was born in New York City in 1915, the third of four children of Louis Hofstadter and the former Henrietta Koenigsberg. He was brought up in New York and attended the College of the City of New York where he received a BS degree *magna cum laude* in 1935. With a Coffin Fellowship and a Proctor Fellowship, Hofstadter pursued graduate studies at Princeton University where he received his AM and PhD degrees in 1938. As a Harrison Fellow at the University of Pennsylvania, Hofstadter helped construct a large Van de Graaff accelerator and was an instructor from 1940 to 1941. There he met L I Schiff who became a lifelong friend and colleague.

During World War II, Hofstadter worked on the photoelectric proximity fuse at the National Bureau of Standards and for three years was a section chief at Norden Laboratories Corporation. He returned to academic work in 1946 as assistant professor at Princeton University. In 1948 he discovered that sodium iodide, activated by thallium, NaI(Tl), made an excellent scintillation counter. The counting of high-energy particles and quanta by photoelectric detection of individual light flashes in fluorescent materials has been developed into an exceedingly powerful tool for physics, medicine and other studies.

In 1950, Hofstadter joined the faculty at Stanford University where he initiated a programme on the scattering of energetic electrons from the linear accelerator, invented by W W Hansen, which was then under construction. He was also concerned with cosmic rays and cascade showers generated by high-speed electrons. He was appointed Max H Stein Professor of physics in 1971. Hofstadter has written several hundred research papers. He has been co-editor of *Investigations in Physics* (1951–) and an associate editor of *Reviews of Modern Physics* (1958–69), *Physical Review* (1951–53), and *Review of Scientific Instruments* (1954–56).

Hofstadter has been described as a modest, easy-going person. He married Nancy Givan in 1942, and they have three children: Douglas Richard, Laura James and Mary Hilda. The family enjoys skiing on Californian slopes. Hofstadter also enjoys photography, reading, and listening to classical music and jazz.

Rudolf Ludwig Mössbauer

1929–

Shared the 1961 Nobel Prize for physics with Robert Hofstadter for his investigation of the resonance absorption of gamma radiation and the discovery of the Mössbauer effect.

An incoming radio message is received only if the receiver is tuned to the same frequency as the transmitter; resonance is then occurring. Attempts had been made to observe the corresponding phenomenon for nuclei by allowing electromagnetic radiation (gamma radiation) from some kind of nuclei to act on other nuclei of exactly the same kind. However, resonance absorption generally did not occur, for the atom emitting a gamma photon experienced a recoil whereby the energy and therefore the frequency of the gamma radiation was decreased. A similar effect occurred at the receiving nucleus.

While working toward his doctoral dissertation at the University of Munich in 1956, Mössbauer discovered that by locking iridium nuclei into the lattice of a crystal he could virtually eliminate their recoil and its influence on wavelength. Mössbauer has said that when scientists at the Los Alamos Laboratory and the Argonne National Laboratory read his papers, published in German in 1958, '. . . they found them so unbelievable that they were making a bet that they were wrong. They correspondingly repeated the experiments and republished them simply in order to announce to the English scientific community the fact that the experiments had indeed been correct.' Later, as important applications became apparent, there was an avalanche of research papers on the Mössbauer effect, and some 15 radioactive isotopes have since been found to exhibit the effect. In June 1960, some 80 scientists held a conference at Allerton Park, Illinois, to compare ideas on how to use the Mössbauer effect.

The Mössbauer effect produces a gamma ray whose wavelength is invariable to one part in 10^9. With it, one can detect variations in wavelength due to gravity between the top and bottom floors of a building. Resonance absorption can be made to occur by moving either the emitter or the target at the proper speed with respect to the other. The speed, which may be as little as a few millimetres per hour, then serves as the indicator of the influence of relativity: the dependence of wavelength upon gravity. In addition to verifying the gravitational redshift predicted by Einstein's theory of relativity, the Mössbauer effect has been used to measure the strong magnetic fields that surround nuclei in magnetic materials and to test Einstein's premise that time moves more slowly as the speed of light is approached. The annual *Mössbauer Data Index* cites thousands of papers, review articles and books written on the Mössbauer effect.

Rudolf Mössbauer was born in Munich in 1929, the son of Ludwig and Erna (Ernst) Mössbauer. He attended schools there and worked for two years at the Rodenstock Optics Factory. He entered the Technische Hochschule in 1949, received his master's degree in 1955 and doctorate in 1958. Influenced in part by 'budget cuts and administrative obstacles,' Mössbauer left Munich to join the faculty of California Institute of Technology (1961–64). Mössbauer has been professor of physics at the Technical University in Munich (1965–71, 1977–), and in the interval (1972–77) director of the Institut Laue–Langevin in Grenoble.

Mössbauer married Elizabeth Pritz, a fashion designer, in 1956; they have two children, Peter and Regine. Mössbauer is light-framed, five feet eight inches tall. He has brown eyes, a thick stock of hair and a serious manner.

Lev Davidovich Landau

1908–1968

Awarded the 1962 Nobel Prize for physics for his pioneering theories of condensed matter, especially liquid helium.

Lev Landau was born of Jewish parents in 1908 in the oil city of Baku on the Caspian Sea in Russia. His father was an engineer, his mother a physician. Lev entered Baku University at the age of 14, and completed his studies at the University of Leningrad in 1927. His 1927 paper on damping in wave mechanics presented the first description of quantum states of systems with the aid of density matrices.

In 1929 Landau studied in Denmark, Switzerland, Germany, the Netherlands and England. In Copenhagen, Landau and Niels Bohr began a friendship and exchange of ideas that was to continue for many years. Landau returned to Copenhagen in 1933 and 1944 and spent much time with Bohr during his visits to the Soviet Union in 1934, 1937 and 1961.

From 1932 to 1937 Landau was head of the theoretical physics department of the Physical-Technical Institute at Kharkov. He exhibited versatility and a talent for solving difficult theoretical problems by ingenious mathematical analysis. One of Landau's students at Kharkov, who became a lifelong friend and collaborator, was Evgeny M Lifshitz, then only 17. Kharkov became the centre for theoretical physics in the USSR.

In 1937 Peter L Kapitza asked Landau to join the Institute for Physical Problems in Moscow, which had been created in 1935 to allow Kapitza to continue the research he had begun at Cambridge. A year later Lifshitz joined Landau and they continued their collaboration on an encyclopedic series of monographs on modern theoretical physics. Published in 1938, the books became classics, were translated into seven languages, and won for the authors the 1962 Lenin Prize. In 1937 Landau married Konkordia T Drobanezva, a Kharkov girl who had trained as a food technologist.

In Moscow, Landau joined in the work Kapitza was conducting in superfluidity. It was for work in this area of low-temperature physics performed in 1940 and 1941 that Landau received the Nobel Prize some 20 years later. Landau succeeded in explaining in mathematical terms why below 2 K liquid helium-4 flows without friction and has a thermal conductivity 800 times greater than that of copper at room temperature. Further, he predicted that in superfluid helium sound would travel at two different speeds: one of a familiar pressure wave, the other of the 'second sound' which is a temperature wave. This prediction was verified in experiments by V Peshkov in 1944.

In 1945 Landau carried out work for the engineering committee of the Soviet Army on shock waves at large distances from their place of origin. During the following year he presented papers on the oscillations of plasmas. For the rare isotope helium-3 he predicted the emergence of special properties near absolute zero, one a unique wave propagation called 'zero sound,' and the other, more bizarre, a spontaneous occurrence of rotational domains in the substance would be capable of causing a suspended vessel containing helium-3 to begin spinning suddenly.

Landau's career had a tragic interruption in a car accident on 7 January 1962, near Dubna. Top USSR medical specialists and neurologists from Canada, France and Czechoslovakia brought Landau back from near clinical death several times; he was in a coma for 57 days. In November when his Nobel Prize was announced, Landau was not yet out of bed but he seemed pleased that he could remember enough English to talk briefly with a Swedish reporter. Landau's wife and his son Igor, an experimental physicist, went to Stockholm to accept the Prize on his behalf. Landau's physical condition did not return to normal; he died on 1 April 1968 after an operation.

Landau was a widely educated man. With Kapitza, he admired and encouraged the abstract sculpture of Ernst Neizvestny. In Copenhagen, Landau had many arguments with James Franck about religion; he considered Franck's religious beliefs outmoded for a scientist. His views on politics were liberal and progressive. Kapitza wrote: 'Landau has done work in all the fields of theoretical physics, and all of it can be described by one word—remarkable. We all love Landau very much. We are proud that his work has now been marked by this worldwide recognition. Seldom can you find another man with such a zest for life, so full of camaraderie, such a wonderful friend, such an attentive teacher of young physicists.'

Eugene Paul Wigner

1902–

Received half of the 1963 Nobel Prize for physics for his contributions to the theory of atomic nuclei elementary particles, especially for his discovery and application of fundamental principles of symmetry.

A citation for Wigner might say: 'To one of the truly great physicists of our time for a lifetime of deep understanding and contributions which have profoundly influenced many fields.'

Eugene Wigner was born in Budapest, Hungary, in 1902, the same year as his brother-in-law, British Nobelist Paul Dirac ('my famous brother-in-law,' Wigner calls him). He earned an engineering doctorate at the Technische Hochschule in Berlin in 1925; there and at Göttingen he became absorbed in physics. 'The whole of quantum physics was being created within my own eyesight,' was his description of physics in Germany in the 1920s. With von Neumann, Wigner developed the theory of energy levels in atoms on the basis of group theory; his book on group theory is a classic. Wigner and Seitz provided a basis for solid state physics in their method of treating electron wavefunctions in a solid. In the theory of chemical kinematics Wigner is a master. His interest in the philosophical implications of quantum mechanics was the background for Wigner's Nobel lecture, 'Events, Laws of Nature, and Invariance Principles,' in which he remarked: 'We have ceased to expect from physics an explanation of all events, even of the gross structure of the Universe, and we aim only at the discovery of the laws of nature, that is the regularities of the events . . . If it is true that there are precise regularities, we have reason to believe that we know only an infinitesimal fraction of these . . . Six years ago here Yang mentioned four interactions: gravitational, weak, electromagnetic and strong, and it now seems that there are two types of strong interactions . . . It is hard, if not impossible, to believe that the laws of nature should have such complexity as implied by four or five different types of interactions between which no connection, no analogy, can be discovered.'

Wigner began his long career at Princeton University in 1930, becoming Thomas D Jones Professor of mathemetical physics in 1938. In 1941 he married Mary Annette Wheeler; they have two children, David and Martha.

Wigner was one of the three Hungarians, with Leo Szilard and Edward Teller, who persuaded Einstein to send the famous letter to President Roosevelt that finally resulted in government support for studies of nuclear reactions, leading to the development of the atomic bomb and nuclear reactors. During World War II Wigner worked on the Manhattan Project at Chicago and in 1946–47 became director of the AEC Laboratory at Oak Ridge, Tennessee. Colleagues noted that Wigner the theorist had a remarkably detailed knowledge of the engineering design of reactors.

Wigner has been influential in scientific societies, and he was one of 33 Nobel Prize winners who sent a telegram to President Podgorny asking that Andrei Sakharov be allowed to receive the Nobel Peace Prize in Stockholm. In 1979, Wigner wrote, 'I am very concerned about the future of our country and of freedom.'

Maria Goeppert-Mayer

1906–1972

Shared half of the 1963 Nobel Prize for physics with Hans Jensen for their discoveries regarding the shell structure of nuclear particles.

Only two women have ever won a Nobel Prize for physics. One of them, Maria Goeppert, was born in Kattowitz, Upper Silesia, the only child of Friedrich and Maria (Wolf) Goeppert. Her father was the sixth generation of university professors. When Maria was four, her father went as professor of paediatrics to Göttingen where she spent most of her life until her marriage. There was only one privately endowed school which prepared girls for the *Abitur,* the entrance examination for the university, and this school closed its doors during the runaway inflation. However, her teachers continued to instruct her and in 1924 Maria was given the *Abitur* exam in Hanover, by teachers she had never seen before.

As a student at the University of Göttingen, Maria intended to become a mathematician, but was soon attracted to physics: 'At the time quantum mechanics was young and exciting.' Except for one term at Cambridge, where she said her greatest profit was to learn English, Maria Goeppert's entire university career was spent at Göttingen. She was especially grateful to Max Born for his educational guidance. When she took her doctorate in 1930 in theoretical physics there were three Nobel Prize winners on her doctoral committee: Born, Franck and Windaus. Also in that year, Maria, 'the beauty of Göttingen,' married Joseph Edward Mayer, an American Rockefeller Fellow working with James Franck.

The Mayers went to Johns Hopkins University in 1930. During the depression years a university would not employ the wife of a professor, so Maria kept working, 'just for the fun of doing physics.' She developed into a chemical physicist, wrote various papers with her husband and with K F Herzfeld, and started work on the colour of organic molecules.

In 1939 the Mayers went to Columbia University. Mrs Mayer taught for a year at Sarah Lawrence College, but mainly she worked at the SAM Laboratory, directed by Harold Urey, on the separation of isotopes of uranium. She recalled: 'Urey usually assigned me not to the main line of research of the laboratory but to side issues, for instance, to the investigation of the possibility of separating isotopes by photo-chemical reactions. This was nice, clean physics although it did not help in the separation of isotopes.'

When the Mayers went to Chicago in 1946 Maria felt it was the first place where she was greeted with open arms. She was immediately named a professor in the physics department and in the Institute of Nuclear Studies and was employed by the Argonne National Laboratory.

Maria Mayer's interest in nuclear stability and models lay in a 'little-bang' theory of cosmic origin that she and Edward Teller developed in about 1945 to explain element and isotope abundances. The liquid drop model of the nucleus current in the 1930s explained the gross features of nuclear stability. The abnormal stability at neutron (or proton) numbers 2 (helium), 8 (oxygen), and 20 (calcium) had been noted and explained (a liquid of as few as 20 neutrons or protons is not a drop), but the natural extrapolation to higher numbers showed no abnormalities. Yet Harkins, Elsasser and others had found abnormalities. Theorists despise unexplained numerology; they showed little interest and applied the somewhat derisive epithet 'magic' to the numbers 2, 8, 20, 28, and later 50, 82 and 126.

When in 1946–47 Maria Mayer tried to assemble the plethora of peculiar experimental nuclear properties at or near the magic numbers she had the advantage that Chicago and the Argonne were fountainheads of nuclear experimentation; not infrequently experimentalists made measurements where data were missing.

Maria Mayer (and independently Hans Jensen) evolved a shell model of the nucleus in which nucleons were assumed to move in orbits arranged in so-called shells. The key idea they introduced was that a nucleon has different energies when it 'spins' in the same or opposite sense as it revolves around the centre of the nucleus, and a strong *coupling* exists between the spin and orbital momentum of each nucleon; the two vectors tend to be parallel. The shell model, plus the concept of spin–orbit coupling, predicted correctly that the magic numbers corresponded to nuclei of greatest stability.

When Maria Mayer learned that Haxel, Jensen and Suess,

whom she had never met, had given the same explanation at the same time, she felt convinced of the usefulness of this shell model interpretation. She met Jensen in 1950, and together they wrote *Elementary Theory of Nuclear Shell Structure* (1955). New concepts often encounter scepticism. Once when Maria Mayer was discouraged about the reception of the nuclear shell theory, Jensen wrote to her, 'You have convinced Fermi, and I have convinced Heisenberg. What more do we want?'

Maria Mayer was a skier in the Göttingen days and was also an avid gardener. She raised orchids, particularly cymbidiums, in the Mayer's third-floor glass porch in Chicago. She had a great interest in archaeology, the American southwest (hypothesis: mesas were built of pot-sherds that women had broken over their husbands' heads), and also in India and in the Near East. Two children were born to the Mayers, both in Baltimore, Maria Ann and Peter Conrad.

In 1960 Maria Mayer and her husband left Chicago to accept professorships at the University of California at La Jolla, she in physics, he in chemistry.

J Hans D Jensen

1907–1973

Shared half of the 1963 Nobel Prize for physics with Maria Goeppert-Mayer for their discoveries concerning the shell structure of the nucleus.

In the 1930s it was found that neutrons and protons each form especially stable structures in an atomic nucleus when the number of either kind of nucleon is one of the so-called magic numbers: 2, 8, 20, 28, and later 50, 82 and 126. Since the model of the nucleus as a liquid drop was of no help in explaining these numbers, attempts were made by Elsasser and others to interpret the magic numbers in an analogy to the successful Bohr–Pauli explanation of the periodic system of the elements. The assumptions were made that nucleons move in orbits in a common field of force, these orbits are arranged in so-called shells, and the magic numbers represent complete shells energetically well separated from the next shell, although this explanation was successful only for light nuclei.

Hans Jensen and Maria Goeppert-Mayer simultaneously and independently found the concepts needed to make the shell model acceptable, beginning in 1948. The key idea is that a nucleon has different energies when it 'spins' in the same or opposite sense as it revolves around the centre of the nucleus. A strong coupling exists between spin and orbital momentum of each nucleon; these two vectors tend to be parallel.

Hans Suess, then a geochemist in Hamburg, was interested in element and isotope abundances, and plotted everything against everything else and examined every kink or dip. He soon spotted the numbers 50, 82 and 126, and consulted Haxel, a nuclear experimentalist, who recognised that he had also been puzzled about peculiar nuclear behaviour at these numbers. Together they consulted Jensen and convinced him that the phenomena were real, and were in need of explanation.

When Jensen hit on the idea of spin–orbit coupling, he wrote it up and sent it to the *Physical Review* adding the names of Haxel and Suess as co-authors, and sending them copies.

Jensen and Goeppert-Mayer collaborated in showing how the magic numbers corresponded to nuclei of greatest stability in the shell model. In a book published in 1955, they also showed that magic nuclei and their nearest neighbours should behave in certain special ways; that magic nuclei have a low probability of capturing slow neutrons; they predicted values for the angular momenta of nuclei, and they predicted that in regions of large values one should find numerous nuclear isomers. Experiments have since verified these predictions of the shell model, and other ideas have been added to it, such as the collective model of Bohr, Mottelson and Rainwater (1975 Nobel laureates).

Hans Jensen was born in Hamburg in 1907, the son of Karl Jensen, a gardener, and Helene (Ohm) Jensen. A teacher recognised Jensen's ability and secured for him a scholarship in the Oberrealschule. He was a student at the universities of Freiburg and Hamburg, where he received his doctorate in 1932. He remained there until 1941 when he went to the Technische Hochschule in Hanover. In 1949 Jensen became a professor at the University of Heidelberg, where he lived in a flat above the Institut für Theoretische Physik on Philosophenweg, with a delightful view of Heidelberg across the River Neckar. He tended the institute garden and kept pet turtles.

Jensen was a guest professor at the University of Wisconsin (1951), the Institute for Advanced Study at Princeton (1952), the University of California at Berkeley (1952), Indiana University (1953), California Institute of Technology (1953), and the University of California at La Jolla (1961). Jensen was co-editor of *Zeitschrift für Physik* from 1955 to 1973.

Charles Hard Townes

1915–

Shared the 1964 Nobel Prize for physics with Nikolai Basov and Alexander Prokhorov for fundamental work in the field of quantum electronics which has led to the construction of oscillators and amplifiers based on the maser–laser principle.

Einstein's photon theory of radiation, the Boltzmann law for energy distribution, and the selection rules of quantum mechanics together describe an atomic system in which it might be possible to obtain microwave amplification through stimulated emission of radiation (maser). This possibility had been recognised in varying degrees of precision by a number of physicists in the 1950s, but the first conception of a workable system was due to Charles Townes who used ammonia gas as the amplifying medium. This was followed by the development of a variety of systems (crystalline, liquid and gas) and different types of excitation. Later the principles of 'optical pumping' and 'stimulated radiation' were extended to higher frequencies. Light amplification . . . (laser) was achieved by T H Maiman in 1960.

Laser beams are very narrow and exhibit very little angular divergence. They can be very intense, delivering enormous power onto very small areas. Practical applications include precision alignment of equipment, surveying, drilling small holes in metals and ceramics, and the performance of certain surgical tasks such as repairing detached retinas. A maser beam modulated with a radio or television signal provides a communication link. A maser amplifies the weak signal from Telstar some 10 000 times.

Charles Townes was born in 1915 in Greenville, South Carolina, one of six children of Henry Keith Townes, an attorney, and Ellen (Hard) Townes. At Furman University in Greenville, Townes specialised in modern languages and physics; he still maintains some competency in French, German, Spanish, Italian, Greek, Russian and Latin. He received his BA and BS degrees *summa cum laude* in 1935, his MA from Duke University in 1937 and his PhD from the California Institute of Technology in 1939.

During World War II at Bell Telephone Laboratories, Townes designed radar bombing systems and navigational devices. He was also one of three physicists who independently discovered microwave spectroscopy of gases.

Isidor Rabi, who brought Townes to the faculty of Columbia University in 1948, remarked, 'He is not interested in science alone but in science to give variety to experience.' Townes and his colleagues used short-wavelength radar, a war surplus tool, to investigate the electrical and magnetic interaction between the rotating motion of molecules and the spinning nuclei within. His initial interest in the maser principle was for oscillators to allow further study of molecules, but after a system was made to work he turned its use almost immediately to a high-precision atomic clock. It was later used to verify some predictions of Einstein's special theory of relativity.

From 1961 to 1966 Townes was provost of Massachusetts Institute of Technology. Since 1967 he has been university professor of physics at the University of California. He has been active in developing microwave and infrared astronomy, using the new quantum electronic techniques for sensitive measurements. In 1968 he and his associates at Berkeley discovered the first polyatomic molecules in interstellar space, NH_3 and H_2O, which helped to open the now active study of interstellar clouds.

In 1941 Charles Townes married Frances Hildreth Brown whom he met on a skiing holiday; they have four daughters: Linda Lewis, Ellen Screven, Carla Keith and Holly Robinson. The Townes enjoy travelling, skin-diving and skiing. Townes is a political independent and an active Protestant layman: 'There is a tremendous emotional experience in scientific discovery which I think is similar to what some people would normally describe as a religious experience, a revelation.'

Nikolai Gennadievich Basov

1922–

Shared with Alexander Prokhorov half of the 1964 Nobel Prize for physics with Charles Townes for their work on the oscillators and amplifiers used to produce laser beams.

In the 1950s it occurred to a number of physicists that one might devise an atomic oscillator or amplifier based on a type of atom which has at least three energy levels with the lifetime in the intermediate level greater than that in higher levels. In this three-level method, the atoms are initially distributed among at least three energy states with the smallest population in the highest state and an intermediate number in the middle state, in accordance with Boltzmann's distribution law. Externally supplied radiation near the frequency of the transition between the two outer states causes atoms to be transferred from the lowest to the highest state by the absorption of energy. These excited atoms quickly lose some energy and fall to the intermediate, long-lived level; here they are trapped because of the low probability of transition from the metastable level to the ground level. Radiation introduced at the frequency corresponding to the transit between the latter two states will trigger downward transitions from the metastable state, amplifying the signal which triggered them. This is called maser or laser action.

By 1958, Basov had proposed the use of semiconductors for lasers, and had realised various types with excitation through p–n junctions, electron beams and optical pumping (1960–65). In 1968 Basov produced thermonuclear reactions by using powerful lasers.

Nikolai Basov was born in 1922 in Voronezh, Russia, the son

of Professor Gennadiy Fedorovich Basov and Zinaida Andreevna Basova. After graduating from secondary school in 1941, he served in the Soviet Army during World War II. He joined the Lebedev Physical Institute as a laboratory assistant in 1948, two years after he graduated from the Moscow Institute of Physical Engineers. During 1958–73 Basov was deputy director of the Lebedev Institute, under Dmitriy V Skobelstyn, and head of the quantum radiophysics laboratory from 1963. He was appointed professor at the Moscow Institute of Physical Engineers in 1963. He became director of the Lebedev Institute in 1973.

In 1956, Basov received a doctorate of physical–mathematical sciences in Moscow. He has been a member of the Communist party since 1951 and was a deputy to the USSR Supreme Soviet in 1974. He served on the Soviet Committee of Defence of Peace, World Peace Council. He is the author of some 300 works.

Nikolai Basov married Kseniya Tikhonovna Nazarova in 1950; they have two sons, Gennadiy and Dmitriy. Basov's leisure interests include photography and skiing.

Basov is editor-in-chief of *Priroda* (Nature), a popular science magazine, and the *Soviet Journal of Quantum Electronics*. He became president of the All-Union Society 'Znauie' in 1978.

Alexander Mikhailovich Prokhorov

1916–

Shared with his colleague Nikolai Basov half of the 1964 Nobel Prize for physics (Charles Townes received the other half) for their work in quantum electronics which led to the construction of masers and lasers.

In 1952 Basov and Prokhorov presented a paper at an All-Union (USSR) Conference on Radio Spectroscopy on the possibility of constructing a 'molecular generator,' which was later realised in a molecular beam of ammonia. In 1955 they published a brief note on a new way to obtain the active atomic systems for a maser.

Masers and lasers generally may be understood from a different example, a single-crystal ruby laser. Ruby is an aluminium oxide crystal in which a small fraction of aluminium ions have been replaced by chromium ions. The absorption of green and blue light by these chromium ions imparts a red colour to ruby. In addition, ruby is fluorescent in the red. When the ruby is illuminated by light of wavelength 5500 Å, the chromium atoms are boosted from their lowest energy level E_1 to a third level E_3. They quickly drop to a lower level E_2 by giving heat energy to the crystal lattice. The final drop from E_2 to E_1 occurs with the emission of light of wavelength 6943 Å, but E_2 is a metastable state, and atoms remain in it for a relatively long time $(3 \times 10^{-3}$ seconds). In the quantum mechanical interpretation, there is a low probability of transition from E_2 to E_1. Hence from 'optical pumping' there may develop a population inversion: more chromium atoms are in the higher-energy state E_2 than in the ground state E_1.

For radiation of a particular frequency and for two given

energy levels, in quantum mechanics the probability of radiation absorption is equal to the probability of radiation emission. So if the excited chromium atoms are irradiated with light of wavelength 6943 Å the net effect is a cascade from the more populous level E_2 to level E_1. The stimulated radiation amplifies the triggering radiation; it is monochromatic (6943 Å); it is coherent, and all the atoms which undergo stimulated emissions give off radiation that is precisely in phase with the exciting radiation (a consequence of conservation of momentum).

In a typical small ruby laser, reflecting coatings (to build up radiation intensity within) are applied to the ends of a ruby rod 2–5 cm long and about 0·3 cm in diameter. The rod is placed within a helical flash lamp much like those used in high-speed photography. When this lamp is flashed (providing the energy for optical pumping) a bright beam of red light emerges from the partially transmitting end of the ruby rod. The fact that this light is 'pure,' monochromatic, intense and coherent, makes it ideal for many applications.

Alexander Prokhorov was born in 1916, the son of Mikhail Ivanovich and Maria Mikhailovna Prokhorova. He graduated from Leningrad State University in 1939 and then served in the Red Army during World War II. He joined the staff of the Lebedev Physical Institute as a junior scientific worker in 1939, became a senior scientific worker in 1946, head of a laboratory in 1954, and deputy director in 1968. He was appointed professor at the University of Moscow in 1954.

Prokhorov became a corresponding member of the Academy of Sciences of the USSR in 1960, a full member in 1966, and a member of its praesidium. He was granted an honorary professorship at Delhi University in 1967, and at Bucharest University in 1971. He is an honorary member of the American Academy of Arts and Sciences. Prokhorov became editor-in-chief of the *Bolshaya Sovietskaya Encyclopedia* in 1969.

Prokhorov shared with Basov the Lenin Prize in 1959 for their work in quantum electronics, and he was honoured as Hero of Socialist Labour in 1970. Prokhorov married Galina Shelepina in 1941, and they have one son, Kerill.

Richard Phillips Feynman

1918–

Shared the 1965 Nobel Prize for physics with Sin-itiro Tomonaga and Julian Schwinger for their fundamental work in quantum electrodynamics which involves profound consequences for elementary particle physics.

The recipients of the 1965 Nobel Prize for physics worked independently to build what is perhaps the most nearly perfect theory in physics. Each provided ideas peculiarly his own, and all three arrived at consistent conclusions. Their theory of quantum electrodynamics (QED) describes electrons, positrons, photons, and their interactions; it has been confirmed with remarkable precision in each experimental test to which it has been subjected. Their work has influenced the style of theoretical physics generally, as is evident from numerous papers published since 1948.

In developing the new techniques of QED, Tomonaga initially proceeded on theoretical considerations, largely independent of experiment, to produce from basic physical principles a structure which was simple, clear, and with little elaboration of detail. Schwinger was concerned with inclusive mathematical formulation, while Feynman, unwilling to take anything for granted, reconstructed most of quantum mechanics and electrodynamics from his own viewpoint, seeking simple rules for the direct calculation of physically observable quantities.

While Tomonaga and Schwinger developed QED from a consideration of electric and magnetic fields, Feynman took the fundamental process to be the propagation of particles from place to place.

His measurable quantities were elements of the scattering or 'S' matrix. Another Feynman innovation was the diagrammatic representation of interactions among elementary particles, including photons, and possible transformation. These 'Feynman diagrams' have come to be widely used.

Richard Feynman was born in New York City in 1918, the son of Melville Arthur and Lucille (Phillips) Feynman. He received his BS degree in 1939, at Massachusetts Institute of Technology, and completed his graduate work as Proctor Fellow at Princeton University, obtaining his PhD in 1942. During 1942–45 Feynman was a group leader at the Los Alamos Laboratory. He then served on the faculty at Cornell University until 1950 when he became a professor at California Institute of Technology, and Richard Chace Tolman Professor of theoretical physics in 1959.

Feynman married Gweneth Howarth, his third wife, in England in 1961; they have two children.

In addition to his many contributions to the understanding of the atom, Feynman has captivated a generation of students, and some imitators, by his originality and showmanship in classroom presentations. The three volumes of his recorded and published *Feynman Lectures in Physics* (1963–65) are still widely quoted.

Julian Seymour Schwinger

1918–

Shared the 1965 Nobel Prize for physics with Sin-itiro Tomonaga and Richard Feynman for their fundamental work in quantum electrodynamics which involves profound consequences for elementary particle physics.

An important result of the work of the 1965 Nobel Prize winners was an explanation of the Lamb shift. The laws of quantum mechanics developed in about 1925 described the behaviour of the simplest atom, hydrogen, accurately enough so that some 20 years passed before any experimental evidence was found for error in that theory. However, in 1947 Lamb and Retherford noted that some energy levels of hydrogen which theory said should coincide were in fact somewhat shifted with respect to each other. Starting in the late 1920s Dirac, Heisenberg and Pauli formulated a theory called quantum electrodynamics (QED) for the interaction of charged particles, in particular electrons, and the electromagnetic field, which was in agreement with the theory of relativity. Discovery of the contradictory Lamb shift generated in some physicists a strong distrust of quantum field theory, while in others a determination to rescue it. Attempts to improve that theory by minor adjustments were unsuccessful. 'All attempts to mutilate the theory have been uniformly unsuccessful,' wrote Schwinger in an early paper.

Added to the problem of the Lamb shift, Kusch and Foley discovered another peculiarity: that the magnetic moment of the electron was somewhat larger than had been assumed. Using his method of renormalisation, however, Schwinger was able to show that a small

203

anomalous contribution should indeed be added to the value of the magnetic moment accepted until then. As Schwinger continued to develop the formalism of the new QED he produced a massive mathematical structure, a monument of formal ingenuity. An irritated critic once said, 'Other people publish to show you how to do it, but Julian Schwinger publishes to show you that only he can do it.' But Schwinger emerged from the mathematical jungle with an experimentally confirmed numerical value for the magnetic moment of the electron and an explanation for the Lamb shift.

Julian Schwinger was born in 1918 in New York City and was marked at an early age by an intense awareness of physics. Guided by I I Rabi, he entered Columbia University, published his first paper at the age of 16, received his BA at 17, his PhD at 21, and at 29 was made full professor at Harvard, one of the youngest in Harvard's history. It was in that year that he married Clarice Carrol of Boston.

For two years (1940–42) Schwinger was at the University of California at Berkeley, first as a National Research Fellow and then as assistant to J Robert Oppenheimer. During World War II, he was at the Radiation Laboratory at MIT. 'Being a confirmed solitary worker,' he wrote, 'I became the night research staff.' A story is told that his fellow workers occasionally at closing time left unfinished work on a blackboard or desk top and were pleased in the morning to find that Schwinger had filled in the solution.

Schwinger was led to QED by several influences. With large microwave power available, he thought about electron accelerators, which led to the radiation of electrons in magnetic fields. He was reminded that classical theory says that reaction of the electron's field alters the properties of the particle, including its mass. These considerations were significant in the comprehensive development of QED which followed.

Subsequent to his Nobel-awarded work, Schwinger has worked on general theoretical questions rather than specific problems of experimental concern. 'A speculative approach to physics has its dangers, but it can have its rewards,' he has remarked. As examples he cites his anticipation, in early 1957, of two different neutrinos associated with the electron and the muon, which have now been experimentally confirmed. Another fruitful speculation concerned magnetically charged particles.

Schwinger's awards include the first Einstein Prize (1951), the US Medal of Science (1964), honorary degrees from Purdue and Harvard, and the Nature of Light Award of the National Academy of Sciences (1949). He is a member of the NAS and a sponsor of the *Bulletin of the Atomic Scientists* and editor of *Quantum Electrodynamics*.

Sin-itiro Tomonaga

1906–1979

Shared the 1965 Nobel Prize for physics with Julian Schwinger and Richard Feynman for their fundamental work in the area of quantum electrodynamics, which carries profound consequences for the physics of elementary particles.

Quantum electrodynamics (QED) is the complicated theory that governs the reactions of electrons, protons and photons. Excluding gravitation and nuclear forces, QED elegantly unifies into a small number of very general principles such diverse phenomena as atomic structure, radiation/absorption, particle creation/annihilation, solid state physics, lasers, microwave spectroscopy, electronics, plasmas and chemistry.

The quantum theory of the 1920s as conceived by Paul Dirac dealt with the interactions of electrons and electromagnetic radiation. It successfully described emission and absorption of light by atoms; the Raman, Compton and photoelectric effects; and pair production. However, this field theory was plagued by difficulties referred to as the 'divergence' problem; in extending it, many computations led to absurd answers, such as zero or infinity. From about 1930 to 1945 many attempts were made to replace this theory, but all were unsuccessful.

Working in wartime isolation, Tomonaga published his fundamental paper on QED in Japanese in 1943 (not available in English translation until 1948), unaware of alternative approaches being developed elsewhere. Tomonaga showed that if one applied the physical ideas of existing theory in an appropriate, consistent manner the theory gave unambiguous and meaningful answers. This was a triumph of conservatism. But getting rid of the 'infinities' in earlier calculations required sophisticated and complicated procedures. One was the 'renormalisation' of mass and charge to take account of the fact that the electronic mass and charge were modified by field reactions. The completed structure of QED is perhaps the most comprehensive theory in physics and agrees with measured properties of electrons to at least six decimal places.

Sin-itiro Tomonaga was born in Tokyo in 1906, and was brought up in Kyoto where his father was an eminent professor of philosophy at the Imperial University. He completed work for his bachelor's degree at Kyoto, under the guidance of Hideki Yukawa, in 1929. After three years of graduate work there, Tomonaga started work on QED with Yoshio Nishina at the Institute of Physical and Chemical Research in Tokyo. They published an important paper on photoelectric production of positrons and electrons in 1934.

While Tomonaga was in Leipzig (1937–39), Heisenberg infected him with enthusiasm for studying field reactions, crucial in meson–nucleon scattering. Tomonaga became professor of physics at Tokyo University of Education in 1941. During World War II he worked on a theory of microwave systems; afterwards he returned to working on QED and developed a renormalisation theory. Tomonaga spent the year 1949 at the Institute for Advanced Study in Princeton. He took the leadership in establishing the Institute for Nuclear Study at the University of Tokyo, in 1955. He was president of Tokyo University of Education (1956–62), and from 1963 to 1969 was president of the Science Council of Japan and director of the Institute for Optical Research.

In 1940 Tomonaga married Ryoko Sekiguchi, daughter of the former director of the Tokyo Metropolitan Observatory. They had a daughter and two sons.

Alfred Kastler

1902–

Awarded the 1966 Nobel Prize for physics for the discovery and development of optical methods for studying Hertzian resonances in atoms.

Aided by Jean Brossel, first his pupil and later close co-worker, Kastler sought to identify the sublevels associated with energy levels in atoms. Their *double resonance* method used both a light beam and a radio-frequency electromagnetic (Hertzian) wave. When a group of atoms is illuminated with a beam of light of suitable wavelength, some of the atoms will absorb light quanta, and will go from the ground or lowest energy state to one of the optical excited states. The average time the atoms spend in the excited state, called the lifetime, may be about 10^7 seconds. They then make a transition back to the ground state, emitting fluorescent radiation.

Assume that we have an apparatus with which we can measure the polarisation and angular distribution of the photons the atoms emit when returning to the ground state. When a group of atoms is excited by a beam of polarised light, not all of the sublevels of the excited state receive equal populations; in general the emitted radiation will not be isotropic and radiation in a particular direction will be partially polarised. Now if a radio-frequency field is applied to cause transitions from one of the populated levels of the excited state to an unpopulated level, the angular distribution of the radiation will change. Thus by studying the re-emitted light one can detect the radio-frequency transitions in the induced state. One then has a precise tool for studying

207

the structure of excited atomic levels.

Kastler also used optical techniques to move atoms in their ground state from one magnetic sublevel to another. For an atom with two or more magnetic sublevels, when irradiated with circularly polarised light, atoms in one sublevel absorb light and go to the excited state, while atoms in the other sublevel do not. The quantum mechanical rules for optical transitions are such that when excited atoms radiate and fall back to the ground state, they make transitions into both of the two magnetic sublevels of that state. So one can use light to pump atoms from the absorbing level to the non-absorbing level. This technique is called *optical pumping.*

If you find Kastler's work on double resonances and optical pumping difficult to comprehend and appreciate, you are in good company. A spokesman for the Royal Swedish Academy of Sciences said: 'It would be almost impossible to explain the work . . . to people other than scientists.' Kastler's award touched off a *New York Times* editorial (6 November 1966) entitled 'Incomprehensible Science.' Yet from Kastler's esoteric work have come valuable practical instruments. These include frequency standards, atomic clocks often accurate to one second in 10 000 years, and a magnetometer used to measure a weak magnetic field such as that surrounding the Earth.

Alfred Kastler was born in 1902 in the town of Guebwiller in Alsace, then a part of Germany, the son of Frédéric and Anna (Frey) Kastler. For his secondary education, he attended the Lycée Bartholdi in Colmar. In 1920 he entered the Ecole Normale Supérieure under a special exemption the government made for a few Alsatians who could not pass the national entrance examination. Kastler has written of the stimulating and fraternal atmosphere of that school, where Eugene Bloch introduced his students to the Bohr atom and to Sommerfeld's *Atombau und Spektrallinien.*

Before beginning his graduate studies, Kastler taught physics at lycées in Mulhouse (1926–27), Colmar (1927–29) and Bordeaux (1929–31). In 1931 he began graduate studies at the University of Bordeaux where his thesis dealt with the step-wise excitation of mercury atoms. When he received his DSc degree in 1936, Kastler became a lecturer at Clermont–Ferrand University, and from 1938 to 1941 he was a professor of physics at the University of Bordeaux. He returned to the Ecole Normale Supérieure in 1941, where he was the director of a research group of some 20 persons in Hertzian spectroscopy. In 1952 Kastler was given the rank of full professor. He has served on numerous educational and scientific commissions.

Kastler is a retiring and modest man, and has acknowledged the research of his colleagues with characteristic generosity. He has expressed his political views forcefully in speaking and writing. He spoke out against the atomic bomb and the war in Vietnam, and supported the rights of conscientious objectors and independence for

Algeria. He was in support of Israel during its 1967 conflict with Arab countries and in support of anti-Fascist causes in general.

While he was still a school teacher, in December 1924, Kastler married a fellow teacher, Elise Cosset; they have two sons, Daniel and Claude-Yves, and a daughter, Mireille. His sons are teachers, and his daughter is a physician. He has seven grandchildren.

Hans Albrecht Bethe

1906–

Awarded the 1967 Nobel Prize for physics for his contributions to the theory of nuclear reactions, especially for his discoveries concerning energy production in stars.

The achievement for which Hans Bethe is most widely known is his theory (1938) of how the Sun and stars use nuclear reactions to supply the energy they radiate. Bethe found that the carbon-12 nucleus has unique properties: it reacts with protons at a sufficient rate to explain energy production in the stars, and it undergoes a cycle of reactions that terminates in the creation of a new carbon-12 nucleus. The carbon nucleus thus acts as a catalytic agent that is regenerated. The net result of the cycle is equivalent to the fusion of four protons with a nucleus of helium; the one per cent difference in mass acounts for the energy released.

Bethe and C L Critchfield made calculations for a proton–proton sequence for the building of the helium nucleus from hydrogen that fit the observed facts equally well. The rates at which this cycle and the carbon cycle proceed are very sensitive to temperature. Bethe concluded that for stars with internal temperatures greater than that of the Sun, the carbon cycle probably predominates; for the Sun and cooler stars with temperatures in the region of 10^7 degrees, the proton–proton reaction is the more important thermonuclear reaction.

Hans Bethe, son of a university professor, was born in Strasbourg (then in Germany) in 1906. He earned his doctorate at the age of 22 at Munich, under Sommerfeld. During 1930–32 he worked

210

with Rutherford at Cambridge and with Fermi in Rome. In 1933 he was dismissed from his assistant professorship at Tübingen (his mother was Jewish). While in England for the next two years Bethe wrote several important papers on nuclear physics and on radiation theory, including one with Heitler on electron–positron pair production.

In 1935, Bethe joined the faculty of Cornell University. Few other physicists have worked as productively as has Bethe on so many different problems. To chemists, Bethe is the father of crystal field theory. Bethe was the first to use the new ideas of renormalisation to account for the electromagnetic shift of atomic levels measured by Lamb and Retherford. He was the first to calculate level densities in nuclear spectra, in 1936. His continuing interest has been the connection between nuclear forces and the structure of nuclei.

During World War II Bethe contributed much to the development of radar (1942), and to military applications of nuclear fission. Convinced that it was feasible to monitor nuclear explosions, he worked for adoption of the 1963 limited test ban treaty. Bethe, with the Federation of American Scientists, fought to get transferred from military to civilian hands the control of the development of atomic energy for peacetime uses.

Victor Weisskopf has written: 'Bethe's strength was that of finding simple and general ways to deal with complicated situations . . . Every paper of Bethe's [there are some 300 titles] bears the characteristic marks of his insight and his special way of attacking problems. He differs from most of us in his universality and his encyclopedic knowledge . . . His warm, straightforward, and simple approach to any human or scientific question has given support and confidence to many people.'

Bethe is a superb expositor. He has often chosen to work on subjects of great topical importance, never far from experiment. Generations of students have learned their nuclear physics from 'Bethe's Bible,' the monumental, lucid review articles Bethe and Bacher published in 1936–37, and from *Elementary Nuclear Theory* written with P Morrison (1956).

Bethe enjoys hiking in the mountains, and he is a stamp collector. Bethe married Rose Ewald, the daughter of one of his professors in Germany, in 1939, and they have two children, Henry George and Monica.

Luis Walter Alvarez

1911–

Awarded the 1968 Nobel Prize for physics for his decisive contributions to elementary particle physics, in particular the discovery of a large number of resonant states, made possible through his development of the technique of the hydrogen bubble chamber and data analysis.

Luis Alvarez was born in 1911 in San Francisco, the son of Harriet (Smyth) Alvarez and Walter C Alvarez, a teacher and Mayo Clinic physician who became a medical journalist. At the University of Chicago, on the advice of a favourite professor, Luis switched from chemistry to physics. He received his BS degree there in 1932, MS in 1934, and PhD in 1936. Then, taking his bride Geraldine Smithwick Alvarez to Berkeley, he joined the Radiation Laboratory of the University of California, which, except for leaves, has remained the site of his research.

By the time the bevatron, a 6·2 BeV proton synchrotron, first operated in 1954, certain particles had been identified which were called 'strange particles' because they lasted much longer (10^{-10} seconds) than the 10^{-23} seconds predicted by theoretical models for their production. To investigate such particles in detail, electronic counters appeared inadequate, cloud chambers had too long cycling periods, and nuclear emulsions could not record neutral particles or provide time resolution.

Alvarez felt he had found the 'big idea' he needed to track particles when, during a fortunate lunch-time encounter at the April 1953 meeting in Washington, Donald Glaser showed him photographs of bubble tracks left by particles which had passed through diethyl ether in a small (2 cm) glass bulb. Alvarez returned to Berkeley to organise elementary particle research in three major levels: the design of a bubble chamber that he felt must use liquid hydrogen; the invention of semi-automatic track-measuring equipment, and programming procedures for computers to reduce the voluminous track data to a physically meaningful form. Alvarez and his group were the pioneers in each of these stages of research.

Scientific papers on the bubble chamber were published by authors who were listed at the Lawrence Radiation Laboratory as technicians. Alvarez has remarked, 'I believe this is a healthy change from practices common a generation ago; we all remember papers signed by a single physicist that ended with a paragraph saying, "I wish to thank Mr . . ., who built the apparatus and took much of the data".'

Alvarez's group quickly increased the size of its liquid hydrogen bubble chambers in stages from the first 1 inch diameter glass chamber to a 2 inch, a 10 inch, a 15 inch, and then the giant 72 inch chamber (1959). Largely from this technique, the number of so-called fundamental particles discovered now approaches 100.

Track-sensitive devices planned by Alvarez used projection microscopes and determined the momentum for each track from its curvature in a magnetic field. These measuring machines (exhibited at the 1958 Atoms for Peace exposition in Geneva) were called 'Franckensteins' after their designer Jack Franck. Next, from a 'kinematics programme,' the computer identified the 'name' of each particle in an event. By 1968 improved 'spiral readers' used by Alvarez's group measured more than one million events per year, a rate nearly equal to that of all other laboratories combined.

While Alvarez may be best known for his work in high-energy physics, he has also made other important contributions in rapid sequence in many areas of physics. While a graduate student at the University of Chicago, he was co-discoverer of the east–west effect in cosmic rays, which indicated the incoming particles to be positive. At Berkeley, he demonstrated orbital electron capture by nuclei. He collaborated in the design and construction of the first proton linear accelerator based on the use of cavity resonators. With Robert Cornog, Alvarez made the discovery that ^{3}He is stable and ^{3}H (tritium) is radioactive, rather than vice versa, as had been expected. In 1941 Alvarez took leave from the University of California to help develop microwave radar at the Radiation Laboratory at MIT. There he developed the GCA (ground-controlled approach) blind landing system for aircraft. In experiments lasting several years, Alvarez used cosmic rays and spark chambers to prove that there are no chambers in Kefren's 'second pyramid' at Giza.

Alvarez moved from MIT to the wartime Manhattan Project in 1943; for six months he worked with Fermi on the first nuclear reactor.

Later he joined with Ernest Lawrence and Edward Teller in urging that the US government embark on a crash programme to develop the H-bomb. This recommendation was opposed by J Robert Oppenheimer and most of the AEC Science Advisory Committee. President Truman decided in favour of making the H-bomb.

Alvarez married Geraldine Smithwick in 1936; following a divorce, he married Janet Landis in 1958. He has four children: Walter, Jean, Donald and Helen. Alvarez is now Emeritus Professor of physics at the University of California at Berkeley. His recreations are flying, golf and music.

Murray Gell-Mann

1929–

Awarded the 1969 Nobel Prize for physics for his contributions and discoveries concerning the classification of elementary particles and their interactions.

Murray Gell-Mann, who became regarded by some as Albert Einstein's scientific successor, was born in 1929 in New York City, the youngest son of Austrian immigrants. He entered Yale University on his fifteenth birthday, earned his PhD degree at MIT when he was 22, and after teaching for four years at the University of Chicago he was appointed professor of physics at CalTech when he was 26. There he became R A Millikan Professor of theoretical physics in 1967.

Gell-Mann's domination of the complex and popular subject of elementary particle physics is illustrated by the following story. For the 1966 International Conference on High-Energy Physics at Berkeley, the organisers planned to have five or six experts give progress reports on special areas of this rapidly growing field. After some wrangling over whom should be asked to present these reports, someone made the inspired suggestion that Gell-Mann do the whole thing. In a 90-minute talk he covered the whole field authoritatively, having worked on almost all aspects of it.

There was a time when the electron, proton and neutron seemed to be the fundamental particles from which all matter was built. Then in the 1940s and 1950s new unstable particles were discovered, first in cosmic-ray events and later produced by high-energy accelerators. Some (mesons) had masses about 1000 times the mass of the electron, and some were 'strange' in having lives 10^{-10} seconds long, as compared to the 10^{-23} seconds expected for strong interactions. Gell-Mann found that nearly all the known particles could be grouped into families or multiplets which showed geometrical patterns corresponding to Lie groups, patterns that had been studied by the Norwegian mathematician Sophus Lie. When his rules of geometry were applied to particle physics, a theory emerged to explain the properties of the particles in the multiplets and to predict the existence of new ones, somewhat analogous to Mendeleev's achievement in constructing the periodic table of the elements. For this grouping Gell-Mann defined a new quantity called the strangeness quantum number, S, related to the multiplet charge (Francis Bacon: 'There is no excellent beauty that hath not some strangeness in the proportion').

In about 1961 Gell-Mann and, independently, the Israeli physicist Yuval Ne'eman progressed to a new theory that Gell-Mann named the eight-fold way (after the eight ways of right living Buddhists recommend to avoid pain). Isotope multiplets were grouped into supermultiplets according to a mathematical structure called the group SU(3). This led to prediction of an eighth meson called η^0, which was subsequently discovered.

The real world is not as symmetrical as the theory; by making assumptions about how symmetry is broken in nature, one can predict relations among masses of the particles. In 1962 Gell-Mann predicted the existence of particles of masses corresponding to energies 1532 MeV and 1679 MeV. The 1964 discovery of these particles, called Σ_{10} and Ω^- respectively, underlined the importance of this theory. It was this SU(3) theory which also led Gell-Mann to speculate on the existence of three(?) entities out of which all the other particles could be built, which he named *quarks* (James Joyce, in *Finnegan's Wake*: 'Three quarks for Master Mark!').

Murray Gell-Mann was married to J Margaret Dow in 1955; they have a daughter, Elizabeth, and a son, Nicholas. Gell-Mann has extended his influence beyond the laboratory; he served on President Nixon's Science Advisory Committee, and in 1969 he helped to organise an environmental study programme sponsored by the National Academy of Science. He is fluent in several languages, and is a birdwatcher and a hiker-camper.

Hannes Olof Gösta Alfvén

1908–

Shared the 1970 Nobel Prize for physics with Louis Néel for his fundamental work and discoveries in magnetohydrodynamics and their fruitful applications in different parts of plasma physics.

Hannes Alfvén has suggested that since theory must remain in touch with experimental data, the centre of gravity of physics moves with the big instruments: spectrographs, cyclotrons, spacecraft, etc. He believes that the main scientific goal of space research, as early identified by NASA, should be to clarify how the Solar System was formed. To this end Alfvén pioneered the field of magnetohydrodynamics (MHD) which is the study of electrically conducting gases in a magnetic field. Plasma— a highly conducting gas—is the state in which some 90 per cent of the matter in the Universe exists and from which Alfvén believes grains, embryos, protoplanets and protosatellites were formed.

Alfvén's ideas were sometimes regarded as eccentric and received delayed acceptance, perhaps because of his extraordinary intuitions and his habit of putting new data into a theoretical picture larger than that required to account for just those observations. In 1942 Alfvén's study of sunspots led him to the discovery of hydromagnetic waves (Alfvén waves) in the ionised gas of the Sun. Since it was 'well known' from Maxwell's theory that an electromagnetic wave could scarcely penetrate a conductor, Alfvén's discovery was initially disregarded. Six years later, when he gave several lectures on hydromagnetic waves in the US, the correctness and importance of his work was recognised. A J Dessler has given an oversimplified account; Fermi heard Alfvén's lecture at the University of Chicago, nodded his head and said, 'Of course.' The next day the entire world of physics said, 'Oh, of course.'

Alfvén collected much of his work in the book *Cosmical Electrodynamics* published by Oxford University Press in 1950, and in the monograph *On the Origin of the Solar System* (1956). Alfvén has also contributed to other fields: in cosmology he offers the view that the Universe is made up of equal quantities of matter and antimatter. He has written a number of popular scientific books, some in collaboration with his wife, and under the pen name Olof Johannesson he has written a social satire: *The Tale of the Big Computer* (1968). In space planning he has campaigned for an unmanned mission to an asteroid or a comet in the belief that more information about the accretion of matter in the Solar System can be obtained from these smaller bodies than from the planets (whose centres are not accessible and whose earliest structures have been disturbed).

Alfvén's work on MHD is important also in the development of controlled thermonuclear reactors, in hypersonic flight, in providing thrust for propulsion in outer space, and in the braking of space vehicles upon re-entry into the Earth's atmosphere.

Hannes Olof Gösta Alfvén was born in Norrköping in Sweden in 1908. His parents, Johannes Alfvén and Anna-Clara Romanus, were both practising physicians. He entered Uppsala University in 1926, received his PhD and became a lecturer in 1934. Alfvén was successively research physicist at the Nobel Institute of Physics (1937), professor at the Royal Institute of Technology (1940), and professor at the University of California, San Diego (1967). He has been a member of science research councils and scientific adviser to the Swedish government. Originally he strongly supported nuclear energy but around 1970 he became convinced that not only nuclear arms but also 'peaceful' nuclear energy were unacceptable, and since 1970 he has taken part in the anti-nuclear campaign.

Alfvén married Kerstin Maria Erikson in 1935; they have five children and nine grandchildren.

Louis
Eugène Félix
Néel

1904–

Shared the 1970 Nobel Prize for physics with Hannes Alfvén for his fundamental research and discoveries concerning antiferromagnetism and ferrimagnetism which have important applications in solid state physics.

By about 1930 three states of magnetism had been identified and explained: dia-, para- and ferromagnetism. In the first two, the elementary magnets of the atoms behave independently of one another when subjected to a magnetic field. In ferromagnetism, which is much stronger, there is a collective alignment treated by Heisenberg (1928) in exchange coupling, a quantum mechanical effect. Louis Néel in 1932 added a fourth type, antiferromagnetism. He presented a model for a crystal built up from two interlaced lattices with magnetic fields acting in opposite directions, all but cancelling out the observable field. He showed that this ordered state should disappear at a temperature now known as the Néel point, in analogy with the Curie point for ferromagnetics.

In 1948 Néel explained the strong magnetism found in ferrite materials, one of which, magnetite, was used by the Chinese to produce the first compass. Néel assumed that in these materials, which he called ferrimagnetic, the lattices could be of different strengths and could produce external fields. In magnetite, which has three atoms of iron and four of oxygen, the effects of two of the iron atoms cancel out, but the third gives the observed magnetic field.

Because ferrimagnetic materials are electrically non-conducting (and hence immune to stray currents) they are highly useful in telephony, the coating of magnetic tape, in computer memory cores, and in low-loss, high-frequency techniques. They also serve as permanent magnets in engines, loudspeakers and microphones.

Born in Lyon, France, in 1904, Louis Néel spent the early part of his scientific career at the University of Strasbourg. There he published two celebrated papers on the basis of antiferromagnetism. In 1945 he became director of the Laboratoire d'Electrostatique et de Physique du Métal and guided it to become a superior centre for scientific research. Néel heads a staff of some 300 at this laboratory. He was director of the Centre d'Etudes Nucléaires de Grenoble which has strong programmes in neutron diffraction, crystal growth and Mössbauer studies. He has been largely responsible for a laboratory for high magnetic fields, high pressures, and very low temperatures, and for the joint Franco–German–British (Institut Max von Laue–Paul Langevin) high-flux reactor laboratory at Grenoble. Néel has accepted broad responsibilities in education; he was a member of the Consulting Committee on Higher Education and president of the Institut National Polytechnique de Grenoble. In 1940 he found a way to protect the French Navy against German magnetic mines.

Néel has a rugged, open face and in conversation he gestures with expressive hands. His leisure activities include hiking in the mountains surrounding Grenoble; reading classics, 'whodunits' and especially eighteenth-century French literature; and carpentry. Néel married Hélène Hourticq in 1931, and they have three children.

Dennis Gabor

1900–1979

Awarded the 1971 Nobel Prize for physics for his invention and development of the method of holography.

The Royal Swedish Academy of Sciences awarded the 1971 prize to a man whose inventions received more than a hundred patents, especially for 'Gabor's achievement of holography which can be referred to both as discovery and invention.'

      Dennis Gabor described his 1948 experiments in 'wavefront reconstruction' as an exercise in serendipity. His original goal was an improved electron microscope, only later attained (1971), but his experiments immediately established exciting possibilities for optical holography, a system of lensless, three-dimensional photography. Holography has since grown into a business that grosses several hundred million dollars a year. In 1971 airborne hologram radar was used to 'photograph' clearly, in spite of cloud cover, three million square miles of the Amazon River basin. Wide-ranging applications of holography, to which Gabor made many contributions, include: photographic storage of several hundred pictures in one emulsion, the recognition of patterns and characters, new microscope methods, production of gratings for optics, viewing through turbulent media, and three-dimensional cinematography. Recently acoustical holography and ultrasonic 'sonaradiography' have found valuable applications in medical diagnosis. As a method of non-destructive testing, holography has mundane but economically important applications in testing tyres and laminated structural materials for faulty bonding.

Dennis Gabor was born in Budapest, Hungary, on 5 June 1900, the first of three sons of Adrienne (Jacobovitz) Gabor and Bertalan Gabor, the director of the Hungarian General Coal Mining Company. His father interested Dennis in invention through the careers of such men as Thomas Alva Edison and visits to the museum of technology in Budapest. Gabor was fascinated by Abbe's theory of the microscope and Gabriel Lippmann's method of colour photography, which was to influence his work 30 years later.

When he reached university age, Gabor opted for engineering (physics was not then a recognised profession in Hungary), and so he aquired his degrees, diploma (at the Technische Hochschule in Berlin, 1924), and Dr-Ing in electrical engineering (1927). But as often as possible, he slipped over to the University of Berlin where physics was in an apogee with Einstein, Planck, Nernst and von Laue.

With thousands of other intellectuals, Gabor left Hitler's Germany in 1933. At the British Thomson–Houston Company in Rugby (1933–48) he wrote his first papers on communication theory, developed a system of stereoscopic cinematography, and carried out the basic experiments in holography. At the start of 1949, he joined the Imperial College of Science and Technology in London. 'This was a happy time,' he wrote, 'With my young doctorands and collaborators I attacked many problems, almost always difficult ones.'

One of Gabor's laboratory assistants at the Technische Hochschule had been Peter C Goldmark, a fellow Hungarian. Goldmark remembers how Gabor built his own research instruments with patience and superlative skill, not satisfied with the commercially available ones. Gabor often rewarded Goldmark's good work with a generous supply of Hungarian salami. After his retirement in 1967, Gabor was elected Emeritus Professor and professorial research fellow at Imperial College in London, and became staff scientist of CBS Laboratories, Stamford, Connecticut, where he collaborated with the president, his lifelong friend, Peter Goldmark, in many new schemes of communication and display.

From about 1958, Gabor devoted much thought to the future of our industrial civilisation. In three books he expressed his conviction that a serious mismatch had developed between technology and our social institutions and that inventive minds ought to consider social invention as their first priority. Gabor was one of the founder-members of the Club of Rome and was co-author of its report *Beyond the Age of Waste* (1978).

In the autobiographical note Gabor wrote for *Les Prix Nobel en 1971*, he included under 'honours': 'Married since 1936 to Marjorie Louise, daughter of Joseph Kennard Butler and Louise Butler of Rugby.' Gabor described his wife to a reporter as '. . . one of those rare people . . . who can make other people happy.' The couple had no children. Gabor was a relatively short and sturdy man with a grey moustache. A

British citizen, he spoke softly with a Hungarian accent. He was meticulous in his dress and had an outgoing, courtly manner. Never long away from work, Gabor found time for swimming, writing and reading. He could quote Rilke and Valery extensively.

Leon N Cooper

1930–

Shared the 1972 Nobel Prize for physics with John Bardeen and John Schrieffer for their theory of superconductivity called the BCS theory.

In 1933 Meissner and Oschenfeld had discovered that in the supercon-ducting state, a superconductor shows perfect diamagnetism. If a magnet is brought near, the lines of force are repelled by the superconductor. In 1935 Fritz and Heinz London showed how for a superconductor Ohm's law is replaced by another which predicts both the diamagnetism and the zero resistance. Independently, E Maxwell and a group working under B Serin found that the critical temperature for the onset of superconductivity varied inversely with the square root of the molecular weight of the specimen. This signalled that the *nucleus* had a role in superconductivity. One might picture the metal lattice as a jungle-gym with nuclei at the joints, through which baseballs (the electric current) are passed. John Bardeen and Herbert Fröhlich independently thought that electron interactions with lattice vibrations (electron–phonon interactions) were involved, but these early attempts (1950) were not successful in explaining superconductivity.

It appeared from the work of B B Goodman on thermal conductivity, and that of Brown, Zemansky and Boorse on specific heats, that another ingredient needed in the theory of superconductivity was the concept of an energy gap. Pauli's exclusion principle, which deter-mines the placement of electrons in orbits or energy levels in an atom, and thus explains the periodic table of the elements, also applies to the cloud of electrons in a metal. Even at absolute zero some electrons will have considerable energy, since the lower levels are filled. If the highest occupied level, the Fermi energy, has no nearby higher levels, a gap exists and electrons must pay an entrance fee to cross it to the higher levels. Bardeen intuitively realised that a superconductor was a normal metal in which an energy gap was introduced; he felt that if one could find the reason for the energy gap one would understand superconductivity. The third ingredient in a theory of superconductivity was felt to be a phase transition called a condensation in velocity. To picture this abstraction, consider children running at random in a playground. They hear the school bell and head for the door; although they are in different places, they have a common velocity. Substitute the electrons in a metal for the children and ask why they should have a common velocity (providing an electron current).

This was the status of superconductivity as Bardeen, Cooper and Schrieffer got together at the University of Illinois for their successful assault on the problem. They recognised that essential to superconductivity were: condensation in velocity space, an energy gap, and interaction of electrons with lattice vibrations.

Leon Cooper had recently received his academic degrees from Columbia University: AB in 1951, AM in 1953 and PhD in 1954. He was recognised as an expert in quantum field theory, and so Bardeen called in this 'quantum mechanic from the east.' His first contribution to superconductivity theory was the discovery of 'Cooper pairs.' Although two electrons repel each other because of their charges, an electron located between two positive ions in a metal lattice brings these ions somewhat closer and provides a small net attraction for a second electron. The two electrons, with their spins oppositely oriented, form a Cooper pair: it is they which are involved in the velocity condensation. We should replace our earlier playground analogy by another in which cars enter a two-way highway and travel at the speed limit; we then have a condensation in two velocities, east and west. This kind of condensation occurs in superconductors. The BCS team next showed how in a superconductor a new cooperative state of *all* the conducting electrons may be formed; the Cooper pairs then have a common momentum which is not affected by random scattering of individual electrons and so the effective electrical resistance is zero.

Cooper is a slightly built, dark-haired native of New York City. He graduated from the Bronx High School of Science before entering Columbia University. Following the BCS collaboration at the University of Illinois, Cooper joined the faculty of Brown University in 1958. He is the Thomas J Watson Senior Professor of science and co-director of the Center for Nuclear Research. Cooper has been a visiting professor at some ten US and European universities and he is a consultant for several industrial and educational organisations.

Cooper has taught a popular course in physics for humanities students, drawing on his interest in art and literature to relate science and the humanities. The textbook he wrote, *An Introduction to the Meaning and Structure of Physics* (1968) has flying buttresses for its cover design, and its preface has a message similar to that expressed at the close of Cooper's Nobel lecture. There, in answer to the question 'What are the practical uses of your theory?' Cooper listed its important applications, and then added, 'But a theory is more. It is an ordering of experience that both makes experience meaningful and is a pleasure in its own right . . . we see columns of remarkable height and arches of daring breadth.'

John Robert Schrieffer

1931–

Shared the 1972 Nobel Prize for physics with John Bardeen and Leon Cooper for their theory of superconductivity called the BCS theory.

John Schrieffer was born in 1931 in Oak Park, Illinois, the son of John H and Louise (Anderson) Schrieffer. For two years he specialised in electrical engineering at the Massachusetts Institute of Technology, and then changed to physics in his junior year. On arrival at the University of Illinois for graduate studies, he started research with John Bardeen, initially working on a problem dealing with electrical conduction on semiconductor surfaces. In his third year, in consultation with Bardeen, Schrieffer chose superconductivity as his thesis topic, working with Bardeen and Cooper.

The BCS collaboration was remarkably close and fruitful. Shortage of office space advantageously resulted in Bardeen and Cooper sharing an office. Schrieffer found a much-prized place with theorists, all graduate students, in the 'Institute for Retarded Study' on the $3\frac{1}{2}$ floor of a neighbouring building.

Bardeen had come to believe that superconductivity involved three critical elements: the existence of an energy gap, the interaction of electrons with lattice vibrations in the metal, and a phase transformation called a condensation in velocity space. The initial step towards a successful theory was made when Cooper showed that although two electrons experience repulsion due to their charges, their attraction to the positive charges in a metal lattice could deform that lattice to make the formation of 'Cooper pairs' of electrons stable.

Bardeen, Cooper and Schrieffer sought to extend Cooper's investigation of a simple two-electron system to the many-body problem of all the electrons in a metal interacting with its lattice. What was needed, Schrieffer has explained, was the wavefunction to choreograph the dance of some 10^{23} couples. One had to find a notation in which this description was manageable. The problem was so refractory that for a while Schrieffer considered changing his thesis problem to one in ferromagnetism. At this time, Bardeen left for Stockholm to receive his 1956 Nobel Prize, urging Schrieffer to continue his work for another month.

By considering a statistical approach to the electron pairs, Schrieffer in an intuitive leap arrived at a manageable form of the wavefunction. Then in about a month of intense work, Bardeen, Cooper and Schrieffer were able to show that their theory did indeed explain all the experimentally known aspects of superconductivity. Frederick Seitz arranged for this achievement to be announced in two special post-deadline papers at the March 1956 meeting of the American Physical Society in Philadelphia. By 1959 the BCS theory of superconductivity was so firmly established that at a Cambridge University conference on superconductivity David Schoenberg introduced some reports with the words, 'Let us see to what extent the experiments fit the theoretical facts.'

The BCS theory did not end, but rather greatly stimulated work in superconductivity, as summarised in Schrieffer's book *Theory of Superconductivity* (1964). He continued research in superconductivity as a National Science Foundation Fellow at the University of Birmingham and at the Niels Bohr Institute, 1957–58. Following appointments at the University of Chicago and the University of Illinois he joined the faculty of the University of Pennsylvania in 1962 where in 1964 he became Mary Amanda Wood Professor of physics. In addition to superconductivity, Schrieffer has also worked on dilute alloy theory, ferromagnetism and surface physics.

Schrieffer was co-author of a report which helped start the Afro–American Studies Programme at the University of Pennsylvania. He is a sturdy, unassuming man known for felicitous phrasing and a quip for any occasion. At Christmas 1960, Schrieffer married Anne Grete Thomsen, a Dane; they have a son and two daughters.

Leo Esaki

1925–

Shared the 1973 Nobel Prize for physics with Ivar Giaever and Brian Josephson for his experimental discovery of tunnelling in semiconductors.

The phenomenon of tunnelling, whereby a charged particle can occasionally get through an 'insurmountable' energy barrier, if it is not too wide, is a bizarre consequence of the wave nature of particles. In 1957, while he led a small research group at the Sony Corporation in Tokyo, Leo Esaki decided to look into the tunnel effect in germanium p–n junctions. Using an extremely narrow junction and heavy impurity doping of the semiconductor, he achieved the successful operation of a 'backward diode,' so called because its polarity is opposite to that of an ordinary diode.

While testing a more heavily doped diode, he observed a fuzziness in the current–voltage curve in the forward direction. The anomaly showed more significantly in a measurement at low temperatures. Then he realised that the diode should have a *negative* resistance region if a large tunnelling current was made possible in the forward direction. Esaki quickly proceeded to make more heavily doped diodes with junctions only 100 Å wide and found the expected negative resistance. Thus the tunnel or Esaki diode was discovered in 1957, opening a new field of research on tunnelling in semiconductors. The method soon became important in solid state physics because it was simple in principle and highly sensitive to many finer details. It was soon recognised that this diode, with hitherto unseen negative resistance, had practical applications for high-speed circuits, such as those used in computers.

Leo Esaki was born in Osaka, Japan, in 1925. He specialised in physics at the University of Tokyo where he received his MS degree in 1947 and his PhD, on the tunnelling study, in 1959. He went to the United States in 1960 to join the International Business Machines Corporation.

Dr Esaki is an IBM Fellow (the highest scientific award granted by IBM) and has been engaged in semiconductor physics research at the IBM Thomas J Watson Research Center, Yorktown Heights, New York, since 1962. His current interests include a man-made semiconductor superlattice in search of predicted quantum mechanical effects.

Esaki is married to the former Masako Araki, and they have three children: Nina, Anna and Eugene. Esaki has retained his Japanese citizenship.

Ivar Giaever

1929–

Shared the 1973 Nobel Prize for physics with Brian Josephson and Leo Esaki for his discovery of tunnelling in superconductors.

'Master of billiards and bridge, almost flunked physics—gets Nobel Prize' is the approximate wording of a headline in an Oslo newspaper. It refers to Ivar Giaever's student days in Trondheim, reasonably accurately, he says.

Ivar Giaever, son of a pharmacist, was born in Bergen, Norway, in 1929, the second of three children. In 1952 he graduated from the Norwegian Institute of Technology with a degree in mechanical engineering. After completing military duty and serving for a year as a government patent examiner, Giaever emigrated to Canada in 1954 where he worked for the General Electric Company. In 1958 he joined the GE Research and Development Center, in Schenectady. He obtained his PhD degree in 1964 at Rensselaer Polytechnic Institute.

His interest in electron tunnelling between two metals separated by a thin insulating barrier goes back to about 1928, in connection with problems relating to electrical contacts. Giaever described his work as 'marrying tunnelling to superconductivity.' He undertook measurement of current–voltage characteristics of aluminium/aluminium-oxide/lead junctions. Lead was chosen because it becomes superconducting at a more convenient temperature, 7·2 K, than does aluminium, 1·2 K. So at around 4 K one of the films would be superconducting. Giaever found that when the lead became superconducting, the tunnel current decreased sharply for voltages below the lead gap parameter but was relatively unaffected above.

Giaever's discovery greatly simplified the previously complicated measurement of energy gaps, and its dependence on various parameters in many superconductors was quickly investigated. Giaever and others found that the current–voltage characteristics contained fine detail which gave information on the phonon structure of superconductors, leading to a solid state spectroscopic technique. Great progress has been made in understanding superconductivity in the last decade, chiefly through tunnelling experiments. The experiments are simple, direct and informative, in a way that reflects Giaever's style.

Giaever concluded his Nobel lecture with the observation: 'I am convinced that often a newcomer to a field has a great advantage because he is ignorant and does not know all the complicated reasons why a particular experiment should not be attempted. However, it is essential to be able to get advice and help from experts in the various sciences when you need it. For me the most important ingredients were that I was at the right place at the right time and that I found so many friends both inside and outside General Electric who unselfishly supported me.'

With that outlook, it may not be surprising that instead of working out further details of physics discoveries, biophysicist Giaever is now doing research in immunology at GE and the Albany Medical Center. He is particularly interested in the behaviour of protein molecules at solid surfaces.

Ivar Giaever married Inger Skramstad in 1952, and they have four children: John, Anne, Guri and Trina. He became a naturalised US citizen in 1964. Giaever says that he enjoys tennis and skiing and has a passion for wind surfing.

Brian David Josephson

1940–

Shared the 1973 Nobel Prize for physics with Leo Esaki and Ivar Giaever for his theoretical prediction of the properties of a supercurrent through a tunnel barrier, and in particular those phenomena which are generally known as Josephson effects.

Each of the three Nobel laureates for 1973 made his decisive discovery while still a graduate student. In 1962 Brian Josephson was conducting experiments in superconductivity in the Mond Laboratory at Cambridge and attending a course in solid state theory given by Philip Anderson of Bell Telephone Laboratories, then in England on leave. Anderson said, 'This was a disconcerting experience for a lecturer, I can assure you, because everything had to be right or he would come up and explain it to me after class.'

Josephson made some calculations of the tunnel current in a junction of superconductors. These predicted that in addition to the electron tunnelling discovered by Giaever, a current due to the bound superconducting electrons (Cooper pairs) occurs. A superconducting current can exist in the junction even when there is no voltage drop across it. In the presence of a voltage, the theory predicts that the supercurrent oscillates at a frequency simply related to the voltage. Dependence upon a magnetic field is also predicted.

After Josephson published these predictions in *Physics Letters*, Anderson and Rowell soon found experimental evidence for the zero-voltage supercurrent (the DC Josephson effect) and S Shapiro observed the oscillating supercurrent (the AC Josephson effect). At the

University of Pennsylvania the AC Josephson effect was used to determine the constant e/h and led to a quantum standard of voltage now used in many national standards laboratories. The SQUID (superconducting quantum interference device) neatly combines quantisation of magnetic flux and Josephson tunnelling. SQUIDS (AC and DC) have been used as voltmeters in low-temperature measurements, as magnetometers in ultra-sensitive geophysical measurements, and as speedy logic elements and memory cells in computers.

When it became known that the Josephson effect had been taken up by IBM research centres in Europe and the United States, *The Times* quoted a Member of Parliament, Ian Lloyd, as suggesting that this might be another case of Britain losing out by not developing ideas originating in the United Kingdom.

Brian Josephson was born in 1940 in Cardiff, Wales. He earned his BA (1960), MA and PhD (1964) degrees at Cambridge University. He was a junior research fellow (1962–69), and senior research fellow (1969) at Trinity College, Cambridge, and spent a year (1965–66) as research assistant professor at the University of Illinois. Returning to Cambridge, Josephson became assistant director of research (1967–72), reader (1972–74), and professor (1974).

Josephson was married to Carol Anne Oliver in 1976 and they have one daughter, Miranda Louise. For recreation, Josephson enjoys mountain walking, ice skating, photography and astronomy. Recently Josephson has worked on a theory of intelligence: 'I am taking a rather unconventional theoretical approach to the phenomenon of intelligence, in that I believe that the most basic concepts underlying intelligence were discovered in ancient times. In particular I am basing my research to a considerable extent on the formulations which have been given in numerous lectures by Maharishi Mahesh Yogi. It is hoped that the usefulness and validity of these concepts can be confirmed by computer simulation.'

234

Antony Hewish

1924–

The 1974 Nobel Prize for physics was awarded to astronomers Antony Hewish and Martin Ryle for their pioneering research in radio astronomy, to Hewish for the decisive role he played in the discovery of pulsars.

We are all familiar with the twinkling of visible stars. Antony Hewish was determined to find out why radio stars also twinkle. He discovered this effect, which he called interplanetary scintillations, in 1964. Using his knowledge of diffraction phenomena, he showed that when radio waves from a small-diameter source, such as a distant quasar, cross plasma clouds in interplanetary space they are diffracted and fluctuations in otherwise steady intensity occur with a period typically of about one second. Hewish exploited interplanetary scintillations to investigate the solar corona, to measure the angular diameter of distant radio sources in the range of 0·1 to 1·0 second of arc, and to map the solar wind far outside the plane of the ecliptic where spacecraft have yet to venture.

The foregoing work put Hewish in a position to discover pulsars. In 1967 he completed a high-resolution radio telescope, an array of 2048 dipole antennae covering an area of 18 000 m² (4·5 acres). Sir Bernard Lovell has called Hewish's grant of £17 000 from the Department of Industrial and Scientific Research for this project 'one of the most cost-effective in scientific history.' As his Cambridge team initiated their survey of more than 1000 radio galaxies, graduate student Jocelyn Bell analysed the paper flow from four recorders on a sky chart. After about two months she noted a weak source apparently scintillating strongly on the 3·7 m recordings around midnight, when normal scintillations are inconspicuous. Detailed investigation of this source using recordings of much higher time resolution were planned and in November 1967 it was discovered that the signals were recurrent pulses. There followed a period which Hewish described as 'the most exciting in my life,' as they established the extraterrestrial and stellar nature of the signals.

By elimination they were led to suggest that the sources of the pulsed signals were vibrating neutron stars, and products of supernova explosions. Some months later Thomas Gold put forward another theory involving a rotating beam from a spinning neutron star. By 1974 some 130 such pulsars had been charted and Gold's neutron star 'lighthouse' model was generally accepted. So Hewish gave evidence for the speculation of theorists of a star collapsed into a body only 20 kilometres in diameter with a density of the order of 10^{15}–10^{16} g/cm^3, and probably with magnetic fields as enormous as 10^{12} gauss.

Antony Hewish was born in Fowey, Cornwall, the youngest of three sons of Ernest William Hewish, a banker, and Frances Grace Lanyon (Pinch) Hewish. He was educated at King's College, Taunton (1935–42) and at Cambridge University (1942–43 and 1946–48). During the war he was concerned with airborne radar counter-measure devices at the Telecommunications Research Establishment at Malvern, and it was there that he met Ryle. Upon graduating from Cambridge in 1948, Hewish joined Ryle's research team at the Cavendish Laboratory. He was a university lecturer in physics from 1961–69, a visiting professor in astronomy at Yale in 1962, and was elected professor of radio astronomy at Cambridge in 1971.

In 1950 Hewish married Marjorie Richards, and they have a son and a daughter. His relaxations are 'listening to music, sailing, gardening, and almost any manual activity.'

The 1974 Nobel awards (the first to be given in any branch of astronomy), denoted the recognition that astrophysics is a fundamental part of physics as a whole. Radio astronomy is providing a means for studying both cosmology at the distant edge of the Universe and the properties of highly condensed matter in neutron stars. It has also revealed 'fossil' radiation from the hot, condensed phase of the Universe near the beginning of time (1978 Nobel Prize).

Martin Ryle

1918–

Shared the 1974 Nobel Prize for physics with Antony Hewish for their pioneering research in radio astrophysics; Ryle for his observations and inventions, in particular in the technique of aperture synthesis.

Martin Ryle and Antony Hewish were the first astronomers to be awarded the Nobel Prize although radio astronomy was started by K G Jansky in 1932. Bursts of radio noise from the Sun received attention during World War II because of their effect on radar systems. With the development of more powerful radio telescopes after the war, many other sources were discovered, most of which turned out to be distant galaxies having radio emission some million times greater than that from our own or neighbouring galaxies.

Radio observations were, in this way, able to supplement and extend optical observations of distant galaxies and hence contribute to the large-scale study of the nature and origin of the Universe as a whole. At the same time, they provided a much increased understanding of our own Galaxy and the radio sources in it. The use of wavelengths some million times greater than optical wavelengths meant that quite different regions—such as those containing high-energy particles or diffused ionised gas—could be studied for the first time.

However, the use of such long wavelengths introduced severe practical problems: the smallest detectable change in the angular position of a distant source, or the finest detail in its structure which a telescope can establish is proportional to the wavelength, and is inversely proportional to the aperture of the telescope. For the unaided

237

human eye the resolution is about one minute of arc. To acquire a radio picture with the same resolution, using wavelengths some million times greater than optical wavelengths, one needs a telescope having a diameter of about 1 km with the shape of its surface true to within several centimetres.

Ryle's inventions side-stepped the engineering difficulties involved in building fantastically large telescopes. He used small aerial elements moved to occupy successively the whole of a much larger aperture plane. A computer controls the telescope, continually updating the position of the map centre selected for viewing, for precession and aberration. The signals from each pair of elements (with electrical delays imposed corresponding to path differences) are combined in the receivers. Outputs of the receivers are sampled by the computer and stored on a magnetic disc. On completion of the observation they are combined and a curve-plotter draws a map of the area observed. The 5 km telescope at Cambridge comprises eight dishes, four on a rail track, which have to be located with an accuracy of 0·3 mm (using a new astronomical surveying method), and provides maps having a resolution of 0·6 second of arc—better than that of the largest ground-based optical telescopes. The detailed radio maps obtained are being used to understand the immensely powerful mechanisms which occur in radio galaxies and quasars, whilst the positional accuracy provided makes it possible to identify the radio sources even when they are very faint optically.

Detailed maps of supernova remnants and their relations to pulsars/neutron stars, and the study of other galactic sources, such as the condensations within large gas clouds which may represent the birthplace of stars, have also benefited from the high resolution obtained with the 5 km telescope. Other instruments have been built at Cambridge using the same technique, (a) to extend the observations to very weak and distant sources for cosmological work, and (b) to study the detailed distribution of atomic hydrogen in our own and other galaxies.

Martin Ryle was the second of five children of Professor J A Ryle, MD, and Miriam Scully Ryle. He was educated at Oxford and for the period 1939–45 was at the Telecommunications Research Establishment at Malvern. In 1945 he joined the Cavendish Laboratory at Cambridge, where he trained many younger scientists, 'Instilling an incredible personal devotion in all who worked with him,' J L Greenstein has said. In 1972 Ryle was named Astronomer Royal of Great Britain. Ryle engaged in a continuing debate with Fred Hoyle over the manner in which the Universe came into being. Hoyle maintained that there is a continuous creation of new matter, replacing old matter, while Ryle supported the big-bang theory that the elements were created in an explosion and that the Universe is still expanding.

In 1947 Ryle married Ella Rowena Palmer; they have a son and two daughters.

Aage Niels Bohr

1922–

Shared the 1975 Nobel Prize for physics with Ben Mottelson and Leo Rainwater for the discovery of the connection between collective motion and particle motion in the atomic nucleus and for development of the theory of the structure of the nucleus based on this connection.

Aage Bohr was the fourth son of Niels Bohr and Margrethe (Norlund) Bohr, born in 1922, the year his father received the Nobel Prize. During his childhood his parents lived at the Institute for Theoretical Physics in Copenhagen. The remarkable coterie of scientists who were attracted to the Institute became for the Bohr children Uncle Kramers, Uncle Klein, Uncle Nishina, Uncle Heisenberg, Uncle Pauli, etc.

In October 1943 Niels Bohr and his family fled from Denmark to Sweden to avoid arrest by the Nazis, and for the next two years Aage assisted his father in work on the atomic energy project in London, Washington and Los Alamos. On their return to Denmark, Aage completed work for his master's degree in 1946, and in 1948 he became a member of the Institute for Advanced Study in Princeton. Through discussions with Isidor Rabi at Columbia, Bohr became interested in evidence which the hyperfine structure in atomic spectra offered about the symmetry of the nucleus.

In the heavier elements, the distribution of charge on the nucleus is far more asymmetric than was predicted by the shell model devised by Goeppert-Mayer and Jensen. Bohr returned to Copenhagen to begin with Mottelson investigation of a model in which there was motion of individual nucleons in the nucleus, while at the same time the nucleus as a whole could change its shape and rotate its orientation. By analogy, in a swarm of bees each bee seems to have its own rapid flight but the swarm moves slowly as a unit.

The collective nuclear motion is strongly influenced by, and in its turn affects, the motion of the individual nucleons, and in 1951 Bohr published a study of this interplay between the two basic types of motion in the nucleus. The consequences for nuclear properties were systematically analysed by Bohr and Mottelson in the following years. Remarkable confirmation was found in that the energy levels of certain nuclei could be explained by the assumption that they formed a rotational spectrum.

Aage Bohr has been associated with the Niels Bohr Institute since completion of his university studies, and he followed his father as director (1962–70). He has since lightened his administrative duties to pursue research, but still serves as director of NORDITA (the Nordic Institute for Theoretical Atomic Physics).

Bohr was married to Marietta Bettina Soffer in 1950, in New York; they had two sons and a daughter. Mrs Bohr died in 1978.

At the Nobel banquet in Stockholm, Bohr addressed his response to 'Dear Students,' and closed with: 'The attempt to explain our understanding to those who come with fresh minds and the experience of community with the creative force of youth is a profound source of inspiration. The constant questioning of our values and achievements is a challenge without which neither science nor society can remain healthy. We live in an age with revolutionary changes, and the inadequacy of old frameworks for our thinking has led to a highly developed disrespect for authority and tradition. This even goes so far that the tradition for disrespect can also be looked upon—disrespectfully.'

Ben Roy Mottelson

1926–

Shared the 1975 Nobel Prize for physics with Aage Bohr and Leo Rainwater for their work on the internal structure of the atomic nucleus.

The 1975 Nobel award recognised the importance of the discovery that the atomic nucleus is generally deformed (not spherical), and the development of an acceptable model for the nucleus, supported by experimental data. Around 1950 a dilemma arose in reconciling two contrasting pictures of the nucleus. The liquid drop model developed in 1936 described the nucleus as a charged liquid drop that could oscillate around its spherical shape. This picture received strong support from the discovery of the fission process (1939) in which the nucleus becomes so strongly deformed that it breaks into two pieces. The shell model of the nucleus developed in 1949 viewed the nuclear structure in terms of the independent motion of the neutrons and protons, each moving in an orbit about the centre of mass. This model had far-reaching success in accounting for a variety of nuclear properties that could be associated with the orbits of individual particles.

Aage Bohr and Ben Mottelson attempted to bring together the two contrasting aspects of nuclear structure, and in their 1953 article presented an encyclopedic collection of experimental data analysed for what information it provided on the interplay between the motion of individual nucleons and deformations of the nuclear shape. Building on this work, a major effort in the following decades aimed at the development of a comprehensive and consistent description of the atomic nucleus.

Highlights in this development were the understanding of how vibrational and rotational motion can be built out of the motion of individual particles, the recognition of the important role of the pair-wise bonding of particles in the nucleus which bears close analogies to the pairing of electrons responsible for superconductivity in metals, and the discovery of a great wealth of new types of vibrations in the nucleus, some of which resemble those of a liquid drop while others involve quantal features of the nucleus that lie outside such classical pictures. In these developments there was a lively cooperative effort involving physicists from many different countries. The Niels Bohr Institute in Copenhagen provided unique opportunities for such international cooperation building on the traditions established by its founder.

Ben Mottelson was the second of three children born to Goodman and Georgia (Blum) Mottelson, in 1926. He has said his childhood home in Chicago was a place where scientific, political and moral issues were freely and vigorously discussed. 'He would have made a great scholar in any field,' said one of Mottelson's colleagues in 1968.

Mottelson entered Purdue University on a US Navy (V12) programme and received a BS degree in 1947. In graduate studies at Harvard he worked on a problem in nuclear physics directed by Julian Schwinger and received his PhD in 1950. He then continued his work in Copenhagen, successively under a travelling fellowship from Harvard, an AEC fellowship, and a research position in CERN. Since 1957 he has been a professor at NORDITA. Of his collaboration with Aage Bohr, begun in 1951, Mottelson has said, 'We feel that in this cooperation we have been able to exploit possibilities that lie in a dialogue between kindred spirits that have been attuned through a long period of common experience and jointly developed understanding.'

Mottelson is known among his colleagues as an excellent lecturer, and as one who can discuss intelligently almost any subject. 'He got me interested in walking the woods for mushrooms,' said a friend recounting Mottelson's interest in nature, cycling, swimming and music.

Leo James Rainwater

1917–

Shared the 1975 Nobel Prize for physics with Aage Bohr and Ben Mottelson for their work on the internal structure of the atomic nucleus.

Leo Rainwater has been associated with the Columbia University Physics Department since 1939, as a graduate student, scientist on what became the Manhattan Project, and full professor, since 1952. His undergraduate study was at the California Institute of Technology where C D Anderson was his instructor when Anderson won his Nobel Prize, R A Millikan was president and T H Morgan was Rainwater's biology teacher. At Columbia he took courses taught by E Fermi, I I Rabi and E Teller. Nobel laureates H Bethe, W Lamb, I I Rabi, C H Townes, T D Lee and P Kusch were his colleagues at Columbia. Laureate Leon Cooper's PhD thesis was related to Rainwater's pioneering muonic atom x-rays studies with Val Fitch, which first established the smaller nuclear charge radius. He and Cooper later wrote a theoretical paper on multiple Coulomb scattering by extended nuclei which refuted cosmic-ray experiments suggesting anomalous muon–nucleus interaction.

From 1948 to 1962 Rainwater taught an advanced nuclear physics course. This led to his belief in early 1949 that nuclear shell models should have considerable validity, so he was pleased and excited with the success of the Mayer–Jensen shell model. In late 1949, C H Townes gave a colloquium on the evidence from nuclear electric quadrupole moments, pointing out the qualitative agreement with the Mayer shell model, but that they were much too large in the rare earth region. During that talk, Rainwater worked out the general features of his argument that valence nucleons should lead to spheroidal shape distortion of such nuclei. This led to a paper in 1950 that was the basis of his Nobel award.

During 1949–50 Rainwater shared an office with Aage Bohr and they had many discussions on the subject which helped to stimulate Bohr, and later influenced Bohr and Mottelson in Copenhagen where their theoretical work filled in the numerous implications for which the Nobel award was given.

Rainwater is basically an experimental physicist, and with Havens and Wu provided most of the neutron cross sections against energy results known by 1948. From 1946 to 1978 he was associated with the Columbia Nevis synchro-cyclotron doing studies of pion, muon and neutron interactions with nuclei.

Leo Rainwater was born in Council, Idaho, in 1917, the son of Leo Jasper and Edna Eliza (Teague) Rainwater. In 1942 he married Emma Louise Smith; their daughter Elizabeth died while young and their sons, James, Robert and William are now grown up. Rainwater enjoys classical music and is interested in astronomy and geology. He is concerned about the world population explosion and resource depletion.

Burton Richter

1931–

Awarded the 1976 Nobel Prize for physics with Samuel Ting for their independent discoveries of a new type of elementary particle known as psi or *J*.

The physicists' search for the smallest, 'fundamental' particles has progressed from atoms via atomic nuclei to numerous types of fermions and bosons, and recently to quarks, tentatively considered to be of three types. Considering the enormous equipment involved and the complexity of their experiments in continuing this search, it is amazing that Burton Richter at Stanford and Ting at Brookhaven should have discovered the ψ/J particle simultaneously, in November 1974. The new particle did not show kinship with any previously known particles; it was drastically new. Its lifetime was found to be 5000 times longer than it reasonably should have been, considering its other properties, indicating that its inner structure was new. The ψ/J particle cannot be constructed from any combination of the known three quarks; it calls for the existence of a fourth quark with special properties called 'charm.' Gösta Ekspong, a member of the Swedish Academy, called the achievement of Richter and Ting 'one of the greatest discoveries in the field of elementary particles.'

Burton Richter was born in Brooklyn, New York, on 22 March 1931, the son of Abraham and Fannie (Pollack) Richter. He became interested in science as a boy through the magnifying glass and the microscope, and he developed a chemistry laboratory in the basement of his home. His interest in physics arose through reading and through the high school's physics laboratory. When about 14, he decided he wanted to go to MIT to study either physics or chemistry. During his freshman year, he decided on physics, and in his junior year he began to work with Francis Bitter in the magnet laboratory. His senior thesis was on the quadratic Zeeman effect in hydrogen. Richter's work with Bitter during his first year of graduate school involved his use of the cyclotron to prepare short-lived isotopes of mercury, to study their hyperfine structure. He became more interested in the cyclotron and spent several months at Brookhaven getting a taste of modern particle physics. Back at MIT, he did his dissertation with Louis Osbourne in the synchrotron laboratory.

As a graduate student, Richter became curious about models of the electron which gave it a structure and which would eliminate the divergences in quantum field theory. To further this interest he obtained a research associate position at Stanford in 1956 to experiment on electron–electron scattering using the 1 GeV Stanford linear particle accelerator. He has been there ever since, in general, 'chasing the same will-o'-the-wisp,' he says. Richter is now a professor at the Stanford Linear Accelerator Center (SLAC).

Richter was married in 1960 to Laurose Becker. They have a daughter Elizabeth, and a son Matthew. Richter has an outgoing temperament, has grey hair, and a build on the plump side. His interests include music, particularly opera; books, particularly history and biography; skiing, hiking and squash.

Samuel Chao Chung Ting

1936–

Awarded the 1976 Nobel Prize for physics with Burton Richter for their independent discovery of a new type of elementary particle known as psi or *J*.

Samuel Ting was born on 27 January 1936 in Ann Arbor, Michigan where his father was studying at the University of Michigan. He spent his childhood in mainland China and his teenage years on Taiwan where his father was a professor at the National Taiwan University. Samuel Ting earned his academic degrees at the University of Michigan: BSE (physics) and BSE (mathematics) in 1959, MS in 1960, and PhD (physics) in 1962. For the next year he was a Ford Foundation Fellow doing nuclear research at CERN in Switzerland. Following a period at Columbia University (1964–69) Ting joined the faculty at the Massachusetts Institute of Technology. His research interests have been experimental particle physics, quantum electrodynamics, and the interaction of photons with matter. An indication of his drive in research is the fact that, with Ulrich Becker, Ting heads three research groups at Brookhaven National Laboratory, at CERN, and at the electron synchrotron facility (DESY) in Hamburg, Germany.

Ting is a quiet and intense man. When he was working in Geneva, a typical day for him started with breakfast at the CERN cafeteria. It ended when he left the laboratory to sleep in his apartment, a ten-minute drive from the laboratory. He would take off alternate weekends to return to his home in Lexington, Massachusetts, to see his wife, the former Kay Louise Kuhne, and their daughters Jeanne and

247

Amy. Ting has a brother John who is a civil engineer in Sommerville, New Jersey, and a sister Susan Ting Yeh who lives in Oak Ridge, Tennessee.

In the summer of 1972, Ting's group set up a massive particle spectrometer adjacent to the 33 GeV synchrotron at Brookhaven. The spectrometer was designed to search for long-lived neutral particles in the region of masses equivalent to energies between 1·5 and 5·5 GeV. It was assumed that if such a particle existed it would decay into electron–positron pairs whose energy would peak at some value corresponding to the mass of the parent particle. The detection equipment had to be sensitive enough to select such a significant event out of a background of some million to 100 million similar but non-significant events. To reduce the background of unwanted particles, the apparatus was shielded by 10 000 tons of concrete and 10 000 lb of borax soap (a cheap neutron shield). Evidence for the J peak first appeared in August 1974. A cautious worker, Ting rechecked until by November he had firm evidence for the existence of the new J particle with a mass corresponding to 3·1 GeV, about three times the mass of a proton.

When Ting attended a committee meeting in Stanford on 11 November he found that Richter's group at SLAC had independently just discovered the same particle, which they had named ψ. Both results were presented to an excited crowd at a memorable session at SLAC. There was immediate worldwide recognition of the importance of the ψ/J particle discovery. Its discovery pushed forward the concept of charm as more than just a label for a fourth quark, and lent some support to the current theory of weak interactions and the possibility of the synthesis of that theory with electrodynamics.

The 1976 Nobel award again raised a question about an aspect of big physics which caused some grumbling over the 1974 award to Antony Hewish. *Science News* remarked: 'Dozens of physicists were involved in the experiments, but only the two leaders (who will share $160 000) were named by the committee. It may tend to increase the touchiness of negotiations over leadership positions in large experimental groups.'

John Hasbrouck van Vleck

1899–

Shared the 1977 Nobel Prize for physics with Philip Anderson and Sir Nevill Mott for their fundamental investigations of the electronic structure of magnetic and disordered systems.

The honour of the 1977 Nobel Prize for physics and $145000 were divided equally among three pioneers in the theory of solid state physics whose contributions together have influenced every part of the physics of condensed matter. This theory has become increasingly abstruse. When asked if he could explain for a layman his theory of magnetism, van Vleck said simply, 'No.'

John van Vleck was born in Middletown, Connecticut, in 1899. He received his AB degree from the University of Wisconsin in 1920, and his AM (1921) and PhD (1922) degrees from Harvard. Van Vleck did research in the old quantum theory and later quantum mechanics during the years American theorists began to attain competence at the level of their European colleagues. His 1926 monograph on line spectra is an historic exposition of the powers and limitations of the old quantum theory. In the late 1920s and early 1930s van Vleck's research was in dielectric and magnetic susceptibilities, culminating in publication of the book *The Theory of Electric and Magnetic Susceptibilities* (1932). He is known as 'the father of modern magnetism.'

In the study of crystals, van Vleck utilised the concepts of the crystal field and the ligand field, which are electric fields experienced by the electrons of a given atom or ion owing to the presence of other ions or atoms in their neighbourhood. The energy states allowed in the system are thereby modified, resulting in changes in electrical, magnetic and optical properties. The underlying ideas are important in understanding solid state lasers, the chemical behaviour of clusters in solution, and the bonding of molecules including the idea of partial covalency. These are all aspects of quantum theory useful to researchers in chemistry, molecular biology and geology, as well as in physics.

During World War II, van Vleck showed that at about 1·25 cm wavelength radar would encounter troublesome absorption due to water molecules in the atmosphere. He showed that there would be even stronger absorption at 0·5 cm because of rho-type triplets of the oxygen molecule. He remarked, 'None of us who worked in molecular spectra in the 1920s dreamed that two decades later some of the results might have military significance, and four decades later important applications to radio astronomy and astrophysics.'

Van Vleck, a lightly built, quiet man with a grasp for details, has been described by his associates at Harvard as charming and 'one of the few true gentlemen and scholars.' Van Vleck says that the anecdotes concerning his knowledge of railways and memorised timetables 'are always exaggerated,' but his interest in railway timetables is indeed mentioned in the citations for honorary degrees he received from Wisconsin and from Oxford.

A measure of the fundamental and durable nature of van Vleck's research is the continuing usefulness of his major book on electric and magnetic susceptibilities. When, as an emeritus professor at Harvard, he recently undertook revision of that text he remarked, 'It does need some revision, but the first edition sold 87 copies last year. Not bad for a 45-year-old science book.'

Sir Nevill Francis Mott

1905–

Shared the 1977 Nobel Prize for physics with Philip Anderson and John van Vleck for their fundamental investigations of the electronic structure of magnetic and disordered systems.

In 50 years of amazing productivity, Nevill Mott developed a theoretical basis for one area in physics after another. *The Theory of Atomic Collisions* (1933) by Mott and Massey included the 'Mott scattering' of charged particles and the role of symmetry. A collaboration of several years' duration resulted in another book by Mott and Jones, *The Theory of the Properties of Metals and Alloys* (1936). This was followed by the exploration by Mott and Gurney of non-metals, leading to another book treating defects, semiconductors and phenomena relevant to the photographic process.

Mott was the first to suggest that in the transition metals, electrons contribute to the electrical conductivity in two ways. One group of electrons is primarily responsible for current, while a second, more sluggish group accounts for the magnetic properties, and gives rise to most of the scattering. Under Mott's leadership, a group that included Sir Charles Frank developed the theory of dislocations, defects and strengths of crystals. From the start of his work as a mathematical physicist, Mott showed a special urge and insight to move from artificial models toward an understanding of real materials. It may have been this faculty in part which in the 1940s led Mott, as president of the British Atomic Scientists' Association, to speak out repeatedly about the perils and opportunities of the emerging atomic age.

While a professor at the University of Bristol (1933–54), Mott's work was of special value to metallurgists and materials scientists. Further, Mott studied 'Mott transitions' by which certain metals may become insulators, and vice versa—processes which are not fully understood even now. He summarised the situation in 1974 in a book *Metal–Insulator Transitions*.

In 1954, Anderson had shown under what conditions an electron in a disordered or amorphous system such as glass could either move through the system or be in effect tied to a specific position. The concept of 'Anderson localisation' was largely ignored; 'Only one person realised its importance,' said Anderson. That person was Mott, whom Anderson visited at the Cavendish Laboratory in 1961. Their collaboration was so fruitful that Anderson returned to Cambridge in 1967 for eight years' work. Mott's contributions were described by Helmutt Fritsche of the University of Chicago: 'He has a tremendous intuition. When he has an idea he sets the whole field of solid state physics in motion.'

Nevill Mott was born in 1905, the son of C F Mott, director of education in Liverpool, and Lilian May Reynolds. In 1930 he married Ruth Horder; they have two daughters.

After working on nuclear problems in Rutherford's Cavendish Laboratory, Mott became professor of theoretical physics at the University of Bristol at the age of 28. During World War II he worked on operational research and explosives, and directed a group which tried to determine the range of German V2 rockets, from Royal Air Force photographs. After the war he succeeded W L Bragg as head of the Cavendish (1954–71); he continues to work there with many colleagues on a variety of problems, particularly non-crystalline materials. He received his knighthood in 1962.

Outside physics research, Mott is deeply interested in secondary education, particularly in science and modern languages; he has served on government and other committees. He is an enthusiastic photographer and is interested in stained glass, Byzantine coins and the history of religion.

Philip Warren Anderson

1923–

Shared the 1977 Nobel Prize for physics with John van Vleck and Sir Nevill Mott for their fundamental investigations of the electronic structure of magnetic and disordered systems.

The ubiquitous tape recorder, the laser, the transistor, the modern computer which runs our lives, and most other gadgets in modern electronics rest on imaginative theories of solid state physics. Anderson, van Vleck and Mott each developed mathematical models to explain how electrons behave in electrical conductors. Each man has had a deep influence on the others.

The Royal Swedish Academy of Sciences cited two of Philip Anderson's many important contributions. In a 1958 publication on wave propagation in random media, he demonstrated that in certain cases the electrons may be trapped in a small region; the concepts developed around this 'Anderson localisation' are vital to an understanding of 'poorly condensed matter.' Anderson's 1961 paper on minimagnets showed the microscopic origins of magnetism in bulk materials. The 'Anderson model' is a quantum model which can explain the basic physics of a host of problems such as superconducting transition temperatures and the effects of impurities.

Anderson's wide-ranging curiosity led to his theoretical study of superfluidity—a flow without friction and with abnormally high thermal conductivity—first found in helium-4 below 2 K and then noted in the 'superconductor' metals and in helium-3. Anderson also clarified the meaning of the Josephson effect and linked it to concepts of symmetry.

Anderson, born in Indianapolis in 1923, interrupted his college education to aid in the war effort as a radio engineer. He received his degrees from Harvard University: BS in 1943, MS in 1947 and PhD in 1949. As a student under van Vleck, he studied pressure broadening in microwave and infrared spectroscopy. Anderson's principal association has been with Bell Telephone Laboratories, where he became assistant director in 1974, but he has also had a long association with Cambridge University, including a sabbatical in 1961–62 and eight years in a unique tenured visiting professorship (1967–75).

A colleague has described Anderson as a 'modest, even shy man with a deep intellect and extremely broad interests.' Beyond physics, these interests include a love of the out-of-doors and hiking, particularly in Cornwall. Anderson commutes to his two jobs, Joseph Henry Professor of physics at Princeton University and consulting director at the Physical Research Division, Bell Telephone Laboratories, from his home on the edge of New Jersey's Great Swamp, New Vernon. He is a certified first-degree master of *Go*, the Japanese board game especially popular with mathematicians. Anderson's wife is the former Joyce Gothwaite; they have one daughter, Susan Osborne.

Peter Leonidovich Kapitza

1894–

Awarded one half of the 1978 Nobel Prize for physics for his basic inventions and discoveries in the area of low-temperature physics.

Peter Kapitza, the son of a general of engineers, was born in 1894 in Kronstadt in Czarist Russia. After graduating from the Polytechnic Institute in Petrograd in 1918, he became a lecturer there. The outbreak of the Red Terror led Kapitza to emigrate to England where, while retaining his Soviet citizenship, he began his long and charmed association with the Cavendish Laboratory of Cambridge University, where he first worked under Sir Ernest Rutherford. When he was appointed assistant director for magnetic research in 1924, Kapitza achieved strong magnetic fields, not surpassed for 30 years, to study alpha particle deflection and magnetostriction. In 1929 Kapitza became the first foreigner in 200 years to be elected to the prestigious Royal Society. From 1930 to 1934 he served as director of the Mond Laboratory built for him by the Royal Society, with a Russian crocodile in bas relief on one wall.

During his years at Cambridge, Kapitza went to Russia each summer to visit his mother, but he encountered increasing pressure to transfer his research to Russia. When he attended a scientific conference in Moscow in 1934, he was permanently detained on orders from Stalin. He was made director of the S I Vavilov Institute for Physical Problems of the Academy of Sciences and in 1939 he was elected a full member of the Academy of Sciences. Starting with his earlier equipment purchased from Cambridge University by the Russian government,

Kapitza engineered a helium liquefier. His design was brought into commercial production after World War II by S C Collins and the Arthur D Little Company. This convenient helium liquefier facilitated research in cryophysics worldwide.

Helium II, the phase of liquid helium that exists at temperatures below 2·17 K, has astonishing properties, one of which is that it defies gravity by flowing up and out of its container. Kapitza investigated effects related to the extraordinarily low viscosity and high thermal conductivity of He II and introduced the term 'superfluid.'

Other fields in which Kapitza has worked are electrical engineering, high-power microwave electronics, nuclear physics, the solid state, hydrodynamics and ball lightning. Most of his publications, interestingly, are without co-authors, but he gathered as colleagues such illustrious men as Khalatnikov, Peshkov, Landau and Lifshitz. Not only a creative thinker, Kapitza also had great engineering and managerial skills. In the laboratory built for him at the S I Vavilov Institute he provided machine shop and apparatus-making instructions for a substantial number of young men. Later in the 1950s he was instrumental in the formation of the 'science city,' Akademgorodok, outside Novosibirsk in western Siberia.

It is thought that Kapitza was under arrest from about 1945 to 1953 for his reluctance to work on the development of an atomic bomb. After the death of Stalin, Kapitza was reappointed director of the S I Vavilov Institute in time to contribute to the successful Soviet effort to launch the first space satellite. His services to the state must have been notable to have been recognised by such honours as the State Prize for physics (1941, 1943); the Moscow Defence Medal (1944); the Order of Lenin (1943, 1944, 1945, 1964, 1971, 1974); Hero of Socialist Labour (1945, 1974); Lomonosov Gold Medal (1959); and the Great Gold Medal, Exhibition of Economic Achievements, USSR (1962). He has received other honours from around the world.

Kapitza used his high stature in the Soviet Union to support his colleague Lev Landau when in 1938 he was arrested as a German spy. In 1970, Kapitza and Andrei Sakharov were among the 20 signatories of an open letter deploring the detention of biologist Zhores Medvedev. Professor R V Pound of Harvard University has said of Kapitza: 'He will be remembered for being an independent thinker in a country where independent thinking is not that easy.'

Kapitza and his wife Anna live in a small country-style house near the Institute. Their sons Sergei and Andrei are also scientists.

Arno A Penzias

1933–

Shared half of the 1978 Nobel Prize for physics with Robert Wilson for their discovery of cosmic microwave background radiation.

Forty years after he and his parents left Hitler's Germany, Arno Penzias was honoured with Robert Wilson for a beautifully simple experiment which was important for the evidence it gave about the origin of the Universe. The two physicists at the Bell Telephone Laboratories used a 20-foot horn reflector antenna originally designed for satellite communication with Echo and Telstar to attempt to measure the intensity of radio waves emitted by the halo of gas which surrounds our Galaxy. They found a persistent noise they could not account for. Even after they evicted a pair of pigeons from the antenna throat and cleaned it, wherever they pointed the antenna they detected noise whose source they concluded was beyond our Galaxy. The intensity of the noise corresponded to that which a black-body source would radiate at a temperature of about 3·5 K.

Fortunately, both Penzias and Wilson were trained as radio astronomers and were able to exploit the serendipity of their unexpected findings. On conferring with theorists Dicke and Peebles at Princeton, they concluded that the cosmic background radiation supported the big-bang theory of the origin of the Universe.

In 1942, George Gamow examined the conditions of temperature and density required if, some 15 billion years ago, the elements were formed in a fireball explosion. Ralph Alpher and Robert Herman concluded that a consequence of this cosmological model was the present existence of cosmic radiation echoing through the Universe. They calculated that the radiation by now would have degraded to correspond to a temperature of 5 K, in fair agreement with what Penzias and Wilson observed.

Arno Penzias was born in Munich in 1933, and was taken to the United States at the age of four, where he attended Brooklyn Technical High School. His motive for going to the City College of New York was, he says, to make a living, and not to be poor any more. When he asked his professor, 'Is physics something one can earn a living at?' the reply he received was, 'Well, you can do the same things engineers can do and do them better.' Penzias was reassured, but remarks that physicists are sometimes arrogant.

Penzias graduated from CCNY in 1954, served in the Signal Corps, and pursued graduate studies at Columbia University. There his adviser was Charles Townes and his thesis (1962) was on a maser radiometer and measurement of emission from free hydrogen in the Pegasus I cluster of galaxies. He was attracted to Bell Telephone Laboratories in 1961 in part by the facilities available for radio astronomy. As director of the Radio Research Laboratory, Penzias heads a group of some 60 people. He and his wife Anne, who is a guidance counsellor, have three children; they live in Highland Park, New Jersey.

Robert Woodrow Wilson

1936–

Shared half of the 1978 Nobel Prize for physics with Arno Penzias for their discovery of cosmic microwave backgroud radiation.

The discovery made by Robert Wilson and Arno Penzias in 1964 'has made it possible to obtain information about cosmic processes that took place a very long time ago, at the time of the creation of the Universe,' stated the Royal Swedish Academy of Sciences. The two radio astronomers at Bell Telephone Laboratories set out to use a horn-like antenna and laser scanner to make accurate measurements of radio waves emitted by the halo of gas which surrounds our Galaxy. While calibrating their equipment, they found something more important: the faint echo of the cataclysmic fireball, or big bang, in which the chemical elements were created some 15 to 20 billion years ago.

In an earlier grand discovery in astronomy in 1929, Hubble had found in his study of the redshift in light from the distant galaxies that the magnitude of the shift was proportional to distance. By Doppler's principle, this means that the more distant the galaxy, the more rapidly it is moving away from the Earth. This led some theorists, notably George Gamow, to propose that the Universe began with a big bang in which the matter now so widely dispersed had its origin in a fireball of intense heat and pressure. The radiation expanded, its temperature falling from 300 to 3 K over a period computed from Hubble's relation to be about 18 billion years. The measurements of Wilson and Penzias confirmed the existence of this background radiation and thus supported the big-bang theory.

Robert Wilson was born in Houston, Texas, in 1936. As an undergraduate at Rice University, his teenage fascination with electronics carried him first into electrical engineering, and then physics. He received his PhD from the California Institute of Technology in 1962, with a thesis on radio astronomy. The following year he was a research fellow in radio astronomy. He is now head of the Radio Physics Department at Bell Telephone Laboratories, whose 14 members work on microwave solid state devices and integrated circuits as well as on radio astronomy. Wilson is especially interested in the investigation of dark clouds in the Galaxy through millimetre wave measurements on interstellar molecules. His wife Betsy says she better understands his work because her father was a scientist. They have three children.

Steven Weinberg

1933–

Shared the 1979 Nobel Prize for physics with Sheldon Glashow and Abdus Salam for contributions to the theory of the unified weak and electromagnetic interaction between elementary particles, including *inter alia* the prediction of the weak neutral current.

The four fundamental forces of nature are gravitation, electromagnetism, and the strong and weak nuclear forces. For many years, there had been a successful theory of electromagnetic forces, in which the interactions of charged particles such as electrons were believed to be due to the exchange of other particles called photons—much as basketball players interact by passing a basketball back and forth. But it seemed to be impossible to understand the weak nuclear forces in this way. The particles that carry the weak force would have had to be enormously heavy, in contrast with the massless photon, and calculations in any such theory seemed to involve unmanageable infinities.

    In 1967, Steven Weinberg proposed a unified quantum field theory of the weak and electromagnetic interactions which solved these problems. The interactions in this theory are joined by an exact symmetry principle, but this symmetry is lost through a phenomenon known as spontaneous symmetry breaking, which Weinberg had previously invoked in exploring the properties of strong interactions in the mid 1960s. In the citation that was read when Weinberg received an honorary degree in recognition of this work from the University of Chicago in 1978, it was noted that 'Weinberg's work on unifying the weak and electromagnetic interactions is one of the major breakthroughs of modern physics and is frequently likened to Maxwell's unification of electricity and magnetism in the nineteenth century.' Similar ideas were proposed independently by Salam in 1968, and the resulting theory is generally known as the Weinberg–Salam theory.

The Weinberg–Salam theory involved a hitherto unobserved kind of weak interaction, called a neutral current interaction, and gave definite predictions for the rates of processes caused by this interaction, worked out by Weinberg in 1972. This interaction was discovered in neutrino experiments in 1973, and subsequent experiments with beams of neutrinos and electrons have verified many of the predictions of the theory. Theorists including Weinberg have also developed a mathematically similar theory of strong interactions, known as quantum chromodynamics, which is increasingly being confirmed by experiment.

Steven Weinberg was born in New York in 1933 to Frederick and Eva Weinberg. His father was a New York City court stenographer. Weinberg received his AB degree from Cornell University in 1954 and his PhD from Princeton University in 1957. Following appointments at Columbia 1957–59, Berkeley 1959–69, and at MIT 1969–73, in 1973 he became Higgins Professor of physics at Harvard and senior scientist at the Smithsonian Astrophysical Observatory. Weinberg and his wife Louise (a professor of law) have been married since 1954, and have one daughter.

Weinberg has published over 130 scientific articles. The Institute for Scientific Information, in a 1978 survey of citations to scientific articles published in 1961–76, found that in that period Weinberg was the most frequently cited physicist in the world.

In addition to his work on many areas of elementary particle physics and quantum field theory, Weinberg has a lively interest in cosmology. He has written a treatise on the subject, *Gravitation and Cosmology—Principles and Applications of the General Theory of Relativity* (1972), as well as a prize-winning popular book, *The First Three Minutes* (1978), which has been translated into more than 15 languages.

Weinberg's government service includes a consultancy to the US Arms Control and Disarmament Agency and membership of the President's Committee on the National Medal of Science. He has served on the council of the American Physical Society, and is a co-editor of the series *Monographs in Mathematical Physics* of the Cambridge University Press. Weinberg has a long-standing interest in medieval history, and is perhaps the only physicist who is a member of the American Medieval Academy.

Abdus Salam

1926–

Shared the 1979 Nobel Prize for physics with Steven Weinberg and Sheldon Glashow for contributions to the theory of the unified weak and electromagnetic interaction between elementary particles, including *inter alia* the prediction of the weak neutral current.

When Abdus Salam's daughter incorporated some of her father's theory in an A-level examination paper, her examiner gave her a failing mark. But for that theory the Royal Swedish Academy of Sciences in Stockholm awarded Abdus Salam a Nobel Prize. While working separately, Salam and Weinberg developed a system of equations known as a 'gauge theory.' A gauge theory changes the scale of one frame of reference so as to compare it with a quite different frame of reference. Their two different frames were electromagnetism, which operates between easily observed objects, and the weak interaction, which is a short-range nuclear force.

The Weinberg–Salam theory predicted that, owing to the weak nuclear force, when electrons are hurled at atomic nuclei and examined as they rebound, there would be a significant difference in the number of electrons with right-hand spin and with left-hand spin. This 'parity violation' was actually found in experiments using the Stanford University linear particle accelerator and was hailed as confirmation of the Weinberg–Salam unified theory relating two fundamental forces of nature.

Abdus Salam was born in Jhang, Pakistan, in 1926. He attended Punjab University and St John's College, Cambridge, where he received a double first in mathematics and physics. In 1952 he earned a PhD in theoretical physics at Cambridge. He was a professor at Government College and Punjab University (1951–54), and a lecturer at Cambridge University (1954–56). Salam became professor of theoretical physics at Imperial College, London, in 1957. Since 1964 he has also served as director of the International Centre for Theoretical Physics at Trieste. He has been the author of some 200 papers on elementary particles and also on scientific and educational policy for Pakistan and other developing countries.

For the United Nations, Salam served as scientific secretary for the Geneva Conferences on Peaceful Uses of Atomic Energy (1955 and 1958) and as a member of the Advisory Committee on Science and Technology (1964–75; chairman 1971–72). He was vice-president of the International Union of Pure and Applied Physics (1972–78). For Pakistan, Salam has served on commissions dealing with education, atomic energy, space and the upper atmosphere. He was also chief scientific adviser to the President from 1961 to 1974.

Sheldon Lee Glashow

1932–

Shared the 1979 Nobel Prize for physics with Steven Weinberg and Abdus Salam for contributions to the theory of the unified weak and electromagnetic interaction between elementary particles, including *inter alia* the prediction of the weak neutral current.

Experiments have increasingly supported proposals developed by Glashow, Weinberg and Salam that two of the basic forces in nature are aspects of the same phenomenon. The forces linked are electromagnetism (which turns electric motors) and the 'weak' force (a nuclear interaction which causes radioactive decay in some atomic nuclei). The new theory may be a major step toward incorporating all physical laws into a single 'unified field theory,' which was the goal of Albert Einstein's later work and that has been sought by other physicists ever since.

The unifying theory, called the Weinberg–Salam theory, was developed independently by them and originally had an undesirable limitation: it applied to only one class of elementary particles. In 1970, Glashow enlarged the conception. He showed that a certain mathematical property of subnuclear particles (a property he named 'charm') enabled the links between electromagnetism and the weak nuclear force to be extended to all elementary particles.

The observation of 'neutral currents' in 1973 supported the unifying hypothesis. A neutral current is a reaction in which no change in electrical charge occurs between particles entering and those of the same type which emerge; for example, an encounter between a proton and a positron from which a proton and a positron emerge. But in a 'charge current,' on the other hand, the electrical charges change; for example, the collision of a high-energy neutrino with another neutrino (each of zero charge) to produce a muon (negative charge) and a proton (positive charge).

Experiments with neutrinos to show neutral currents in weak force reactions were performed both at the Fermi National Accelerator Laboratory in Illinois and at CERN, the European high-energy physics centre near Geneva. In 1978, 20 physicists from five institutions working with the Stanford University linear particle accelerator performed experiments which established the existence of neutral currents under the control of the weak force, supporting the Weinberg–Salam–Glashow theory.

Both Glashow and Weinberg are native New Yorkers, both began their study of physics at the Bronx High School of Science where they were classmates, both received degrees from Cornell University, and after a period of diverging careers, at the age of 46, both are professors of physics at Harvard University. Despite these similarities, the two physicists have worked largely independently. Their friends describe them as quite different people: Glashow is an extrovert and Weinberg is more reserved.

After graduating from Cornell University in 1954, Sheldon Glashow went to Harvard where he received his MA in 1955 and PhD in 1959. He was a National Science Foundation Fellow at the Institute of Theoretical Physics, Copenhagen (1958–60), and was a member of the faculty at the University of California at Berkeley from 1961 to 1967, when he joined the Harvard University faculty.

Bibliography

Cole, Jonathan R and Cole, Stephen 1973 *Social Stratification in Science* (Chicago: Chicago University Press)

Elsasser, Walter M 1978 *Memoirs of a Physicist in the Atomic Age* (New York: Science History Publications/Neale Watson, and Bristol: Adam Hilger)

Farber, Eduard 1963 *Nobel Prize Winners in Chemistry 1901–1961* rev. edn (New York: Abelard–Schuman)

Gillespie, Charles E (ed) 1974 *Dictionary of Scientific Biography* (New York: Scribner) 15 vols

Heathcote, Niels Hugh de Vaudray 1953 *Nobel Prize Winners in Physics 1901–1950* (New York: Schuman)

Heyn, Ernest V 1976 *Fire of Genius: Inventors of the Past Century* (New York: Anchor Press/Doubleday)

Kaplan, Flora (comp.) 1941 *Nobel Prize Winners: Charts–Indexes–Sketches* 2nd edn (Chicago: Nobelle)

Levitan, Tina 1960 *The Laureates: Jewish Winners of the Nobel Prize* (New York: Twayne)

Nobelstiftelsen Stockholm 1904– *Les Prix Nobel en 1901–* (annual volumes) (Stockholm: Imprimerie Royale)

Nobelstiftelsen Stockholm 1951 *Nobel, the Man and His Prizes* H Schuck and others (Norman: University of Oklahoma Press)

Nobelstiftelsen Stockholm 1964, 1972 *Nobel Lectures including Presentation Speeches and Laureates' Biographies: Physics 1942–1962; 1963–1970* (Amsterdam: Elsevier)

Opfell, Olga S 1978 *The Lady Laureates: Women Who Have Won the Nobel Prize* (Metuchen, NJ: Scarecrow Press)

Price, Derek J de Solla 1963 *Little Science, Big Science* (New York: Columbia University Press)

Sarton, George 1956 *History of Science and the New Humanism* 3rd edn (New York: Braziller)

Weber, Robert L 1973 *A Random Walk in Science* (London and Bristol: The Institute of Physics, and New York: Crane Russak)

Whitehead, Alfred North 1967 *Science and the Modern World* (New York: Macmillan)

Zuckerman, Harriet 1977 *Scientific Elite: Nobel Laureates in the United States* (New York: Free Press/Macmillan)

Index

Names of the Nobel Prize winners in physics are the only entries in this Index. For each, the location of his portrait and biography is given in bold type. The other page numbers are for references to him in other biographies. The date of the award appears in parentheses.

Dalén, Nils Gustaf (1912), **45**
Davisson, Clinton Joseph (1937), **109,** 92, 113
Dirac, Paul Adrien Maurice (1933), **97,** 99, 107, 120, 132, 133, 175, 177, 188, 203, 205

Einstein, Albert (1921), **64,** 27, 30, 33, 49, 58, 59, 60, 70, 89, 96, 100, 115, 119, 121, 125, 133, 151, 153, 168, 173, 185, 189, 195, 215, 222, 265
Esaki, Leo (1973), **229**

Fermi, Enrico (1938), **114,** 106, 176, 178, 192, 217, 243
Feynman, Richard Phillips (1965), **201,** 157, 159
Franck, James (1925), **75,** 78, 126, 131, 187, 190
Frank, Ilya Mikhailovich (1958), **171,** 170

Gabor, Dennis (1970), **221**
Gell-Mann, Murray (1969), **215**
Giaever, Ivar (1973), **231,** 233
Glaser, Donald Arthur (1960), **179,** 212
Glashow, Sheldon Lee (1979), **265**
Goeppert-Mayer, Maria (1963), **190,** 239
Guillaume, Charles-Edouard (1920), **62**

Heisenberg, Werner Karl (1932), **95,** 76, 98, 101, 143, 150, 159, 192, 203, 206
Hertz, Gustav Ludwig (1925), **78,** 75
Hess, Victor Franz (1936), **104,** 86
Hewish, Antony (1974), **235,** 237, 248
Hofstadter, Robert (1961), **182**

Jensen, J Hans D (1963), **193,** 239
Josephson, Brian David (1973), **233,** 160

Kapitza, Peter Leonidovich (1978), **255,** 137, 186
Kastler, Alfred (1966), **207**
Kusch, Polykarp (1955), **157,** 203, 243

Lamb, Willis Eugene Jr (1955), **155,** 157, 203, 243
Landau, Lev Davidovich (1962), **186**
von Laue, Max Theodor Felix (1914), **49,** 52, 54, 119, 222
Lawrence, Ernest Orlando (1939), **117**
Lee, Tsung Dao (1957), **167,** 243
Lenard, Philipp (1905), **26,** 61
Lippmann, Gabriel (1908), **34,** 222
Lorentz, Hendrik Antoon (1902), **12,** 13, 29, 65

Marconi, Guglielmo (1909), **36,** 39, 129
Mayer, Maria Goeppert (1963), **190,** 239
Michelson, Albert Abraham (1907), **31,** 65